African Histories and Modernities

Series Editors
Toyin Falola
The University of Texas at Austin
Austin, TX, USA

Matthew M. Heaton
Virginia Tech
Blacksburg, VA, USA

This book series serves as a scholarly forum on African contributions to and negotiations of diverse modernities over time and space, with a particular emphasis on historical developments. Specifically, it aims to refute the hegemonic conception of a singular modernity, Western in origin, spreading out to encompass the globe over the last several decades. Indeed, rather than reinforcing conceptual boundaries or parameters, the series instead looks to receive and respond to changing perspectives on an important but inherently nebulous idea, deliberately creating a space in which multiple modernities can interact, overlap, and conflict. While privileging works that emphasize historical change over time, the series will also feature scholarship that blurs the lines between the historical and the contemporary, recognizing the ways in which our changing understandings of modernity in the present have the capacity to affect the way we think about African and global histories.

More information about this series at
http://www.palgrave.com/gp/series/14758

Sebabatso C. Manoeli

Sudan's "Southern Problem"

Race, Rhetoric and International Relations, 1961–1991

Sebabatso C. Manoeli
Columbia University
New York City, USA

African Histories and Modernities
ISBN 978-3-030-28773-3 ISBN 978-3-030-28771-9 (eBook)
https://doi.org/10.1007/978-3-030-28771-9

Cover illustration: Keystone Press / Alamy Stock Photo

This Palgrave Macmillan imprint is published by the registered company Springer Nature Switzerland AG.
The registered company address is: Gewerbestrasse 11, 6330 Cham, Switzerland

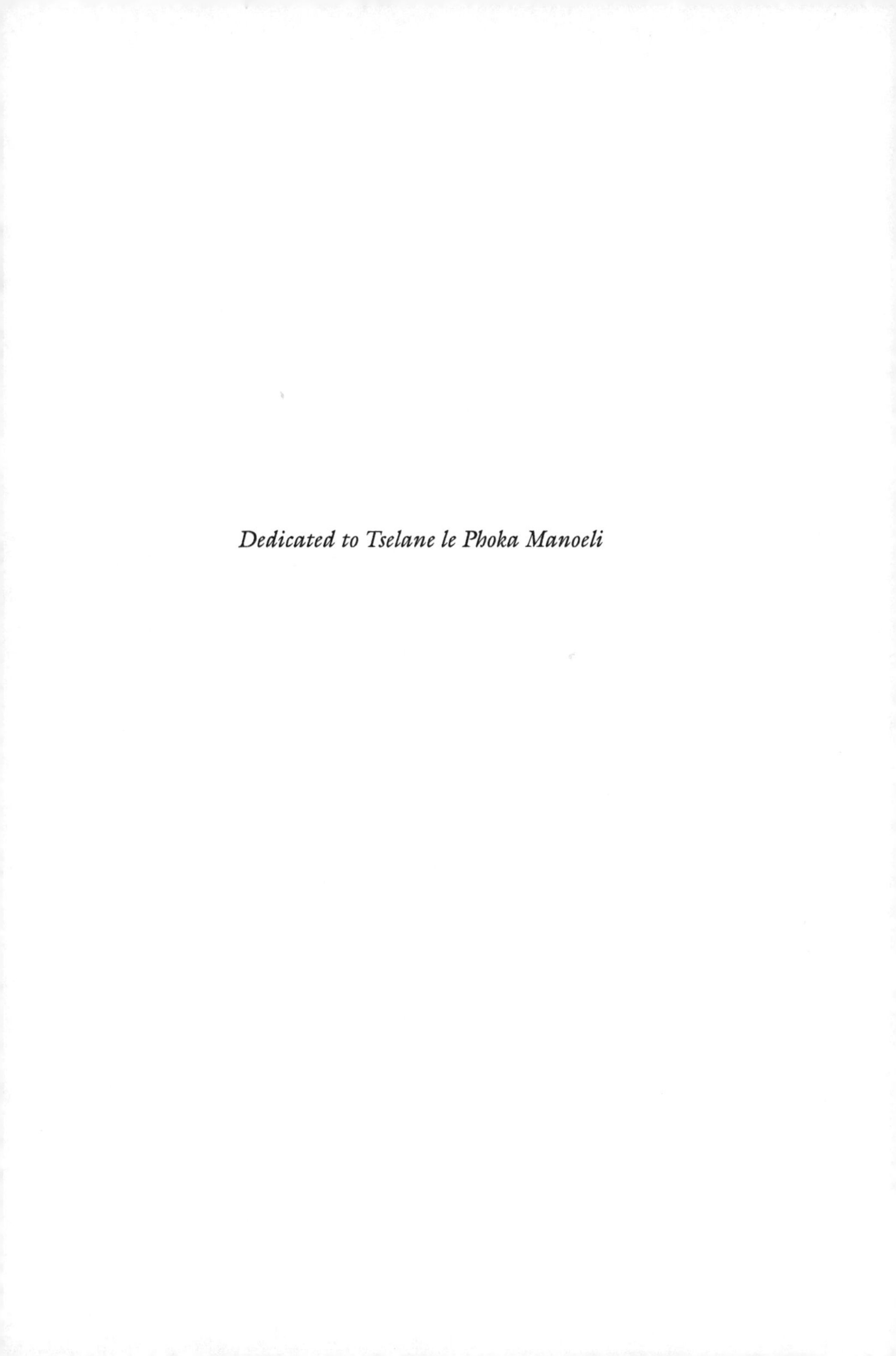

Dedicated to Tselane le Phoka Manoeli

Acknowledgements

Many thanks to my interviewees for entrusting me with their stories. I would also like to express my gratitude to Jocelyn Alexander, for her rigorous guidance and constant encouragement. I am grateful for the community of scholars at the African Studies Centre at the University of Oxford whose instruction, trust and advice have been tremendously enriching—thank you Miles Larmer, William Beinart, Jonny Steinberg, David Anderson and Ahmed Al-Shahi. Many thanks to Douglas Johnson and Wendy James for their wisdom and time. I am thankful for the indispensable intellectual camaraderie of the scholars of Sudan and South Sudan at Durham University who welcomed me into their vibrant community—thank you Zoe Cormack, Nicki Kindersley, Cherry Leonardi, Jane Hogan, Justin Willis, Sarah Marriot, Ade Brown and Matthew Bensen. I am thankful to the wider community of academics and practitioners who enabled and supported my research—thank you David Ambrosetti and the team at the Centre for Ethiopian Studies in Addis Ababa, Sylvain Perron, Brice Garnier and others at the Medicins Sans Frontières (MSF) teams in Addis Ababa and Gambella, and the team at the Centre for Social, Legal and Economic Studies and Documentation in Sudan (CEDEJ) in Khartoum, David Kenrick, Miles Tendi, Dan Hodgkinson and others in the Southern Africa Discussion Group at Queen Elizabeth House, as well as Anne Heffernan and Annette Joseph Gabriel for their invaluable advice. This work would not hve been possible without the support of Rebecca Fradkin and Malebogo Ngoepe. Special thanks to Keagile Lesame. Lastly, I cannot thank my family enough for their selfless love and unceasing support—kea leboha 'M'e Tselane, Ntate Phoka le Abuti Moeketsi Manoeli.

Contents

About the Author

Sebabatso C. Manoeli is a research associate in the Department of History at the University of Johannesburg, South Africa. She leads programme strategy at the Atlantic Fellows for Racial Equity at Columbia University, USA, and previously, she held a lectureship in African history at the University of Oxford, UK.

Abbreviations

AAPSO	Afro-Asian People's Solidarity Organisation
ACR	Archivio Comboniani Roma
ALC	African Liberation Committee
ALF	Azania Liberation Front
ANC	African National Congress
ANF	African National Front
ANO	Anyanya National Organisation
ASA	Azania Secret Army
BADEA	Arab Bank for the Development of Africa
CAR	Central African Republic
EPLF	Eritrean People's Liberation Front
EPRDF	Ethiopian People's Revolution Democratic Front
FRELIMO	Frente de Libertação de Moçambique
GPLM	Gambella People's Liberation Movement
IRR	Institute of Race Relations
MEDU	Middle East Documentation Unit, Durham University
MOD	Ministry of Defence (Ethiopia)
MP	Member of Parliament
MPLA	Movimento Popular de Libertação de Angola
NCFSP	National Council for Friendship, Solidarity and Peace
NPG	Nile Provisional Government
NUP	National Union Party
OAU	Organisation of African Unity
OLF	Oromo Liberation Front
OLS	Operation Lifeline Sudan
PAC	Pan Africanist Congress
PAIGC	Partido Africano da Independência da Guiné e Cabo Verde

PDP	People's Democratic Party
PLO	Palestine Liberation Organization
PMHC	Political-Military High Command
RCC	Revolutionary Command Council
RoAPE	Review of African Political Economy
RSS	Rumbek Secondary School
RTC	Round Table Conference
SACDNU	Sudan African Closed Districts National Union
SAD	Sudan Archive Durham
SAF	Sudan Armed Forces
SANU	Sudan African National Union
SCA	Sudan Christian Association
SCP	Sudan Communist Party
SF	Southern Front
SP	Southern Problem
SPLA	Sudan People's Liberation Army
SPLM	Sudan People's Liberation Movement
SSA	Southern Sudan Association
SSLM	Southern Sudan Liberation Movement
SSPG	Southern Sudan Provisional Government
SSU	Sudanese Socialist Union
SWAPO	South West Africa People's Organization
TANU	Tanganyika African National Union
TPLF	Tigray People's Liberation Front
UDS	University of Dar es Salaam
UN	United Nations
UNSG	United Nations Secretary General
UPC	Uganda People's Congress
USSY	Union of Southern Sudanese Students & Youth
WCP	World Council of Peace
ZANU	Zimbabwe African National Union
ZAPU	Zimbabwe African People's Union

CHAPTER 1

Introduction

On 9 July 2011, South Sudan's Independence Day, the spokesperson of South Africa's ruling party, the African National Congress (ANC), Baleka Mbete, led a delegation to Juba to participate in the festivities. In her subsequent media briefing, she spoke about how the commemoration 'reminded' her of South Africa's historic Freedom Day 'when Comrade Nelson Mandela was inaugurated as the first president of the democratic and free South Africa'.[1] Mbete not only equated the liberation of South Sudan to that of South Africa, she went much further. In the statement, Mbete proceeded to describe the 'historic good party-to-party relations forged over many years of heroic struggle for self-determination and freedom for the people of South Africa and South Sudan'.[2] Specifically, the shared history included their 'progressive' values and the exchange of ideas regularly between the leaders of the movements '[s]ince the founding of the [Sudan People's Liberation Movement] SPLM (1983)'.[3] The ANC and the SPLM, Mbete recalled, 'shared offices in the dark days of our struggle against Apartheid' while their representatives were exiled in Harare, Zimbabwe. Upon gaining liberation, 'the ANC handed over its offices and property to the SPLM'.[4]

This press release, communicating a history scarcely recorded, invokes a moment in time when the leading South African liberation movement stood in solidarity with a Southern Sudanese-led rebellion against the Sudanese government. Their relations are striking considering that in

S. C. Manoeli, *Sudan's "Southern Problem"*, African Histories and Modernities, https://doi.org/10.1007/978-3-030-28771-9_1

January 1986, on the 74th anniversary of the ANC's founding, instead of condemning Sudan, the ANC's National Executive Council publicly commended the Sudanese government for its major role in isolating Apartheid South Africa through sanctions.[5] In fact, Sudan was the only African country the ANC recognised as a vanguard alongside New Zealand, Australia, the United Kingdom (UK) and Scandinavia.

Sudan subscribed to Africa's regional consensus on normalising racial equality in the international system as the Organisation of African Unity (OAU) advocated for sanctions against white settler states in southern Africa.[6] The concerted efforts led to the shaming of Apartheid South Africa as a pariah state and its supporters. This context inadvertently created an international environment—especially in Africa—in which states could accrue reputational currency on the basis of their position on South Africa. Thus, on the edges of the global politics of Apartheid, a succession of Sudanese governments and Southern Sudanese rebels competed for international legitimacy. The period between 1960, when international uproar around Apartheid began, and 1994, when the regime fell, overlaps with the period of the Cold War's escalation and denouement. Including the litmus test of Apartheid, the global Cold War enabled a broad set of political modalities of signalling credibility and respectability. During this period, Sudan's rebels and governments alike deployed a range of discursive signalling practices in order to justify the wars in Southern Sudan and shape world opinion. This is a book about the competition for Sudan's reputation during its civil wars in the South.

The International Dimension of Sudan's Civil Wars

The literature on the international dimension of Sudan's civil wars tends to focus on the military involvement of foreign powers. Specifically, it highlights the Southern rebels' involvement in regional proxy wars.[7] This scholarship frames the relationships the rebels had with Sudan's neighbouring countries in a framework of reciprocated interference between governments through insurgencies.[8] Revealing the existence of transnational alliances in the region, Lovise Aalen examines the multiple factors that led Ethiopia to support Southern Sudanese rebels in the 1960s and 1970s.[9] She argues that in addition to tit-for-tat diplomacy with Sudan, Ethiopia held several influences in tension, ranging from wider Cold War concerns to Middle Eastern interests in the Horn of Africa, and the need to control Ethiopia's Western region, Gambella, where large numbers of Southern rebels and refugees had found sanctuary. Examining the retaliatory politics of successive Ethiopian governments towards Sudan, Belete Yihun extends the analysis to 1991, from a diplomatic angle.[10] Works authored by members of the rebel movements such as Wani Igga's account of the SPLM's relationship with the Ethiopian government have also provided insight into aspects of their host relations.[11]

Not unlike Aalen, Khalid Mustafa Medani argues that Sudan's first civil war was impacted by the complex dynamic created by the Arab Cold War.[12] He holds that the Arab-Israel War of 1967 transformed the relationship between the Middle East and the Horn of Africa[13] and introduced 'Israel as an important actor in these linkages'.[14] Scopas Poggo sheds light on Israel's critical role as a military backer of the Southern rebels in the last three years of Sudan's first civil war (1969–1972).[15] Drawing similar conclusions about Israel, Edgar O' Ballance also highlights the significance of foreign mercenaries in the Southern barracks.[16] Despite its significance, Israel's clandestine military support for Southern rebels will not form part of this book, as my key concern is the Sudanese government's and rebel forces' countervailing pursuits of public legitimacy abroad.

In the scholarship on the second civil war, Southern Sudan's foreign relations tend to be wholly situated within humanitarian and aid discourses.[17] Major foreign NGOs and multilateral organisations such as the United Nations (UN) provided food and supplies to the victims of the war and famine, the vast majority of whom were Southern Sudanese.[18] This literature concentrates on rebels as an obstructing force to the delivery of services to those in need, and it uncovers the important phenomenon of aid militarisation and politicisation.[19] Moreover, how the millions of refugees and persons displaced by Sudan's civil wars fashioned innovative identities in foreign locations has rightly attracted a great deal of scholarly attention.[20] However, beyond the involvement of rebels in regional proxy wars and humanitarian interventions, as well as the roles that international actors played in Sudan's peace processes, little is known about Southern Sudanese diplomatic relations with the outside world.[21]

Although important, these literatures neglect questions regarding the intellectual and socio-historical aspects of rebel transnational relations. I address this lacuna, particularly for the period between 1961 and 1991, which overlaps with the Cold War. The book is not about the internationalisation of the civil wars per se, but about the history of the international discourses surrounding the civil wars, their diplomatic implications and their echoes in the lives of non-elite Southerners in exile. It is concerned with the international networks and imaginaries marshalled by the Sudanese state and the rebels from the South as they made competing claims to legitimacy abroad.

Third World Ideoscapes and Internationalisms in the Cold War

Sudan, I argue, is an important but obscured site through which to analyse the political appropriation and application of Third World internationalisms on the margins of the Cold War. The Sudanese state and Southern rebels variously made claims to legitimacy through the language of Third World politics, and they appealed to various spheres of belonging under the Third World banner. For example, as I will show in Chap. 3, in the 1960s, Southern rebels framed their calls for self-determination in the rhetoric, debates and logics of Black internationalism and a racially exclusionary conception of Pan-Africanism. In contrast, in Chaps. 8 and 9, I show that the Sudanese government refuted these claims by invoking Afro-Arab and broader Afro-Asian solidarities and socialist ideals. Their competing strategies transformed over time, but continued to be situated in the intellectual milieu of Third World internationalisms throughout the duration of the Cold War.

Therefore, the book will help us understand the *ideoscapes* of the Third World, particularly on the margins of the Cold War. A term Arjun Appadurai coined, *ideoscapes*, refers to global cultural flows of political ideas.[22] Expounding on the processes the term entails, Jutta Bakonyi explains that '[a]s they travel, political ideas are adapted to local conditions, interact with locally predominant narratives and are thereby reproduced in multiple forms with divergent contents'.[23] Accordingly, I will chart the ways in which competing Sudanese political actors and intellectuals 'continuously inject new meaning-streams into the discourse'[24] of the "Southern Problem"—a pliable set of arguments that became the focal point of competing propaganda campaigns marshalled to explain the inequalities and discrepancies in socio-economic and political experiences of Southern Sudan and the rest of the country. Even though it participated in overlapping Third World communities, Sudan neither occupied the centre of Pan-Africanism, Pan-Arabism, anti-imperialism or socialist internationalism, and its civil wars were located on the peripheries of Cold War politics. Yet, margins tend to be creative spaces. In the same vein, the book provides a distinctive perspective on the liberation struggles in Africa, and on the identity—and particularly racial—politics of the global Cold War from the margins.

The Cold War was more than the rivalry of superpowers or a 'long peace' that pivoted on the Atlantic world.[25] Across the world, it was a war between a divided but imperial global North and a global South that oscillated between subversion and tactical compliance, but had its own, varied agendas.[26] New histories of the Cold War in Africa reveal the West's support for southern African settler regimes and the Portuguese colonies, and the Eastern Bloc's corollary support of the liberation movements that challenged the same colonial and settler regimes.[27] In light of the overlap of the Cold War and decolonisation, the then emergent Third World represented an intellectual project dedicated to the development of new political subjectivities.[28] Internationalism represents a particularly evocative dimension of Third World politics. It produced solidarity and influenced foreign relations. Socialist internationalism, in particular, featured significantly in the interactions between the Second and Third Worlds in the Cold War. As a community that birthed new imaginaries through its internationalisms, this generative and explicitly anti-colonial community of political leaders, activists and intellectuals was simultaneously riddled with inconsistencies such as the membership's elite status, as well as their tolerance of authoritarian and military regimes.[29] Despite their clear opposition to white supremacist states, the racial fault line remained salient.[30]

While anti-colonial solidarities based on shared experiences of imperialism did lead to the establishment of new trans-geographical connections, they also threw ideological and identity differences within the Third World into sharp relief. Southern Sudanese rebels and, in response, Sudanese governments took advantage of and shaped these cracks in the Third World community. This book thus explores the limits of Third World solidarity. There is little research on the tensions within the Afro-Asian network, particularly between Pan-Africanism and Pan-Arabism. It thus contributes towards our understanding of how elites from the North and the South in Sudan represented their local realities in discourses that had international and internationalist appeal.

Conceptualising Sudan's Political Identities

The category "Southerner" and its antithesis, "Northerner", elide important ambiguities and complexities, and they are historically contingent. I have nevertheless taken the ontological decision to use these labels as they are widely used in Sudan, suggesting that while they were invented, they have real meaning and effect.[31] I use them not to reinforce the artificial binary they represent, but to conform to the self-designation of the actors in question in order to understand and analyse the dichotomised world that they discursively constructed. While I realise that it is possible to challenge a sectarian paradigm by using language that emanates from outside its terms of reference, in this case the main alternative is deeply implicated in a state-led political strategy. By referring to the same groups as "people from the Northern provinces" and "people from the Southern provinces", I would reproduce a labelling technique that the Sudanese government employed to moderate divisive politics as well as to deny the existence of discrimination against the Southern Sudanese.[32] If "Southerners" did not exist—the pernicious logic held—then the allegations of discrimination against them also could not. The Sudanese government used these seemingly neutral alternative classifications expressly to conceal anti-"Southern" prejudice in Sudan. Thus, this book seeks to highlight both the veiled and overt politics of these phrasings and framings.

By adopting these terms, I do not mean to suggest that all Southerners or all Northerners self-identified in terms of these territorial labels or that these categories consisted of politically, socially or culturally homogenous populations. It was Sudan's lack of a common conception of the nation in the post-independence period that gave rise to sub-nationalism in the South (and in other parts of the Northern periphery, in less pronounced ways).[33] Revealing the synthetic quality of the Southern identity category, Justin Willis has persuasively argued that Southern politicians 'collectivized "the south"' such that it became 'a community that always seemed more tangible to the external observer than it did from within'.[34] These identities were, to a certain extent, fictions. Yet, they remain useful terms of reference as an 'imagined community' does not begin with the complete assent of its imagined membership.[35] Thus even though I appreciate the fictitious nature of these groupings, they remain valid analytical frames not unlike other social constructions such as "nation", "tribe" or "race" because they had political power. However, I disaggregate the "Southerners" and "Northerners" as far as I can and where relevant to the political analysis of discursive strategies.

Taking a Discursive Diplomacy Approach

While a great deal of scholarly attention has been paid to Sudan's bi-lateral and multilateral foreign relations, the Sudanese state's diplomacy has yet to be placed in the same frame as that of its rebels.[36] By defining diplomacy as 'an ensemble of practices, power struggles and truth contestations that develop into a dominant discourse of dealing with the other', it becomes possible to conceive of it in expansive enough terms to include non-state actors, such as rebels.[37] I share Reyko Huang's view that '[a]rmed confrontation is one dimension of a civil war; diplomatic confrontation is another, one in which states and rebels battle it out for external support'.[38] It is important to note that, although I frame the Sudanese state and successive generations of Southern rebel organisations as diplomatic rivals, I realise that they sought different ends. The diplomacy of dissidents is aimed at obtaining recognition whether for the purposes of attaining self-determination or for reforming the state. The state aims to protect its reputation and to secure international legitimacy, which constitutes a form of soft power.[39] Unlike states, rebels lack institutional technologies and access to state resources, and as a result, the shape of their diplomatic strategies and linkages is limited but nimble. Solidarity-building efforts by rebels can also function as the guerrilla-style diplomacy of under-resourced, non-state political actors. Herein, I chart the uneven networks of international political actors that Southern exiles and the Sudanese government sought to influence.

Exile often represents a *generative* site in which ideas and identities are crafted, debated and deconstructed. Indeed, '[a]mbiguity, uncertainty, and the ceaseless questioning of identity – these are resources of the exiles'.[40] Other resources include writing—one of the 'dissident practices' of exiles that provides a means through which they can challenge the representational practices of a state.[41] This challenge is significant because sovereignty can be partially understood in terms of a state's ability to 'represent its domestic community in global politics' through the spoken word and symbolic representation.[42] These state forms of representation acquire set meanings. When rebels contest these meanings and publicise alternative narratives abroad, purporting to speak on behalf of a constituency neglected by the state, they disturb the state's authority by challenging its right to hold the monopoly on representational meaning. Through a process of discursive diplomacy, the Southern Sudanese exiles functioned as the discursive aggressors and the primary claimants in the narrative battle against the Sudanese state.

The book takes the rhetorical efforts of both parties—the government and Southern rebels—seriously, recognising the power play inherent in the dynamics of competitions over discursive dominance.[43] Since '[r]hetoric is central to politics, even when politics takes the form of war', this lens can be productively employed in the context of the Sudanese civil wars.[44] By engaging 'narrative and language games'—what is said by whom and in what context—we can observe and unpick processes that reveal how discursive framings and arguments were marshalled to construct competing realities.[45] As David Carr posits, '[n]arrative requires narration; and this activity is not just a recounting of events but a recounting informed by a certain kind of superior knowledge'.[46] There is authoritative power in the point of view that *can* narrate, and find audiences too. These discursive rebels did not act as chroniclers, simply conveying events in the sequence in which they happened. They functioned as narrators, identifying what they considered the most pertinent incidents, relegating certain pieces of information that they deemed irrelevant, making causal claims and inferring motive, in order to provide the audience 'an organized, coherent account'.[47] Indeed, as John Peel argues, 'narrative is an expression of power' for 'those who can achieve it'.[48] The discourses explored in this book focus on the narrativisation of Sudan and its "Southern Problem".

The book focuses on a 30-year window of time in which the bi-polar international system made a wide array of rhetorical claims possible, given the multiple communities that existed between the competing centres of global power. It thus aims to reconstruct the history of how these divergent accounts were constructed, disseminated, consumed and reproduced abroad. It is not only about different ways of remembering the past and framing the causes and nature of the crisis in Sudan, it is also about how these narratives were performed and represented to international audiences, and the subsequent diplomatic implications.

Methods, Sources, Structure

A mixture of archival and oral history methods has made my reconstruction of the history of Sudan's narrative battle possible. I have conducted extensive archival research in the Sudan Archives at Durham, UK; the Bill Bryson Library in Durham, UK; the Comboni Archives in Rome, Italy; the Sudan National Library Archive; the Institute of African and Asian Studies at the University of Khartoum; the National Archives and Library of Ethiopia, the Ministry of Defence Archives of Ethiopia; the French

Centre for Ethiopian Studies' Newspaper Archive; the African National Congress Liberation Archives in Alice, South Africa; the Anti-Apartheid Movement Archives, and the Bodleian Library Archive, at the University of Oxford, UK; the British Library's Newspaper Archive and the personal collections of Douglas H. Johnson. Moreover, I have conducted 21 in-depth interviews with former SPLM soldiers in Ethiopia, Uganda and the UK; members of the host community in Gambella, Ethiopia; as well as former Sudanese diplomats in Khartoum, Sudan. Through this diverse array of sources, I chart the shifts in the narrative and diplomatic strategies of the rebels and the state over three critical decades.

Through archival research, I have found a rich corpus of documentary sources that have illuminated rebel and government discursive and diplomatic interactions. Given the centrality of the Southern actors as diplomatic threats to the Sudanese government, the book primarily gives voice to these political actors, particularly as they remain marginal in narratives of Sudanese international history. However, having read both along and against the archival grain when dealing with the propaganda material and other documents pertaining to both actors, the book does not provide a heroic account of either of these protagonists.[49] Press releases, newspapers and other official publications of both Southern rebels in exile and the Sudanese state served as an important set of resources for this book. As the most important external backer for the SPLM from 1983 to 1991, Ethiopia served as an appropriate case through which to study the Movement's host relations in the 1980s. I therefore spent time in Ethiopia researching the nature of the relationship between the SPLM and Ethiopia and how the South Sudanese combatants were received by the host society. I also conducted research in Uganda, Sudan, South Africa, Italy and England.

The book offers a simultaneously chronological and thematic account of the battle for international legitimacy. Following Chap. 2's brief examination of the "Southern Problem's" colonial provenances, Chap. 3 traces its uses in the discursive rebellion waged by Southern politicians in exile in the early 1960s. Chapter 4 charts the corollary development of the "Southern Problem" through the government's rebuttals. In a bid to ascertain the efficacy of these competing discourses, Chap. 5 highlights the varied reception rebel discourses had in neighbouring countries and international institutions, and Chap. 6 examines the first international convention devoted to addressing the "Southern Problem", the Round Table Conference. Examining the aftermath of this important gathering, Chap. 7 focuses on the legacies of rebel discourses in the latter half of the

1960s after the disintegration of the South's most influential exile political organisation. With the state as the primary actor, Chap. 8 highlights Sudan's robust diplomatic relations through which it outmanoeuvred rebels in the tenures of the most significant prime minister of the 1960s: Mohamed Mahgoub. Building on these reputational gains, Chap. 9 details the strategies that the Sudanese government employed to consolidate international legitimacy in the eyes of African and socialist audiences during the first three years of Ja'afer Nimeiri's premiership, which preceded the end of the first civil war. Highlighting the evolution of the discursive battle, Chap. 10 reveals how the emergent Southern-led rebellion in the 1980s developed a new narrative that reconfigured the discursive terrain of the "Southern Problem" and enabled them to construct a credible image abroad during the second civil war. Finally, following the conclusion chapter, the epilogue demonstrates the interplay of 'narratives-as-told' and 'narratives-as-lived' in the experiences of exiled rebel soldiers.[50]

Notes

1. 'Media briefing statement by ANC National Chairperson, Comrade Baleka Mbete, following the occasion of the Republic of South Sudan's 9th July Independence Day Celebration, July 12, 2011', cited in Baleka Mbete, 'The ANC and the SPLM go back a long way – Baleka Mbete'. Politicsweb. Accessed 9 July 2016. http://www.politicsweb.co.za/party/the-anc-and-the-splm-go-back-a-long-way%2D%2Dbaleka-mb
2. Ibid.
3. Ibid.
4. Ibid.
5. 'January 8th Statements – Statement of the National Executive Committee on the Occasion of the 74th anniversary of the ANC'. 8 January 1986. South African History Online. Accessed 10 July 2016. http://www.sahistory.org.za/archive/january-8th-statements-statement-national-executive-committee-occasion-74th-anniversary-anc-
6. A. Klotz, *Norms in International Relations: The Struggle against Apartheid* (Ithaca, 1995).
7. G. Prunier, 'Rebel Movements and Proxy Warfare: Uganda, Sudan and the Congo (1986–99)', *African Affairs* 103/412 (2004): 359–383; G. Kibreab, 'Eritrean–Sudanese Relations in Historical Perspective', in *Eritrea's External Relations: Understanding Its Regional Role and Foreign Policy*, ed. Richard Reid (London, 2009), 71–97.
8. A. de Waal, 'The Politics of Destabilisation in the Horn, 1989–2001', in *Islamism and its Enemies in the Horn of Africa*, ed. A. de Waal (London:

Hurst Publishers, 2004): 182–230; P. M. Atlas and R. Licklider, 'Conflict among Former Allies after Civil War Settlement: Sudan, Zimbabwe, Chad, and Lebanon', *Journal of Peace Research* 36/1 (1999): 35–54.

9. L. Aalen, 'Ethiopian state support to insurgency in Southern Sudan from 1962 to 1983: local, regional and global connections', *Journal of Eastern African Studies* 8, 4 (2014): 626–641.
10. B. Yihun, 'Ethiopia's Role in South Sudan's March to Independence, 1955–1991', *African Studies Quarterly* 14/1–2 (2013): 35–54.
11. W. Igga, *Southern Sudan: Battles Fought and the Secrecy of Diplomacy* (Kampala, 2008); A. Madut-Arop, *Sudan's Painful Road to Peace: A Full Story of the Founding and Development of SPLM/SPLA* (Charleston, SC, 2006); L. Akol, *SPLM/SPLA: Inside an African Revolution* (Khartoum, 2001).
12. The Arab Cold War represents the conflict between the Pan-Arabist, nationalist republics (under the leadership of Gamal Nasser's Egypt) and the traditionalist monarchies of the Gulf (led by Saudi Arabia). The divergence had little to do with traditional economic orientation, and instead hinged on wider alliances. The Pan-Arabist camp (with the exception of Lebanon) aligned with the Soviet Union, while the monarchies received military aid from the United States. For more on the Arab world's experience of the Cold War, see M. H. Kerr, *The Arab Cold War, 1958–1967: A study of ideology in politics* (London, 1971).
13. The Horn of Africa generally comprises Sudan, Ethiopia, Eritrea, Somalia and Djibouti.
14. K. M. Medani, 'The Horn of Africa in the Shadow of the Cold War: Understanding the partition of Sudan from a regional perspective', *Journal of North African Studies*, 17, 2 (2012): 280.
15. S. Poggo, *The First Sudanese Civil War: Africans, Arabs, and Israelis in the Southern Sudan, 1955–1972* (Basingstoke, 2009).
16. E. O' Ballance, *The Secret War in the Sudan, 1955–1972* (London, 1977). Others include: 'Africa South of the Sahara: Internal Conflict and External Involvement', *Strategic Survey*, 72/1 (1971): 63–63; J. Abadi, 'Israel and Sudan: The Saga of an enigmatic relationship', *Middle Eastern Studies*, 35/1 (1999): 19–41; K. Adar, 'A State under siege: The internationalisation of the Sudanese Civil War', *African Security Review*, 7/1 (1998): 44–53; O. Dak, *Southern Sudan: The Internationalisation of the Problem* (Khartoum: Ministry of Southern Affairs, 1971).
17. A noteworthy exception, Yaniv Voller's work offers a fascinating window into the discourses of the Egyptian Muslim Brotherhood about the Southern Sudanese rebellion. Y. Voller, 'The Egyptian Muslim Brotherhood and the South Sudan Question: Reconsidering moderation', *International Affairs*, 92/3 (2016): 665–682.

18. D. Large, 'The International Presence in Sudan', in *The Sudan Handbook*, ed. J. Ryle, J. Willis, S. Baldo, and J. M. Jok (London, 2011), 64–176; A. Karim et al., *Operation Lifeline Sudan: A Review* (Geneva, 1996); J. Prendergast, *Crisis Response: Humanitarian Band-aids in Sudan and Somalia* (London, 1997); M. F. Massoud, *Law's Fragile State: Colonial, authoritarian, and humanitarian legacies in Sudan* (New York, 2013); L. Clark, *Relief Operation in SPLA Controlled Areas of Southeastern Sudan* (Washington, DC, 1989).
19. See African Rights, *Facing Genocide: The Nuba of Sudan* (London, 1995), which highlights the SPLM's complicity in the abuses of human rights ranging from unruly soldiers, to the killing of prisoners of war and assassinations of chiefs. D. Keen, *The Benefits of Famine: A Political Economy of Famine and Relief in Southwestern Sudan, 1983–1989* (Princeton, 1994); L. A. Fast, 'Mind the Gap: Documenting and explaining violence against aid workers', *European Journal of International Relations*, 16/3 (2010): 365–389.
20. J. Merkk, 'Refugee identities and relief in an African borderland: a study of northern Uganda and southern Sudan', *Refugee Survey Quarterly*, 21/1–2 (2002): 113–146; J. Boddy, 'Managing Tradition: "Superstition" and the making of national identity among Sudanese women refugees' (paper delivered presented at the 26–30 July 1992, ASA IV Decennial Conference, The Uses of Knowledge: Global and local relations, St Catherine's College, University of Oxford, 26–30 July 1992); D. J. Shandy, *Nuer-American Passages: Globalizing Sudanese migration* (Gainesville, 2007); M. Kustenbauder, 'The politicization of religious identity in Sudan, with special reference to oral histories of the Sudanese diaspora in America', in *Religion on the Move! New Dynamics of Religious Expansion in a Globalizing World*, ed. A. Adogame and S. Shankar (Leiden, 2012).
21. This literature goes beyond the wars in the South. For Canada's role in the Darfur peace processes, see A. Bones, 'Canada as an international actor in Sudan', *African Security Review*, 15/1 (2006): 109–114. For more on the Nuba Mountains, see M. Bradbury, 'Sudan: International responses to war in the Nuba Mountains', *Review of African Political Economy* 25/77 (1998): 463–474. For a general view, see D. Petterson, *Inside Sudan: political Islam, conflict, and catastrophe* (Boulder, CO, 1999); H. Johnson, *Waging Peace in Sudan* (Brighton, 2011); S. Wöndu and A. Lesch, *Battle for Peace in Sudan: An Analysis of the Abuja Conferences 1992–1993* (Lanham, 2000); J. Young, *The Fate of Sudan: The Origins and Consequences of a Flawed Peace Process* (London, 2012); M. G. Jumbert, 'The

Internationalization of the Sudanese conflicts: from South Sudan to Darfur: Agenda setting, mobilization and qualifications' (PhD, Science Po, Paris, Institut d'études politiques, 2010); and D. H. Shinn, 'Addis Ababa Agreement: Was it destined to fail and are there lessons for the Current Sudan Peace Process?', *Annales d'Ethiopie*, 20/1 (2004): 239–259.
22. A. Appadurai, *Modernity at Large: Cultural Dimensions of Globalization* (Minneapolis, 1996).
23. J. Bakonyi, 'Ideoscapes in the World Society: Framing Violence in Somalia', *Civil Wars*, 17/2 (2015): 242.
24. Appadurai, *Modernity*, p. 37.
25. J. L. Gaddis, *The Cold War: A New History* (New York, 2005).
26. O. A. Westad, *The Global Cold War: Third World Interventions and the Making of Our Time* (Cambridge, 2005), 396; M. Berger, 'The real Cold War was hot: The global struggle for the Third World', *Intelligence and National Security*, 23/1 (2008): 112–126.
27. V. Shubin, 'Unsung Heroes: The Soviet Military and the Liberation of Southern Africa', *Cold War History*, 7/2 (2007), pp. 251–262. Also see V. Shubin, *ANC: A view from Moscow* (Sunnyside, 2008); V. Shubin and V. G. Shubin, *The hot "Cold War": The USSR in Southern Africa* (London, 2008); P. Gleijeses, 'Cuba and the Independence of Namibia', *Cold War History*, 7/2 (2007): 285–303. Also see P. Gleijeses, *Visions of Freedom: Havana, Washington, Pretoria and the Struggle for Southern Africa, 1976–1991* (Chapel Hill, 2013); P. Gleijeses, *Conflicting Missions: Havana, Washington and Africa, 1969–1976* (Chapel Hill, 2002).
28. L. James and E. Leake (eds), *Decolonization and the Cold War: Negotiating Independence* (London, 2015).
29. V. Prashad, *The Darker Nations: A people's history of the third world* (New York, 2008); B. Anderson, *Imagined Communities: Reflections on the Origin and Spread of Nationalism* (London, 1991).
30. Q. Slobodian (ed), *Comrades of Color: East Germany in the Cold War World* (New York, 2015); C. Lee (ed), *Making a World after Empire: The Bandung Moment and Its Political Afterlives* (Athens, OH, 2010).
31. For an exploration of race as both an intersubjective consensus and as a social construct, see C. W. Mills, '"But What Are You Really?" The Metaphysics of Race', in *Blackness Visible: Essays on Philosophy and Race*, C. W. Mills (Ithaca, NY, 1998), 41–66.
32. See Chap. 4.
33. *The Black Book: Imbalance of Power and Wealth in the Sudan* (Milan, 1964).
34. J. Willis, 'The Southern Problem: Representing Sudan's Southern Provinces to c. 1970', *Journal of African History*, 56 (2015): 282, 300.

35. B. Anderson, *Imagined Communities: Reflections on the Origin and Spread of Nationalism* (London and New York, 1991).
36. A. M. Lesch, 'From Fragmentation to Fragmentation?: Sudan's Foreign Policy', in *The Foreign Policy of Arab States: The Challenge of Globalization*, ed. B. Korany and A. E. H. Dessouki (Cairo, 2010), 397–420; H. Abdelwahab, *Influence: (Supremacy) of religion on Sudan's foreign policy decision-making* (Bloomington, IN, 2010); L. Rubin, 'The Power of a Weak State: Sudan's Relations with Saudi Arabia and Egypt', in *Islam in the Balance: Ideational Threats in Arab Politics* (Stanford, 2014), 62–95.
37. J. Der Derian, *On Diplomacy: A Genealogy of Western Estrangement* (Oxford, 1987), 6.
38. R. Huang, 'Rebel Diplomacy in Civil War', *International Security*, 40, 4 (2016): 124.
39. J. Wang, 'Managing national reputation and international relations in the global era: Public diplomacy revisited', *Public Relations Review*, 32, 2 (2006): 91–96; R. Jervis, *The Logic of Images in International Relations* (Princeton, 1970); J. S. Nye Jr., *Soft Power: The Means to Success in World Politics* (New York, 2004).
40. R. K. Ashley and R. B. J. Walker, 'Introduction: Speaking the Language of Exile: Dissident Thought in International Studies', *International Studies Quarterly*, 34, 3 (1990): 263.
41. Ashley and Walker, 'Introduction', p. 262.
42. C. Weber, *Simulating Sovereignty: Intervention, the State and Symbolic Exchange* (Cambridge, 1995), p. 6.
43. Some scholars insist on conceiving of rhetoric as only serving to either conceal true motive or to persuade. The former is rooted in a suspicion that seeks to ward off Machiavellian-style deception. The latter suggests that rhetoric is only useful for drawing a causal link between words and actions. I am agnostic as to how persuasion operates, but I hold that resonant rhetoric has usefulness beyond concealing motive and causing action. When we concentrate on true motive, we reduce rhetoric to an informational instrument. Instead, here I hold that a combination of interests and ideas, or calculated costs and convictions, shaped how Sudan interacted with African liberation movements and governments during this period.
44. R. R. Krebs and P. T. Jackson, 'Twisting tongues and twisting arms: The power of political rhetoric', *European Journal of International Relations*, 13, 1 (2007): 46.
45. Ibid, p. 36.
46. D. Carr, *Time, Narrative, and History* (Bloomington, IN, 1986), 59.
47. Ibid.

48. J. Peel, 'For Who Hath Despised the Day of Small Things? Missionary Narratives, Historical Anthropology', *Comparative Studies in Society and History*, 37, 3 (1995): 593.
49. A. L. Stoler, *Along the Archival Grain: Epistemic anxieties and colonial common sense* (Princeton, 2009).
50. J. Peel, 'For Who Hath Despised', 606.

CHAPTER 2

The Origins of the "Southern Problem"

As with many popular terms, it is unclear when the phrase the "Southern Problem" first came into usage. It has nevertheless had an enduring presence in and a profound influence on Sudan's political imagination. The phrase came to describe the debates surrounding the place of the Southern region of Sudan in both the colonial and post-independence eras. Would the South be a part of a unitary Sudan, or maintain autonomy in a federal arrangement, or would it secede? This exploration of the emergence of the "Southern Problem" as a political discourse begins with the colonial era and continues into the post-independence period, when it had seismic implications for Sudan's political cohesion.

The slaving systems of the nineteenth century, both during the Turko-Egyptian occupation of Sudan and the Mahdist era, opened the Southern region of Sudan to violent extraction.[1] As such, the entangled histories of the conflict and subjugation involving the Southern region preceded the Anglo-Egyptian Condominium.[2] However, as a political discourse, the "Southern Problem" has colonial provenances. Established in 1898, the Anglo-Egyptian Condominium government centred its activities in the Northern region. However, it did not govern the broader Northern region evenly. For example, it only conquered regions in the far west, such as the Kingdom of Dar Fur in 1916, almost two decades after the founding of the Condominium.[3] Yet despite this variegated approach to ruling the Northern peripheries, largely due to logistical limitations imposed by

S. C. Manoeli, *Sudan's "Southern Problem"*, African Histories and Modernities, https://doi.org/10.1007/978-3-030-28771-9_2

the vast stretches of desert in the region, the Condominium government followed a largely bifurcated administrative approach towards the Northern and Southern provinces of Sudan. The occupation followed the overthrow of the Mahdiyya regime that had previously governed parts of Northern Sudan.[4] Subsequently, the colonial administration used an elaborate set of policies to co-opt its recently conquered subjects, prevent the re-emergence of the Mahdiyya and entrench its rule.[5] These policies included enlisting certain inhabitants of the region to serve in the police and military, as well as providing educational and employment opportunities for them.[6] In light of Egypt's shared history, religion and language with Northern Sudan, the Condominium government concentrated its activities there.[7] In contrast, the South's weak ties to the North and Egypt meant that the government had less of an incentive to establish a consequential presence and to invest in the region. The government did not in fact establish an administrative system in the South until the late 1920s, when it managed to 'pacify' resistant polities in that region.[8]

Beyond the political dynamics that led to this dual approach, the British-led Anglo-Egyptian Condominium dealt with the two regions differently because it conceived of their people as discrete. Reflecting on the Condominium's governing practices throughout its occupation of Sudan, the Governor General of Sudan in 1945, Sir Hubert Huddleston, stated that the government had aimed

> to act upon the fact that the peoples of the Southern Sudan are distinctively African and Negroid, and that our obvious duty to them is therefore to push ahead as fast as we can with their economic and educational development on African and Negroid lines, and not upon the Middle Eastern and Arab lines of progress which are suitable for the Northern Sudan.[9]

The colonial governing philosophy of this period was unequivocally racialist. The colonial government created categories based on each region's 'racial stock' and institutionalised these identities based on a racial hierarchy that deemed those categorised as African as different and inferior to those categorised as Arab. The colonial census powerfully reinforced a binary of racial identities, composed of the Arabs of the North and Africans from different regions—the South, the West (Darfur) and the East (Beja territory and Nuba Mountains), the far North (Nubia), as well as the Fulani around the North.[10] Despite the wide dispersion of Sudan's various ethnic groups, due to the preponderance of Islam and Arabic in the North, a colonial discourse emerged that collapsed religion and culture into race, and then conflated it with geography. Thus, the Condominium increasingly acknowledged two broad categories: the "Negroid" or "Africans" of the South who were generally categorised as animist or Christian and the Muslim "Arabs" of the North. Adding to the reductionism inherent in racial categorisation, the racialisation of territories further restricted the colonial government's political imagination of heterogeneity in Sudan.[11]

The colonial government's zeal for totalising categories encouraged the conceptualisation of separate regional, racial and religious identities, and thereby elided overlapping or ambiguous identities and spaces. The British bureaucracy in Sudan, as in other parts of the world, functioned through a modernist logic of classifications. Benedict Anderson and Charles Hirschman have argued compellingly regarding the ways in which colonial census categories in particular not only created ethno-racial classifications, but also systematically quantified them.[12] In so doing, these categories gained political currency and salience.[13]

This system of colonial classification created political identities that had a tenuous footing in Sudan's various social organisations that existed prior to the Condominium era. They were nonetheless powerful. These emerging political identities were further entrenched by government policies. From the 1920s, the government legally made the Southern region a Closed District, monitoring the movement of non-native people in the South to diminish Northern Arab influence.[14] In 1930, the government introduced the Southern Policy, which the then Civil Secretary of Sudan described as a 'comprehensive plan to build up a series of self-contained racial and tribal units with structure and organisation based ...upon indigenous customs, traditional usage and beliefs'.[15] The Policy 'mobilised the social resources (e.g. religion, language) to construct separately bounded social identities'.[16] It has also been described as a 'tidying up' of practices that were already in use.[17]

These policies gave the South an ambiguous political status. Reflecting on this uncertainty, the then Governor of the Southern Province of Equatoria, B. V. Marwood, imagined the government's role in shaping the South's political trajectory as follows:

> It is only by economic and educational development that these people can be equipped to stand up for themselves in the future, whether their future lot be eventually cast with the Northern Sudan or with East Africa (or partly with each).[18]

Up until the mid-1940s, the Condominium government remained undecided of the prospect of adjoining the South to British East Africa.[19] Furthermore, despite the cordoning off of the South, there was little to no 'economic and educational development' to speak of due to the lack of government investment. As late as 1945, the Condominium government noted that '[t]he problem of the South is the biggest human difficulty in the country. ... On all grounds, the South ought not be united to the Arab North. In human terms it belongs to Africa south of it'.[20]

The imperatives of 'colonialism on the cheap' contributed to the rise of the segmented policies that produced the possibility of the South's tentative political future as a separate entity.[21] In Sudan, as in other British colonies, the administration relied on indirect rule, called 'native administration', as a means of governing the countryside. Institutionalising (and, as others have argued, partially inventing) tradition complemented the indispensable role of co-opted chiefs and sheikhs in the expansion of the colonial state.[22] The drive to "preserve" indigenous cultures also helped to frame and entrench ethno-racial compartmentalisation as a social good. Christian missionary efforts to convert those living in non-Muslim areas of Sudan further fuelled "preservationist" policies as they aimed at 'building up an indigenous [tribal] culture under Christian influence', preferably without interference from competing Islamic proselytisers.[23] These interests, among others, converged to buttress the binary system.

At the end of World War II, the British post-imperial strategy mandated the end of the social experiment of administrative segmentation. The Condominium government framed its end as a teleological imperative that would benefit the South. British officials rationalised the decision to unite the regions as follows:

> Since 1945 there have been developments both economically and educationally in the south, and it has begun to be clear I think, that the southern Sudan, by its history and by the accidents of geography, river transport and so on, must turn more to the north rather than to Uganda or to Congo.[24]

In reality, pragmatic concerns such as preserving Britain's access to the Suez Canal impelled the British administration to maintain amicable relations with Egypt.[25] In order to do so, Britain abandoned the plans to disaffiliate Southern Sudan from the North as Egypt had vested interests in retaining access to as much of the Nile Valley as possible. Thus, in 1946 the government repealed the Southern Policy. With increasing calls for self-determination among the Northern elite, the Condominium prepared an exit strategy that included rapidly pursuing the political integration of the two regions.

Robert Collins maintains that despite the 'dogmatic' design of the Southern Policy, the Condominium Government was unable to effectively implement it. Instead, he argues that

> [t]he real importance of the Southern Policy was not so much what it was as what it became to the Sudanese nationalists years after its promulgation. At that point the Southern Policy ceased to be a solution and became a symbol.[26]

In the post-independence era, the Southern Policy came to represent the colonial government's divisiveness. Despite this awareness, the enduring colonial legacy of racialised political categories is far less often acknowledged. The Condominium's racial thinking not only made its policy approaches justifiable, but it also presented the approach as if it were beneficial for each region's people. These essentialising ways of framing Sudan as dualistic and its regions as discrete made it possible to conceive of them as potentially politically incompatible. What later became the "Southern Problem" owes its ancestry to the Condominium government's discursive practices, which include its classifications and dualistic governing policies.

The drive to unify Sudan thrust the South into national politics, and political resentment arose in the South in the aftermath of the Condominium's newfound integration policy. Following the annulment of the Southern Policy, a series of political events, including the controversial Juba Conference of 1947, secured the participation of Southerners in the National Legislative Council in preparation for the post-independence parliament.[27] By 1952, the Condominium parliament had passed the self-government statute, and Egypt had relinquished its claim to sovereignty over Sudan. Elections were held for Sudan's first self-governing parliament in 1953.[28] After Britain extricated itself from the colony in January 1956, Sudan gained full independence.

The Southern political experience of the nine years in between the Condominium's decision to unite the country and its independence was characterised by suspicion.[29] The exclusion of Southern politicians from the 1953 independence negotiation and the signing of the Anglo-Egyptian Agreement undermined efforts to unite the representatives of the two regions.[30] Despite the range of diverse political perspectives among Southern politicians, Southern self-rule in a federal system was 'the major policy issue' for Southern legislators and parliamentarians in the 1950s.[31] By 1951, politicians from the region mobilised and established the Southern Party with the explicit aim of protecting Southern interests in the post-independence period. Initially a political movement, the Southern Party only sought official recognition in August 1953, and changed its name to the Liberal Party in December of the same year, in a bid to widen its appeal to the North.[32] By the mid-1950s, the Liberal Party sought to build a coalition of non-Arab minorities in the rest of Sudan.[33] The Liberal Party, partly due to its failure to attract sizable support from Northern minorities and due to the rise of a competing Federalist Party (founded by a former member of the Liberal Party in 1956) from the South that took a firmly Southern line, did not maintain its broad church politics, but reverted to a Southern-oriented politics in order to secure support from constituencies in the South.[34] Southern political parties, unable to hold a united front, 'viewed themselves more as competitors than as allies in a common cause vis-à-vis the north'.[35]

Other experiences of marginalisation from political processes compounded the grievances of Southern politicians of various political persuasions. For instance, the "indigenisation" of government posts, dubbed Sudanisation, led to Northerners—more specifically, the riverain elite who had access to formal education—occupying the overwhelming majority of government posts, including those in the South. Consequently, in October 1954, a group of Southern politicians and chiefs hosted another conference in Juba in which they agreed to reserve the right to pursue self-determination if their Northern counterparts failed to endorse the establishment of a federal political system.[36] Moreover, the conference called for 'all Southern MPs, regardless of party, to form one Southern Bloc' in order to champion a Southern federal agenda.[37] A year later, in August 1955, only months before Sudan's Independence Day, a Southern division of the army mutinied. The subsequent clashes, concentrated in a two-week period, led to over 300 deaths.[38] The violence, occurring mainly in urban settings, added to the sense of insecurity about the South's political position in a post-colonial state.[39] Fuelling a sense of embattlement, the Sudanese government subsequently imprisoned about 1000 mutineers and executed 121 Southerners.[40]

With escalating state repression in the South, during this period, the Northern-dominated parliament repeatedly stalled and opposed the requests various Southern members of parliament made for regional autonomy.[41] The new administration of General Ibrahim Abboud, ushered in by a bloodless military coup of 1958, ended the central government's ambivalence regarding the status of the South: under his leadership, Sudan would not adopt a federal system. Abboud dissolved the parliament, instituted a ban on all political parties, and suppressed political agitation for Southern rights.[42]

The military junta's ruthless targeting of Southern intellectuals radicalised many of the region's leaders and they increasingly took a secessionist stance. In this hostile political climate, exile became the safest space for effective political mobilisation for Southern elites who could no longer participate in representational or electoral politics inside Sudan.[43] By the end of 1960, the South's bourgeoning cadre of intellectuals and ex-parliamentarians began to flee the country to avoid imprisonment and government intimidation. These exiles were largely scattered across Uganda, Congo, the Central African Republic, Kenya and Ethiopia. In 1961, a small group in Uganda founded the Sudan Christian Association, 'a diplomatically chosen title designed to enlist the support of Christian and other benevolent organizations on an international basis'—signalling their awareness of international audiences.[44] It was, however, later overshadowed by more explicitly political organisations.

Three political rebels in particular, Joseph Oduho, Marko Rume and William Deng, formed the exile liberation movement called the Sudan African Closed Districts National Union (SACDNU) in 1962, and they established the Union's headquarters in Leopoldville (now Kinshasa). Father Saturnino Lohure served as the movement's patron and advisor. SACDNU President Joseph Oduho had served as an MP for a Southern district and as the Assistant Secretary-General of the Liberal Party.[45] Also a former member of the Liberal Party and an elected official in the House of Representatives, Vice-President Marko Rume served as the 'chief propagandist for the liberation movement'.[46] Secretary-General William Deng had served in various government posts, including Assistant District Commissioner and Magistrate of the 2nd Class.[47] Father Saturnino Lohure was widely considered the most influential Southern leader in exile throughout the early to mid-1960s.[48] He had access to clandestine Catholic financial resources, which he used to smuggle arms into Southern Sudan for the armed movement.[49] These leaders changed the political organisation's name to the Sudan African National Union (SANU), and moved the head office to Kampala, while continuing operations in Leopoldville as well as Dar es Salaam. By emulating two key independence movements in East Africa, namely the Kenya African National Union

(KANU) and the Tanganyika African National Union (TANU), SANU aimed to associate itself with respected political parties in the region.

Throughout the 1960s, SANU functioned as the leading mouthpiece for the Southern Sudanese cause abroad. Its main objective was to popularise the cause and to mobilise moral, political and financial support from African governments and international institutions for the Southern rebellion against the Sudanese government.[50] Between 1961 and 1962, the exiles began touring African cities in pursuit of political sympathy.[51] In his capacity as Secretary-General, William Deng travelled further afield to 'Rome, Geneva, Brussels, London, Bonn, New York, Washington, Paris and Bangui to lobby for support'.[52] During these trips, and subsequent ones, the SANU representatives and their allies distributed the movement's publications and sought media interviews. Meanwhile, in 1963, a group of ex-soldiers inside Southern Sudan formed an armed resistance organisation, Anya-Nya.[53] By 1963 the violence that escalated from the 1955 mutiny had developed into full-scale civil war. With the South as the theatre of war, a refugee crisis ensued. The emergency constituted yet another grievance against the Sudanese government. SANU aimed to represent the tens of thousands of Southern Sudanese refugees who poured into Sudan's neighbouring countries.[54] These events brought international attention to Sudan, thus giving the exile movement an opportunity to capitalise on the attention and offer the world an interpretation of the conflict in Southern Sudan.

Conclusion

The "Southern Problem" stemmed from both colonial racialism (i.e. the belief that race is a natural, biological system of categorising human beings) and racism (i.e. that which turns a racialist spectrum into a hierarchy).[55] Although both represent unsurprising modus operandi of colonial governments, British racial thought and practice in Sudan distinctively entertained geopolitical separation, which had implications for both regions' international relations. Moreover, the discourse of the Southern difference and inferiority, as well as the material realities it enabled, led to the emergence of a powerful language of self-identification and dispossession. Both proved useful fuel for Southern political organising. The discourse of the "Southern Problem" outlived the Condominium era, and posed a threat to the newly independent Sudan. The political, economic and social neglect that the discourse normalised also continued into the independence period, further entrenching the "Problem" and enabling it to be framed as racial animosity.

Notes

1. For more on the ways the nineteenth-century institution of military slavery in Sudan contributed to Sudan's social stratification prior to the Condominium period, see A. A. Sikainga, 'Military slavery and the emergence of a southern Sudanese diaspora in the northern Sudan, 1884–1954', in J. Spaulding and S. Beswick (eds), *White Nile, Black Blood; war, leadership and ethnicity from Kampala to Khartoum* (Asmara, 2000) and D. H. Johnson, 'Sudanese Military Slavery from the Eighteenth to the Twentieth Century', in L. J. Archer (ed), *Slavery and Other Forms of Unfree Labour* (London, 1988), pp. 142–156; J. R Willis (ed), *Slaves and Slavery in Muslim Africa*, 2 vols (London, 1985).
2. Being a Condominium, the Anglo-Egyptian Sudan was not officially a colony, as the British Consul General in Cairo managed it. The Consul served under the British Foreign Office (FO), and thus the FO rather than the then Colonial Office administered Sudan. Nonetheless, for all intents and purposes, it was a colony.
3. For more on Darfur's distinctive colonial experience within the Condominium, see C. Vaughan, *Darfur: Colonial Violence, Sultanic Legacies and Local Politics, 1916–1956* (Oxford, 2015). For more on other groups in the Northern periphery, see M. C. Jedrej, 'The Southern Funj of the Sudan under Anglo-Egyptian Rule, 1900–1933, *Critical African Studies*, 8/1 (2016): 8–22.
4. P. M. Holt, *The Mahdist State in the Sudan: 1881–1898: A study of its origins, development and overthrow* (Oxford, 1970); D. H. Johnson, 'Prophecy and Mahdism in the Upper Nile: An examination of local experiences of the Mahdiyya in the southern Sudan', *British Journal of Middle Eastern Studies*, 20/1 (1993): 42–56.
5. M. W. Daly, *Imperial Sudan: the Anglo-Egyptian Condominium, 1934–1956* (Cambridge, 1991).
6. It is important to note that the establishment of the Condominium government in the Northern provinces of Sudan did not represent the imposition of uniform modes of governance. Instead, innovative forms of local authority and cultures of governance emerged that were unprecedented and unintended. For example: J. Willis, 'Hukm: The Creolization of Authority in Condominium Sudan', *Journal of African History*, 46 (2005): 29–50.

7. For insights into the complex relations that Sudan experienced with Great Britain and Egypt, see Eve M. Troutt Powell, *A different shade of colonialism: Egypt, Great Britain, and the Mastery of the Sudan* (Berkeley, CA, 2003).
8. D. H. Johnson, *Empire and the Nuer: Sources on the pacification of the Southern Sudan, 1898–1930* (Oxford, 2016); D. H. Johnson, *The Root Causes of Sudan's Civil Wars: Peace or Truce* (Kampala, 2011), pp. 9–19; Ø. Rolandsen and M. W. Daly, *A History of South Sudan: From slavery to independence* (Cambridge, 2016), 10–31.
9. Cited in M. O. Beshir, *The Southern Sudan: background to conflict* (London, 1968), 122.
10. Khartoum, 'Morning News', 18 January 1958. *1956 Census*, published 18 January 1958. The group referred to as the Fulani or Fellata originates from West Africa but settled in various parts of Northern Sudan after completing Hajj in Mecca.
11. The Condominium forcefully imposed these classifications and what it deemed to be the fitting spatial parameters of the groups in question. Heather Sharkey's work shows that the Condominium government viewed 'detribalised' Southerners in urban spaces as a "destabilising" threat to the tribal groupings it envisioned. H. Sharkey, 'African Colonial States', in J. Parker and R. Reid (eds), *Oxford Handbook of Modern African History* (Oxford, 2013), p 156. To further illustrate this point, in addition to charging the 'negroid but detribalised' as vagabonds, a Condominium governor of the Southern Rumbek district once wrote that 'the majority of the Dinka, fast becoming "townees", will be sent outside to live their lives in their proper environment'. C. Leonardi, *Dealing with Government in South Sudan: Histories of chiefship, community and state* (Woodbridge, 2013), p. 82. E. T. Powell, *A Different Shade of Colonialism*, p. 209.
12. C. Hirschman, 'The Meaning and Measurement of Ethnicity in Malaysia: An Analysis of Census Classifications', *Journal of Asian Studies*, 46/3 (1987): 552–582. B. Anderson, 'Census, Map, Museum', in *Imagined Communities*, pp. 163–186.
13. For an example of a post-independence African country similarly collapsing complicated social realities into quantifiable categories for state purposes, see D. R. Peterson and E. C. Taylor, 'Rethinking the state in Idi Amin's Uganda: The politics of exhortation', *Journal of Eastern African Studies*, 7/1 (2013), pp. 58–82.
14. The Closed Districts Ordinance was applied to most of the Southern provinces, Southern Kordofan, Darfur, and the Blue Nile region. It also conversely abetted the rise of the economic and political hegemony of riverian Northerners in the country. See A. A. Gallab, *The First Islamic Republic: Development and Disintegration of Islamism in the Sudan* (Burlington, VT, 2008), p. 31.

15. Beshir, *The Southern Sudan*, 115–118.
16. A. Abdelhay, B. Makoni, and S. Makoni, 'The Politics of Linguistic Indigenousness in the Sudan', in J. Spaudling, S. Beswick, C. Fluehr-Lobban, R. A. Lobban, Jr. (eds), *Sudan's Wars and Peace Agreements* (Newcastle upon Tyne, 2010), p. 28.
17. R. O. Collins and F. Deng, *Civil Wars and Revolution in the Sudan: essays on the Sudan, Southern Sudan and Darfur, 1962–2004* (Hollywood, 2005), p. 280.
18. 'Khartoum Secret Despatch No. 89', 4 August 1945, quoted in B. V. Marwood, Governor, Equatoria, to M. B. Stubbs, District Commissioner, Western District, 23 December 1946, Bahr al-Ghazalm II 112, SGA. Cited in Collins, *Civil Wars*, p. 197.
19. R. O. Collin, *The Southern Sudan 1883–1898* (New Haven, 1962), pp. 11–12.
20. 'The Sudan: the road ahead', *Fabian Colonial Bureau* (London, 1945), p. 25.
21. Martin L. Kilson, *Political Change in a West African State: A Study of the Modernization Process in Sierra Leone* (Cambridge, MA, 1966), p. 24.
22. For an example of the complex histories of the pliable institution of chiefship in Sudan, see Leonardi, *Dealing with Government in South Sudan*. Leonardi holds in tension the creative roles that colonial powers and locals in the South played in shaping chiefship. She offers an agency-driven narrative that examines both chiefship and statehood as malleable ideas as well as enduring institutions.
23. Cited in A. K. Abdelhay, 'The politics of writing tribal identities in the Sudan: the case of the colonial Nuba Policy', *Journal of Multilingual and Multicultural Development*, 31/2 (2010), p. 205.
24. B. V. Marwood, Governor of Equatoria, cited in J. Merkx, 'Refugee Identities and Relief in an African Borderland: A Study of Northern Uganda and Southern Sudan', *Refugee Survey Quarterly*, 21/1–2 (2002), p. 121.
25. Great Britain Foreign Office, *Anglo-Egyptian Conversations on the Defence of the Suez Canal and on the Sudan, December 1950–November 1951* (London, 1951).
26. Collins, *Civil Wars*, p. 280.
27. The various narrativisations of the Juba Conference of 1947 are discussed in greater detail in Chap. 6.
28. P. M. Holt and M. W. Daly, *The History of the Sudan: From the Coming of Islam to the Present Day* (London, 1979), pp. 159–161. P. Woodward, *Sudan, 1898–1989: The Unstable State* (London, 1990), pp. 63–95. R. Collins and F. Deng (eds), *The British in the Sudan, 1898–1956* (London, 1984), pp. 216–242.

29. B. M. Said, *The Sudan: Crossroads of Africa* (London, 1965), pp. 72–84. M. O. Beshir, *The Southern Sudan: Background to Conflict* (London, 1968), pp. 61–73. O. Albino, *The Sudan: A Southern Viewpoint* (London, 1970), pp. 28–35.
30. Collins, *Shadows in the Grass*, p. 442.
31. It is important to note that two Southern legislators, having received bribes from a Northern-based political party, opposed a motion for the creation of a Ministry of Southern Affairs, during a Legislative Assembly session. The incident signals the lack of solidarity among Southern politicians, even though they generally favoured a federal arrangement. J. Sulton, 'Regional Autonomy in the Southern Sudan: A Study in Conflict Regulation (PhD thesis, the John Hopkins University, 1980), pp. 115, 118.
32. K. Okeny, 'The rejection of federalism and emergence of Southern Sudanese nationalism, 1950–1972 (PhD thesis, University of California, Santa Barbara, 1992), pp. 105, 107.
33. Woodward, *Condominium and Sudanese Nationalism*, p. 150. This was not the first non-Arab, minority coalition in Sudanese political history. Nuba Member of Parliament Phillip Abbas recalls that a burgeoning political alliance that took the moniker *Kutla as-Suda*, an Arabic name meaning the Black Bloc, consisting of the Fur, the Nuba, the Fulatta and Southerners who had relocated to the North, emerged in the 1940s. The Condominium government did not issue the group a licence to function as an official political party; as a result of the suppression these constituencies were 'directed through the Arab parties'. *Kutla as-Suda* was allowed to operate strictly as a social organisation. Politically, the group reinvented itself as the Socialist Republican Party. Abbas, "Growth of Black Political Consciousness in Northern Sudan", *Africa Today*, 20:3 (1973), pp. 32–33. Sulton, 'Regional Autonomy in the Southern Sudan', p. 115.
34. Willis, 'The Southern Problem', p. 289; Okeny, 'The rejection', p. 108.
35. Sulton, 'Regional Autonomy in the Southern Sudan', p. 121.
36. Minutes of the Juba Conference, 18–21 October 1954, cited in Johnson, *The Root Causes*, p. 27. D. H. Johnson, 'The politics of remember and forgetting: the Juba Conferences of 1947 and 1954' (unpublished paper, delivered 9 February 2016, Lecture, University of Durham). Rolandsen and Leonardi, 'Discourses of Violence', p. 614. Okeny, 'The rejection', pp. 135–136.
37. C. Eprile, W*ar and Peace in the Sudan, 1955–1972* (London, 1974), p. 39.
38. Ø. Rolandsen, 'A False Start: Between War and Peace in the Southern Sudan', *Journal of African History*, 52 (2011), p. 110.
39. R. Collins, *The Southern Sudan: In Historical Perspective* (Tel Aviv, 1975), pp. 67–68. Eprile, *War and Peace*, pp. 39–48. The violence was based, in

part, on localised grievances including the unfair dismissal of 300 workers from the South at the Northern-run factory in Nzara a month earlier, and the subsequent police brutality when the workers protested.

40. Rolandsen and Leonardi, 'Discourses of Violence', p. 609.
41. For more on later calls for federalism made by Sudan's other non-Southern minorities, see Y. Ajawin and A. de Waal (eds), *When Peace Comes: Civil Society and Development in Sudan* (Asmara, 2002), pp. 221–239.
42. M. O. Beshir, *Revolution and Nationalism in the Sudan* (London, 1974), pp. 202–227.
43. This did not, however, signal the death of Southern political life. As Cherry Leonardi has shown, although it constituted the periphery of political power in Sudan, the South has never been marginal to processes of state formation, in no small part due to the institution of chiefship. Similarly, Nicola Kindersley has shown, in the absence of legal party politics, that ordinary Southern migrants in Khartoum in this period expressed themselves politically through associations and networks. Leonardi, *Dealing with Government*. Kindersley, 'The Fifth Column?'
44. Sulton, 'Regional Autonomy in the Southern Sudan', p. 128.
45. Sudan African National Union (SANU), 'SANU Personalities', *Voice of Southern Sudan*, 1/2 (1963), p. 21.
46. A. K. Kuyok, *South Sudan: The Notable Firsts* (Bloomington, IN, 2015), pp. 369–370.
47. SANU, 'SANU Personalities', p. 22.
48. Sudan Archive, Durham (SAD) 803/5/19-35, J. Howell, 'Political Leaders in the Southern Sudan' (unpublished paper, delivered 1972, 8th Annual Conference of the Social Science Council of East African Universities, University College, Nairobi).
49. 'S. Sudan: Who controls what?', *Africa Confidential*, no. 12 (17 June 1966), p. 4; S. McCall, 'The Rise of a Provisional Government in Southern Sudan' (unpublished paper, delivered December 1969, University Social Sciences Council Conference, University of East Africa, University College, Nairobi), Sudan Archive Durham (henceforth SAD) 803/4/26-34.
50. Rolandsen, 'The Making of Anya-Nya', p. 216.
51. Ibid. Also, A. M. Yangu, *The Nile Turns Red: Azanians Choose Freedom Against Arab Bondage* (New York, 1966), p. 101.
52. Ibid.
53. Chapter 7 includes a discussion on the relationship between the exile political movement and the armed movement.
54. By 1964, around 50,000 Southern Sudanese refugees had relocated to Uganda, and by the end of the war, Uganda hosted 200,000. Other countries in the region hosted similar numbers. Y. Wawa, *Refugee Aid and*

Development: A Case of Sudanese Refugees in West Nile, Uganda (Kampala, 2008), p. 24; A. Ylönen and J. Záhořík (eds), *The Horn of Africa since the 1960s: Local and International Politics Intertwined* (Abingdon and New York, 2017), pp. 189–230.

55. Kwame Anthony Appiah, "Racisms", in *Anatomy of Racism*, ed. David Theo Goldberg (Minneapolis, 1990), pp. 4–5. George M. Fredrickson, Racism: A Short History, Princeton: Princeton University Press, 2002, pp. 153–154.

CHAPTER 3

'Apartheid' Sudan: Rebel Narratives of the "Southern Problem"

With war erupting in 1955 and repression mounting in the latter half of that decade, an exile movement of politicians from the South emerged. During the early 1960s, they mounted a discursive rebellion against the Sudanese government. Having exhausted the routes to recourse domestically, the rebels pursued international legitimacy for the Southern cause. The beginning of the 1960s consequently represents a critical and complex period for the discursive construction of the Southern cause. Therefore, it would be insufficient to reflect on Sudan's first civil war merely militarily or through the prism of high politics since separate nationhood became the pivotal aim of the rebels. After all, nationalism revolves around affective ideas of belonging and association. This war was, at its core, the outworking of an intellectual disputation—an argument between rebels and the state—about the meaning of the differences between groups within Sudan.

By focusing on this rivalry of ideas, specifically the rebellion mounted by the rebel politicians in exile, this chapter holds that an intellectual history approach offers a vital reading of this separatist war. This method is also necessary as race constituted a dominant mode of thought in this discursive conflict. As Robert Miles and Malcolm Brown have shown, race is principally about the 'production and reproduction of meanings' about categories of human beings.[1] Since identity paradigms such as race and nationality are not analytically distinct, but overlap and intersect in mutually reinforcing ways,[2] competing claims to nationhood made through

S. C. Manoeli, *Sudan's "Southern Problem"*, African Histories and Modernities, https://doi.org/10.1007/978-3-030-28771-9_3

arguments based on racial thought doubly lend themselves to discursive analysis. Consequently, here, I chart the development of the "Southern Problem" in the literature of the leading Southern Sudanese exile movement of the early 1960s, the Sudan African National Union (SANU). In its pursuit of legitimacy abroad, SANU relied on internationally resonant lexicons and logics that rendered the "Southern Problem" legible to various audiences abroad. Drawing from literary artefacts including a booklet, newspapers and open letters that SANU politicians produced and disseminated abroad, this exploration contributes to our understanding of competing Sudanese nationalisms, and to the broader literature that problematises the constructed North and South binary.[3] It also contributes to Sudan's intellectual and international histories, particularly regarding the literary construction and evolution of the idea of the "Southern Problem".

A Critical Comparison: Apartheid and Sudan

An internationally circulated publication authored by SANU's President and Secretary-General, Joseph Oduho and William Deng, became the foundational text for the Southern Sudanese discourses of legitimacy formulated in exile. Launched on 13 June 1963, *The Problem of Southern Sudan* was published by the British educational charity, the Institute of Race Relations (IRR) through Oxford University Press. In its other propaganda platforms, SANU described the book as 'a statement by the Southern Sudanese exiles'.[4] In this way, without explaining what qualified them, these SANU representatives claimed the authority of being the primary spokespersons of the South.

The policy-oriented IRR offered SANU access to an international discursive space. It circulated the movement's narrative through its established channels of distribution across the UK as well as to a wide international audience of English speakers. In addition to the IRR's networks, SANU mailed the book along with its letters to various heads of states and governments, as well as to the leaders of international organisations such as the United Nations (UN), the Organisation of African Unity (OAU) and the African Liberation Committee (ALC).

Having published and disseminated reports on race relations concerning Apartheid South Africa, anti-Tamil pogroms in Ceylon and Angola's independence war, the IRR functioned as a site of knowledge production about race and political crises.[5] Mere association with the IRR emphasised the racial dimension of the Sudanese conflict. In the preface, the IRR's director, Philip Mason, compared the book to the Institute's 1960 publication *South Africa: Two Views of Separate Development*, by S. Pienaar and A. Sampson, which captured two opposing perspectives on the policy of Apartheid. Mason explained that the Institute had aimed to provide a platform for representatives of the North and the South to debate the merits of unity and self-rule, respectively, as potential solutions to the conflict in Southern Sudan. However, the Institute was unable to find Northern Sudanese politicians who were willing to participate in the book project, and as a result, the book only documented the views of Southerners.[6] The brief preface thus sought to give the book an air of scholarly objectivity to avoid it being labelled political propaganda.

Apartheid South Africa serves as more than a structural template for the book. In the introductory chapter, the historian of Southern Sudan and a former lecturer of history at the University of Khartoum, Richard Gray, explicitly compared the discrimination in Sudan to that of the white settler states of southern Africa.[7] Gray suggested that although Sudan's racial discrimination stemmed from only slight physical differences, they still produced considerable enmity. He averred that

> Often these two groups are thought of as racially distinct, though in fact the physical differences between them are far slighter than, for example, those between Afrikaner and Xhosa.[8]

Gray posited that

> the Southerner feels himself to be an African, while the ruling Northerner is proud of his Arab connexions. This is why Southerners see the problem today as a fight for racial equality: a struggle no less tense and difficult than that in which black and white are engaged in the southern half of the continent.[9]

Gray also adopted Apartheid South Africa's lexicon to describe Southern Sudan's experience of inequality. For example, he described the Condominium's Southern Policy as 'separate development'.[10] In addition to providing SANU a legitimate international platform from which to publicise its cause, validating this comparison to white settler racism was perhaps the IRR's most significant contribution to the discursive development of the "Southern Problem".

In an attempt to prove that the Southern Policy, in particular, was more than a relic from the Condominium period, Oduho and Deng made a case that it de facto continued in Sudan's independence period. In the same publication, the exile leaders portrayed the asymmetrical relations in explicit terms:

> Open segregation marks the relationship between Northern and Southern Sudanese. The reason for this segregation seems to arise from the fact that the Northerner considers himself as belonging to a privileged class, while the Southerner occupies the lower stratum of Sudanese society. In the South, Northerners have separate clubs[11]

The description of a caste-like system suggested that the two regions' identities were ordered on a rigid hierarchy producing privilege and subjugation, respectively.

Like Mason and Gray, Oduho and Deng took the differences between the people of the two regions for granted as a normative structure of the society. A table dividing the population of Sudan into two racial categories introduced their section of the book. According to the table, which was drawn from the 1956 national census, 'Arabs' constituted 39 per cent of the national population, followed by 'those of African stock' who constituted 58 per cent. At 30 per cent on a national level, 'Southerners' were listed as the second largest population group in Sudan.[12] The quantification of these ethno-racial and territorial identities was aimed at demonstrating the considerable size of the population SANU claimed to represent, and therefore to imbue significance to its cause. By reproducing the statistics that used colonial categories, the leaders of the Southern cause reinforced colonial discursive practices. SANU reified a dichotomised understanding of race by not challenging the colonial framing of Sudan's identities. Yet, at the same time, it implicitly challenged the colonial assumptions regarding the construction of Sudan's racial hierarchy. Specifically, SANU did not accept that 'Africans' were innately inferior to 'Arabs'.

As a point of contrast, it is important to note that the Sudanese government from the moment of Independence did not include the racial breakdown of the census in the almanacs it produced for diplomatic purposes.[13] SANU had deliberately re-racialised the census data for international audiences when the government had abandoned the colonial practice. Whether the government omitted this information from public view to conceal the composition of its population for fear of reopening questions of Southern separatism, or to render the racial categories insignificant, remains unclear. Details about the ways the Sudanese government purposefully framed group differences in its diplomatic propaganda are explored in greater detail in Chap. 4.

To further emphasise the existence of severe racial discrimination, Oduho and Deng tangentially mentioned the ways in which Northern-based Africans experienced marginalisation by stating that they were rendered as mere 'cotton-pickers'.[14] The highly developed cotton industry has been described as 'one of the defining institutions of colonialism in Sudan'.[15] Ethnic minorities and domestic migrant workers (typically from the Darfur region and the Nuba Mountains) often provided labour to the cotton plantations in the North.[16] In the minds of Western readers, the characterisation of Africans as 'cotton-pickers' was reminiscent of the role of Black slaves in the American south. It is plausible that the authors expected readers to decode the reference in these terms.[17]

Besides such intimations, Oduho and Deng also explicitly constructed the "Southern Problem" in highly racial terms that fit Sudan into a larger post-colonial discursive landscape.

> Here is a clear case of Africans being oppressed for no other reason than because their skin pigment differs, slightly in some cases, and because they belong to a different race, from that of the people who at present are wielding power.[18]

This strategy made the Southern Sudanese cause recognisable and understandable to international audiences. The authors listed a variety of injustices that could have been framed in non-racial ways, such as human rights violations, which included the government's scorched earth campaigns, violent seizures of livestock, as well as 'intimidation, burning, prison, public executions and arbitrary arrests', or as religious persecution in light of, inter alia, mass forced conversions of non-Muslim Southerners, intimidation of Christian clergy and the destruction of Christian places of worship.[19] In the book, however, the authors fit these incidents into the discourse of racial oppression. In the political context of decolonisation and Third World solidarity, focusing on the racial fault line was an effective means of arousing sympathy, owing to a growing Pan-African as well as global antipathy towards racism evinced by the international solidarity mobilised against Africa's intransigent white settler states.[20]

In light of the international outrage that the Sharpeville Massacre of March 1960 sparked, and how it strengthened the international anti-Apartheid movement and catalysed international condemnation of the Apartheid regime, SANU sought to obtain similar currency abroad.[21] Increasingly seen as the prototype for racial discrimination in this historical moment, South Africa (and to some extent the American South in the Antebellum Period) served as an expedient shorthand that could be used to brand the Sudanese state as unjust and illegitimate.

Next, we turn to an exploration of how SANU developed these and other analogies in an attempt to evoke sympathy abroad, targeting African leaders as well as the UN, through its publications and letters.

The Anatomy of the "Southern Problem": SANU Discursive Strategies

The Case for Southern Sudanese Exceptionalism

In light of the OAU's commitment to territorial integrity and to the principle of non-interference in the affairs of member countries, SANU had to construct an argument that would convince OAU member states to grant the population in Southern Sudan self-determination. SANU's texts therefore framed Southern Sudan as 'very singular in the African scene' and 'strangely unique'.[22] A series of open letters from Sudan African Closed Districts National Union (SACDNU) and later SANU addressed to international leaders and institutions reveals this exile movement's creative arguments for Southern Sudan's exceptionalism among groups seeking self-determination in Africa. I focus on the significant discursive strategies they employed to this end, which included comparing Sudan to exceptions in the international political system.

The rebels often employed the evocative analogy of Apartheid South Africa. This discursive strategy looms large in an open letter addressed to the Southern Sudanese people written in 1962. Titled 'Report to Azania', this SACDNU open letter was addressed to Southern constituencies. However, given that the Southern Sudanese population had extremely low levels of literacy during this period,[23] this six-page document seems to have been written with international English-speaking audiences in mind.[24] It is worth noting that during the colonial era, a very small cadre of Southern literati occasionally wrote letters to colonial officials making claims to civic rights, even in the limited political context of colonialism 'as experiences of oppression became the grounds for the active negotiation of citizenship'.[25] While these literate citizens certainly comprised an important readership, the report also gave exile politicians the opportunity to perform leadership before international audiences who read SACDNU's exhortations to the population they claimed to represent. It is unclear what channels SACDNU used to circulate the letter, but its bases in Kampala, Dar es Salaam and Leopoldville may have served as key sites in which the movement used the document to make its debut on the international political landscape.

In this letter, SACDNU urged the Southern Sudanese, in emphatic capital letters, to 'NOT CONSIDER YOURSELVES ANY LONGER AS SUDANESE BUT AS AZANIANS – THAT IS YOUR TRUE NAME'.[26] Taken to mean 'land of the blacks', the term Azania originates from the writings of first-century Greek geographers who used it as the name for 'the coast of East Africa and its hinterland'.[27] Its associations were increasingly tied to the anti-Apartheid struggle in South Africa from 1965 when the Pan Africanist Congress (PAC) adopted the term as the appellation for post-Apartheid South Africa.[28] The Black Consciousness Movement (BCM), the Azanian People's Organization (AZAPO) and other groups increasingly recognised and adopted the name in the 1970s.[29] Given this earlier usage by the Southern Sudanese exiles in 1962, it is unclear if the term Azania was used elsewhere at the time. Nevertheless, its Afrocentric meaning remained central to how SACDNU deployed it. It is ironic that these exiles would urge Southerners to dissociate themselves from the name "Sudan" since, according to its etymology, it also means 'land of the blacks' in Arabic. In fact, Arab nationalists in Khartoum did not identify with the name "Sudan" on these grounds until the late 1920s.[30] Contemporaneous to SACDNU's usage of the term "Azania", a group of resistance fighters inside Sudan began organising and calling themselves the Azania Secret Army (ASA), suggesting that the name had currency not only among the exile politicians.[31] However, the exile movement abandoned the name 'Azania' after 1962, only to revive it again at the end of 1965 when a faction of SANU renamed itself the Azanian Liberation Front (ALF).[32] But by May 1969, the leaders of the exile movement rejected the name, 'because of its remote relevance to Southern Sudan'.[33] They felt that 'the South African liberation movements which had already opted for this ancient name appear to have more legitimate claim'.[34] The volte-face of the Southern Sudanese liberation movement suggests that they were aware of the name's association with South Africa by the end of the decade.

Even though it is unlikely that SACDNU's use of the term "Azania" in the early 1960s was linked to the South African liberation struggle, the group did explain the urgent need for Southerners to abandon their Sudanese identity as follows: '[i]f therefore we give the Arabs time to accomplish their task of colonising the entire South, we will in future find ourselves like the Blacks of Soth Africa [sic].'[35] In order to make the case that the oppression Southern Sudanese people faced in a united Sudan warranted the analogy to South Africa, SANU texts had to counter a prevailing characterisation of the "Southern Problem" in the international press at the time. Due to the Abboud regime's imposition of Islam on the South which culminated in the expulsion of all Western missionaries from Sudan in 1964,[36] a narrative of religious persecution developed in the Western press in the early 1960s.[37] SACDNU sought to disabuse local and international audiences of the notion that religion was the root cause of the "Southern Problem". Instead, it posited:

> No, the question is not that of religion, [it] is a racial question that faces us in the Sudan today. The racial issue in the Sudan today is akin to that of the Boers of South Africa, it is an apertheid [sic] which must be fought tooth and nail now before the Arabs put firm roots in our land.[38]

It is unclear why SACDNU sought to distance itself from the religious persecution narrative. Regardless, Apartheid South Africa represents a carefully chosen analogy that had mileage.

By 1963, having changed its name, SANU presented itself as a 'Nationalist Movement' that stood for 'African Unity' (as opposed to division) in an open letter titled 'An appeal to African leaders'.[39] SANU had to justify undermining the sovereignty of an independent African state (Sudan), and here South Africa and other white settler states in Africa became useful tools of comparison once again. Through its texts, SANU reasoned:

> [b]ut south Africa [sic] became independent in the first quarter of this century, did and does that independence mean anything to Africans who are no better than slaves in their own country? In the Sudan, the powers, political, economic and military that were held by the Colonialists were bequeathed to the Arabs whose policy is no different from the apartheid of South Africa,

> or that of a white-dominated Southern Rhodesia. The Arabs in the Sudan seriously believe that they have to civilise, educate, islamise [sic] and arabise [sic] the Africans before they can claim to hold responsible posts. ... To us colonialism has no colour. It is a system based on racial superiority, political domination and economic subjection.[40]

The text challenged the limits of international non-interference. The analogy enabled SANU to describe its interpretation of the civic relations between the two groups. It alleged that

> it is obvious that the relationship between the Northern and Southern Sudan is not based on freedom and equality but on exploitation and subjection of one racial and cultural group by another, and is no different from that of South Africa and Southern Rhodesia.[41]

The ultimate objective of the analogy, stated explicitly in the open letter, was to cause the international audiences to ask themselves the question: 'South African racialism has been condemned, what about racialism practiced by the Northern government against the Africans of Southern Sudan?'[42] The equivalence enabled SANU to request intervention, because if Sudan was like South Africa, it would be indefensible for the world to treat the "Southern Problem" as merely a domestic political issue. SANU thus requested intervention from the OAU in exactly these terms in a letter to the Organisation's Secretary-General. The movement contended that 'what is happening in the southern Sudan needs examination by an international or semi-international Body as it has been done for Angola, Mozambique, South Africa and other trouble area [sic]'.[43] In a 1964 open letter to the United Nations Secretary General (UNSG), SANU reiterated that '[t]he question of South Africa was at one time considered internal but on closer examination it became international', suggesting that paying attention to the Southern Sudanese case would yield a similar change of heart among international audiences, and most importantly, a change of status for Southern Sudan.[44]

The analogy had limits and did not yield the desired outcome. A SANU text, in an expression of resignation, suggested that international organisations did not respond to their claims to being oppressed 'perhaps because the Arabs are not white'.[45] In an outburst of frustration, SANU stated in the 1964 open letter to the UNSG:

> It would be better if the Sudan Government could come out openly and clearly as the South African Government by establishing a racialist elected government in the North; this could enable liberal-minded Northerners to criticise the government. In this respect the Sudan Government is worse off than the South African Government because it is deceiving its own people, for whom it claims to assimilate the Southern Sudan.[46]

Compensating for the ostensible subtlety of the Sudanese state that precluded a neat and straightforward comparison, the letter added that

> [a]lthough there are no formal segregation laws as in South Africa, Northerners and Southerners in the Sudan live in strict segregated groups and this is most apparent in town clubs.[47]

SANU struggled to articulate what critical race theorists understand, that 'racism does not require the full and explicit support of the state and the law', indeed racial oppression 'can long persist and even flourish under the illusion of nonracism'.[48]

It is perhaps because of the looseness of this analogy that SANU employed alternatives. To the UNSG, SANU cautioned against likening the "Southern Problem" to 'the Kurdish problem of the Northern Iraq' which 'is considered an internal matter'.[49] Instead, the letter suggested: 'the present Arab massacre of the Southern Sudan Africans is a premeditated genocide, as Hitler's action against the Jews only a decade ago'.[50] The Holocaust was a more fitting comparison than Iraq's Kurdish problem not because the former allowed for a literally more precise comparison. It fit because it illustrated the status and appeal to legitimacy that SANU sought, as well as the resultant global antipathy the movement sought to elicit towards the Sudanese state. The discursive strategy of broadening the repertoire of comparisons enabled SANU to equate Sudan with two of the world's most demonised states at the time (Nazi Germany and Apartheid South Africa). These examples of demonising rhetoric depoliticised the Sudanese government's engagement with the South.[51] It cast the state's abrasive nation-building policies as purely racist oppression. Such invocations of evil are an effective legitimation strategy because they serve as a trump card that limits tolerable engagement.

In light of the fine line between seeking self-determination based on experiences of *racial exclusion* from the Sudanese national project, and seeking it based on a *racially exclusivist* conceptualisation of Southern Sudanese nationalism, SANU urged in a petition to the UN that

> [w]e would like to assure the United Nations that we are not against racial harmony, for indeed we are all human beings but we are against harsh and unfair treatment or system [sic] which is usually associated with colonial practice.[52]

It further used the language of positive racialism by affirming its belief that 'each race has a mission to fulfil in this world', in an attempt to deflect the negative connotations of racial separatism.[53] In so doing, SANU inadvertently echoed the supposedly positive, "preservationist" governance approach of the Condominium government.

SANU used different discursive strategies for different audiences and institutions. In another attempt at avoiding a conspicuous depiction of the "Southern Problem" as a problem of secessionism, SANU invited the international community to think of Sudan in different terms. To African leaders, SANU alluded to Sudan as a federation:

> It would be unjust, therefore, and unrealistic to consider the Southern movement for freedom as contrary of African Unity. The failure of the Mali Federation between the Senegal and French Sudan did not mark an end to Pan-Africanism nor did it affect the strive for African Unity. Similarly, the withdrawal of Nyasaland and Northern Rhodesia from "white man imposed Federation of Central Africa" has not proved contrary to African Unity.[54]

The rhetorical strategy of highlighting acceptable instances of fragmentation and the reorganisation of borders was designed to make the call for Southern self-determination palatable and non-threatening to Africa's territorial integrity.[55] These discursive strategies of reframing Sudan and analogising it to exceptional cases requiring international intervention raised questions regarding the exact nature of the differences between "Northerners" and "Southerners". The following section uncovers the ways SANU's open letters sought to answer them.

Immutable Differences and Political Incompatibility

SANU used racial nationalist discourses to underpin its claims to self-determination. To solidify its allegations of racial oppression, SANU aimed to convince international audiences that immutable racial differences existed between the people of the two regions, and to prove their fundamental political incompatibility. Three particularly revealing open letters are analysed here in which SANU argued along these lines. The movement employed a variety of dissemination strategies for these pieces of propaganda. The first was addressed to the African Liberation Committee (ALC). Also called the Committee of Nine, the ALC was formed by the OAU and was based in Tanzania to support the liberation movements that the Organisation deemed legitimate. The members of the Committee represented nine countries: Algeria, Congo-Leopoldville (now the Democratic Republic of the Congo), United Arab Republic (now Egypt), Ethiopia, Guinea, Nigeria, Senegal, Uganda and Tanzania.[56] The benefits of ALC endorsement included receiving the near-unequivocal support of the African political community that would also secure the exile movement's recognition in the broader international system. In light of the weight of the ALC's estimation, SANU representatives hand-delivered this open letter to the ALC in anticipation of the Committee's meeting in Tanzania in December 1963.[57] The other two were published in a periodical called *Voice of Southern Sudan* that SANU launched in April 1963, which widened the audiences exposed to the open letters while signalling SANU's diplomatic activism to its supporters.[58] SANU sent carbon copies of all the letters to African heads of state, the Secretary-Generals of the OAU, the UN and the International Commission of Jurists, as well as to the United Nations High Commissioner for Refugees (UNHCR). Addressed respectively to the African Liberation Committee (ALC), the Foreign Missions in Uganda and the Ugandan Prime Minister, Milton Obote, the three open letters formed part of SANU's plan to obtain the political support of African and other international leaders. SANU also used the location of its headquarters in neighbouring Uganda to deliver copies of its letter to foreign representatives in the country.

The London-based SANU member Lawrence Wol Wol produced *Voice of Southern Sudan* with the aim of fostering a readership that SANU imagined included the Southern Sudanese, 'the African world and the world at large'.[59] Wol Wol was an intellectual who, in the 1960s, was based in Switzerland for his Bachelor's degree, in Uganda for his Masters, in the UK as a representative of the exile movement, and in France for his PhD, which he earned in 1972.[60] In addition to serving as the editor-in-chief of *Voice of Southern Sudan*, Wol Wol also co-founded the London-based Southern Sudan Association (SSA). Sold at the affordable rate of ten shillings sterling for an annual subscription,[61] *Voice of Southern Sudan* functioned as a leading Southern Sudanese periodical in the 1960s. SANU used it as an instrument for fighting for self-determination and performing nationhood. In the first issue, William Deng explained that

> [w]riting is one of the methods of judging national maturity because it puts to the world our ideas in permanent form. All modern nations have had to write before they achieved their independence.[62]

Thus, with every edition, SANU sought to script the Southern Sudanese national identity, word by word. Moreover, through *Voice of Southern Sudan*, SANU framed itself as a paragon of Pan-Africanism, thereby distancing itself from the view that all secessionist groups were divisive and could weaken African unity. The publication carried the tagline 'Negritude and Progress' and it was, according to its first edition, avowedly 'dedicated to self-determination for the Southern Sudanese who are an unseparable [sic] part of Black Africa by race and culture'.[63] As the platform for SANU's nationalist propaganda, *Voice* became another vehicle through which SANU attempted to insert Southern Sudan into transnational Black liberation politics.

The case for Sudan's indisputable racial differences began with the semblance of objective facts. Specifically, SANU's letters typically began with an introductory paragraph that naturalised the racial binary. The letter to the African Liberation Committee is a case in point. In it, SANU representatives used dispassionate academic language to pass a contested position as factual and objective:

> The Sudan, the largest single area in Africa measuring nearly one million square miles is in two distinct parts; the North which is predominantly Arab by race and culture and the South which is exclusively inhabited by Black Africans... Southern Sudan is in fact part of the East, Central and West Africa by race, culture, geography, outlook and economic potential, while the North is linked by similar factors to the Arab Middle East.[64]

The text gives the impression that the numerical precision used to quantify the size of Sudan's geographical terrain can be applied to the political and social division of the country into 'two distinct parts'. The characterisation takes this duality for granted and represents the differences as fixed and natural. The letter also stated that 'the Sudan ... is described by geographers as being equal to half the size of Europe and the South alone being just under the size of Tanganyika',[65] thus suggesting that Sudan is too large, comparable with half a continent, while the South is comparable with a country. The geographical description implied that the Southern region was suitable for statehood.

SANU's letter to the foreign embassies in Uganda acknowledged the slightness of the phenotypical differences between Northern and Southern Sudanese people, by describing the Northerners as 'no browner than some Bantu people'.[66] The latter refers to a group that makes no claims to an Arab identity even though they are fairer than some darker skinned Africans from Southern Sudan. The letter suggests that, nevertheless, Northerners 'boast of their Arab blood, culture and heritage with the Arabs of the Middle East'.[67] The letter further racialised Sudan's geopolitical affiliations, alleging that pride in Arab identity ought to weaken Sudan's allegiance to Africa, since 'Sudan is officially a member of the Arab League and is generally written off as an Arab country politically'.[68] According to the letter, this resulted in the Southerners feeling excluded as their primordial and familial 'cultural and blood ties' were not to the Arab world.[69] In this way, the text naturalised the potential alliances between Black Africa and Southerners by referring to the divergent spheres of belonging that both regions claim. Thus, the reader was to understand that the racial differences between the 'Arab' Northerners and the 'Black' Southerners necessarily led to political incompatibility.

Further shifting the tone from "scientific" objectivity to impassioned language, another letter addressed to Prime Minister Obote urged:

> We therefore consider that the resistance of Southern Sudanese to Arab domination is the resistance of the Negro to any domination. Such resistance is thus part and parcel of the great struggle for liberation in Africa. It is part and parcel of the movement of the African Negro peoples to reassert themselves and show to the world that they are not meant to be only hewers of wood and drawers of water. It is not only a fight against European domination and European imperialism, but it is a fight against any one [sic] who looks down at the Negroes, be he a European, an Asian or an Arab. As such therefore, our movement needs to be supported by all the Negro governments of Africa because it is our part of the Africa which first comes face to face with the Arab menace.[70]

SANU's letter aligned the Southern Sudanese exile movement with 'Negro Africa', based on a racialised conception of African identity in a time when debates were raging about the place of Berber and Arab people in Pan-Africanism.[71] It reaffirmed a racial agenda behind the political emancipation of African countries. The reference to 'hewers of wood and drawers of water' is biblical, but it is also a phrase in Kwame Nkrumah's seminal book on Pan-Africanism, *Africa Must Unite*, in reference to the emancipation of Africans 'from colonial rule and imperial exploitation'.[72] This highly literate group of exiles that had been pleading for ALC recognition were likely aware of Nkrumah's use of the evocative phrase.

SANU's texts also argued that the colonial invention of the boundaries of Sudan violated the natural order of political affiliation, and thus logically 'we the Negro people are determined to revise it and cut the Negroes out of the Sudan to be free peoples once and for all'.[73] These open letters argued that by forcing the integration of the two regions, the Condominium government enforced 'the destruction of our personality and national identity as Africans'.[74] Yet again, the notion of an African 'personality' and 'identity' reiterated SANU's belief in racial essentialism.

Conclusion

The key rebel publications that popularised the "Southern Problem" during the 1960s enable us to understand the post-independence rebel discourses of legitimation. As we have seen, in its publications to various audiences, SANU used a range of techniques to defend and justify its claims to secession, including cartographical comparisons based on Sudan's size, to constructing diametrically opposed identities, as well as naturalising the racial binary. SANU thereby extrapolated political incompatibility from these claims. By inference, a united Sudan was unnatural.

The details of the strategies used to direct international attention towards the war in the South provide insight into the ways SANU grappled to explain the grievances of Southerners. SANU confronted the slippery nature of explaining racialisation and racism to international audiences. Analogising Sudan to Apartheid South Africa served two purposes. Through it, SANU aimed to spark international outrage for Sudan akin to the kind that the government of South Africa received at the time. That condemnation, in turn, represented a vehicle that would enable the South to legitimately claim its right to self-determination. As we have seen, South Africa served as more than an outcomes-based analogy. It also formed part of SANU's attempts at describing racism in Sudan, and framing it as similarly egregious. Drawing on the parlance of period—influenced by Negritude and Black Nationalism—SANU used racial essentialism to make the case for Southern secession. For SANU, this discourse signified political morality in the Third World.

Notes

1. R. Miles and M. Brown, *Racism*, 2nd edn (London, 2003), p. 112.
2. Glassman discusses nationalism as a 'form of ethnic thought' not unlike race in: J. Glassman, *War of Words, War of Stones* (Bloomington, IN, 2011), p. 12.
3. See Introductory Chapter for a discussion of this literature.
4. SANU, *Voice of Southern Sudan*, 1/2 (1963), p. 23.
5. Before 1970, the British Left considered the IRR a credible institution. In 1963, the Nuffield Foundation commissioned the IRR to conduct a five-year survey of race relations in the UK, and in 1969, the IRR published the findings of the study in *Colour and Citizenship: A Report on British Race Relations* authored by E. J. B. Rose. Leftist critics in Britain deemed the report controversial and allegedly reacted to the 'partiality and pro-government stance' in the book, accusing the Institute of serving Britain's ruling classes and 'spying on behalf of capitalism'. The confrontation was significant and threatened the Institute's reputation in the British public and its very survival. http://www.irr.org.uk/irr_history/ (11 June 2015).
6. P. Mason, 'Foreword', in J. Oduho and W. Deng, *The Problem of the Southern Sudan* (London, 1963). No reasons are provided in the book to explain why Northern politicians declined to participate.
7. SANU, *Voice of Southern Sudan*, 1/3 (1963), p. 3.
8. R. Gray, 'Introduction', in Oduho and Deng, *The Problem*, p. 1.
9. Oduho and Deng, *The Problem*, p. 2.
10. Ibid, p. 4. "Separate development" was the South Africa government's official moniker for Apartheid.
11. Ibid, p. 53.
12. Ibid, p. 8.
13. See Sudan Diplomatic Press, 'The Peoples of the Sudan', *The Directory of the Republic of the Sudan*, 1957–1958, 1959, 1960, 1961–1962, 1963, 1964, 1965, 1966–1967 (London).
14. Oduho and Deng, *The Problem*, p. 8.
15. S. Mollan, 'Business, State and Economy: Cotton and the Anglo-Egyptian Sudan, 1919–1939', *African Economic History*, 36 (2008), p. 95.
16. See A. A. E. Elageed, *Weaving the Social Networks of Women Migrants in Sudan: The Case of Gezira* (Berlin, 2009); Mollan, 'Business', p. 107; A. Quereshi, *Insurgency and International Law: The Case of Darfur* (Wembley, 2006) p. 55.
17. See S. Hall, 'Encoding/Decoding', in S. Hall, D. Hobson, A. Lawe and P. Willis (eds), *Culture, Media, Language* (London, 1980), pp. 128–138.

18. Oduho and Deng, *Problem*, p. 59.
19. Ibid, pp. 41, 56.
20. A. Klotz, *Norms in International Relations: The Struggle against Apartheid* (Ithaca, NY, 1995); B. Boutros-Ghali, *The United Nations and Apartheid* (New York, 1996).
21. On 21 March 1960, the Apartheid government opened fire on 5000–7000 Black protestors who opposed the pass laws in the Vereeniging township of Sharpeville, killing 69 people. The massacre led to demonstrations in townships across the country, leading to a national state of emergency by the end of the month, and the detention of 18,000 citizens. Internationally, allies protested in solidarity and the UN publicly condemned the massacre by issuing a Security Council resolution. Sharpeville shifted international opinion concerning the Apartheid regime, and precipitated its international isolation.
22. SANU, 'Southern Sudan Nationalist Movement and Call for African Unity: An appeal to African leaders', 1963, p. 1, Archivio Comboniani Roma (ACR), A/90/7/.
23. The region only had two secondary schools for boys and a handful of university graduates. L. Sanderson and N. Sanderson, *Education, Religion and Politics in Southern Sudan, 1899–1964* (London, 1981). L. Sanderson, 'Education and Administrative Control in Colonial Sudan and Northern Nigeria', *African Affairs*, 74 (1975), pp. 427–441.
24. I do not mean to suggest that political literacy did not exist in Southern Sudan at the time. To the contrary, the political culture of active citizenship that exile leaders demonstrated within the broader international community of nations through their political letters may very well have stemmed from the late colonial period during which the 'Condominium government was promoting ideas and discourses of representative government and national citizenship', throughout Sudan, including among the missionary-educated elites of the South. C. Leonardi and C. Vaughan, '"We are oppressed and our only way is to write to higher authority": the politics of claim and complaint in the peripheries of Condominium Sudan', in E. Hunter (ed), *Citizenship, Belonging, and Political Community in Africa: Dialogues between Past and Present* (Athens, OH, 2016), p. 75.
25. Ibid, p. 97.
26. SACNU, 'Report to Azania', 15 May 1962, p. 7. ACR, A/90/6/10. Emphasis in original. In the 1962, the exile movement occasionally used the acronym SACNU but later used SACDNU more consistently.
27. G. W. B. Huntingford, 'Azania', *Anthropos*, 35/1 (1940), pp. 208–220. The following source attributes the etymology of the name to Arabic: 'Azania', in K. A. Appiah, and H. L. Gates Jr. (eds) *Africana: The Encyclopedia of the African and African American Experience, Second*

Edition (New York, 2008). The following ascribes it to Persian traders: M. D. W. Jeffreys, 'Book review: M. Shinnie, *Ancient African Kingdoms* (London, 1965)', *African Studies*, 27/3 (1968), p. 145. The Huntingford text makes the most compelling and thorough case for Greek derivation.

28. Using Azania to refer to South Africa may have been the idea of PAC theoretician Peter Raboroko. Email correspondence with Professor Tom Lodge, 28 March 2017.
29. C. R. D. Halisi, *Black Political Thought in the Making of South African Democracy* (Bloomington, IN, 1999), p. 63.
30. H. Sharkey, *Living with Colonialism: Nationalism and Culture in the Anglo-Egyptian Sudan* (Berkeley, 2003), pp. 16–38.
31. J. Lagu, *Anya-Nya: What we Fight For* (London, 1972) p. 4.
32. J. Howell, 'Political Leaders in the Southern Sudan', 1972, p. 33, SAD 803/5/19-35.
33. Nile Provisional Republic, 'Editorial: It is now the NILE REPUBLIC', *Voice of Southern Sudan*, No. 5, 15 May 1969, p. 1.
34. Ibid.
35. ACR, A/90/6/10.
36. See Istituto Artigianelli, *The Black Book of the Sudan on the Expulsion of the Missionaries from Southern Sudan: An Answer* (Milan, 1964).
37. For example, see 'Mission Superior Tells of Troubles in Sudan', *The Tidings* (7 October 1960); 'Sudan Court tries Priest for Treason: Protested school classes on Sunday', *The Catholic Standard and Times* (11 November 1960); 'Anti-Catholic Persecution Reaching Final Stages in the Sudan, Reporter finds', *NCWC News Service* (16 October 1961); 'New Threat to Missions in the Sudan', *The Tablet* (21 July 1962); 'Sudan Threat to Slaughter Christians', *Catholic Herald* (14 February 1962); 'Priests Expelled from Sudan', *The Times* [London] (28 December 1962); 'The Church in Sudan: Sudan steps up Attack', *Leadership* [Uganda] (January 1963); 'Sudan Consul Denies Missionary Murders', *Uganda Nation* (January 1963); 'Sudan Expels Missionaries', *The Christian Century* (2 February 1963); 'Sudan Expels 5 Missionaries', *Daily Telegraph* (11 January 1963); 'Vatican Plea Fails', *The Observer* (13 January 1963); 'Priest Tells of Life in Sudan Jail – Campaign of Persecution Continues', *Irish Weekly* (9 March 1963); 'Freedom of Worship', *Daily Nation* (24 August 1963); Editorial, 'A Restive South', *The Times* [London] (13 March 1964); 'Revenge for Rome', [Translation], *Der Spiegel* [Hamburg] (19 March 1964).
38. ACR, A/90/6/10.
39. SANU, 'Southern Sudan Nationalist Movement and Call for African Unity: An appeal to African leaders', 1963, p. 1, ACR, A/90/7/3.

40. Ibid, p. 2.
41. Ibid, p. 5.
42. Ibid, p. 6.
43. Letter from William Deng (SANU) to the Secretary General of the OAU, 16 December 1963, in Yosa Wawa draft manuscript, 'The Southern Sudanese Pursuits of Self-determination: documents in political history', p. 141, D. H. Johnson Personal Papers (henceforth DHJ-PP).
44. Sudan African Closed Districts National Union (SACDNU), 'Petition to the United Nations', 1963, p. 2. ACR, A/90/7/4.
45. ACR, A/90/7/3, p. 2.
46. ACR, A/90/7/4, p. 7.
47. Ibid, p. 13.
48. Fredrickson, *Racism*, p. 4. See, Eduardo Bonilla-Silva, *Racism without Racists: Color-blind racism and the persistence of racial inequality in America*, Lanham: Rowman, 2003. France Winddance Twine, *Racism in a Racial Democracy: The Maintenance of White Supremacy in Brazil*, New Brunswick, NJ, 1998. George Reid Andrews, *Blacks and Whites in Sao Paulo, Brazil, 1888–1988*, Madison, 1991.
49. Letter to the Secretary General, UN, from SANU, 30 March 1964, p. 1, ACR, A/90/7/7.
50. Ibid.
51. For more on the use of evilisation discourse in international relations, see A. Geis and C. Hobson, 'The existence and use of "evil" in international politics', *International Politics*, 51/4 (2014), pp. 417–423.
52. ACR, A/90/7/4, p. 2.
53. Ibid, p. 4.
54. ACR, A/90/7/3, p. 6.
55. P. Nugent, *Arbitrary lines and the people's minds: a dissenting view on colonial boundaries in West Africa* (Edinburgh, 1993).
56. D. H. Humphries, 'The East African Liberation Movement', in International Institute for Strategic Studies, *Adelphi Paper: Africa, Vol. 1* (Abingdon, 2006), p. 36.
57. Letter from W. Deng, N. Lore and P. M. Beit (SANU) to the African Liberation Committee (ALC), 5 December 1963, in Yosa Wawa draft manuscript, 'The southern Sudanese pursuits of self-determination: documents in political history', pp. 134–140, DHJ-PP.
58. The letter to Prime Minister Milton Obote was reproduced in the first edition of the *Voice of Southern Sudan*, 1/1 (1963), pp. 16–18. The letter to the Foreign Missions in Uganda was also reproduced in *Voice of Southern Sudan*, 1/2 (1963), pp. 7–15.
59. W. Deng, 'Official Statement by the National Executives on the Sudan African Closed District National Union', *Voice*, 1/1 (1963), p. 1.

60. Kuyok, *South Sudan*, p. 364.
61. SANU, *Voice of Southern Sudan*, 3/2 (October 1965), p. i.
62. SANU, *Voice of Southern Sudan*, 1/1 (April 1963), p. 2.
63. W. Deng, 'Official Statement', p. 1.
64. Letter from W. Deng, N. Lore and P. M. Beit (SANU) to the ALC, 5 December 1963.
65. Ibid.
66. Letter from I. Nyigilo to Foreign Ministers in Uganda, 1963, in Yosa Wawa draft manuscript, 'The Southern Sudanese Pursuits', p. 127, DHJ-PP.
67. Ibid.
68. Ibid.
69. Ibid.
70. Letter from SAC[D]NU to Milton Obote, 1963, in Yosa Wawa draft manuscript, 'The Southern Sudanese Pursuits', p. 124, DHJ-PP.
71. A. Kasanda, 'Exploring Pan-Africanism's theories: from race-based solidarity to political unity and beyond', *Journal of African Cultural Studies*, 28/2 (2016), pp. 179–195.
72. Joshua 9:23. Also, K. Nkrumah, *Africa Must Unite* (London, 1963).
73. Letter from SAC[D]NU to Milton Obote, 1963, p. 123.
74. Letter from I. Nyigilo to Foreign Ministers in Uganda, 1963, p. 127.

CHAPTER 4

'[A] Nation Is Not Physically of One "Blood"': Portraying Sudan as Non-racial

Building on the emergence of rebel narratives in the early 1960s, this chapter charts the development of the "Southern Problem" in the oppositional literature of the Sudanese government. By unpacking the Sudanese government's response to this discursive attack, we will see the rhetorical strategies the government used in two complementary publications aimed at undermining the Sudan African National Union (SANU)'s accusations. This exploration will show the resultant framing competitions that took place in rival propaganda texts, specifically two booklets the government published through the Ministry of Information precisely to counter the claims that the rebels made. It completes the picture set out in Chap. 3 by placing the competing discursive nationalist projects in the same frame. By tracing their logomachy, the chapter reveals how the Sudanese government deliberately competed against SANU to sway international audiences. The subsequent diplomatic duel between the Sudanese government and Southern exiles, with words as their weaponry, constituted a crucial terrain of the first civil war.

Government Rebuttal

The vitriolic reactions of the government of Sudan and its allied media in Khartoum to SANU's publications suggest how much of a threat the government thought the exiles represented. According to a report by a Nairobi-based SANU correspondent, the day after the book launch of

S. C. Manoeli, *Sudan's "Southern Problem"*, African Histories and Modernities, https://doi.org/10.1007/978-3-030-28771-9_4

Joseph Oduho and William Deng's *The Problem of the Southern Sudan*, the Sudanese media accused the British government of seeking to take back Sudan, the Institute of Race Relations of being an instrument of Britain's imperialism and the exile politicians of spreading lies abroad.[1] The Sudanese government proceeded to ban the book from the country and reportedly confiscated copies mailed through the Khartoum Post Office.[2]

The government subsequently produced texts intended to counter SANU's international campaign. In 1964, the Central Office of Information published a noteworthy response in the form of a booklet titled *Basic Facts about the Southern Provinces of the Sudan*.[3] The booklet noticeably refers to the 'Southern provinces', rather than "the South", thereby depicting it as a composite part of Sudan rather than as a discrete entity. As an official government document, the booklet's authors are unnamed. That an Arabic-speaking country positioning itself to be seen as an Arab state would write to English-speaking audiences attests to the government's sensitivity to SANU's diplomatic rivalry, primarily in its Anglophone neighbours in Africa, but also further afield in the West. Divided into three chapters, the booklet focused on the role of the colonial administration in the South and the development of the Southern provinces after independence and framed Sudan as 'An African Experiment in Social Cohesion'. The booklet targeted African leaders as its audience, as well as other Anglophone audiences sympathetic to the challenges of post-colonial nation-building.

The booklet offers a narrative explaining why Sudan's nationhood ought not to be based on racial homogeneity. It justifies the government's policy choices, such as the strict application of Arabic as the lingua franca even in the South, and the adoption of Islam as the national religion, as a part of nation-building efforts aimed at facilitating societal unity. It even broaches the differential remuneration Northerners and Southerners received, framing it as a legacy of colonialism. It blames the "Southern Problem" and the mutiny that ushered it into Sudan's post-colonial political imaginary as 'a culmination of a protracted policy designed since the inception of the condominium regime to drive a wedge between the North and the South'.[4] The booklet makes two central claims. Firstly, in order to challenge SANU's racial binary argument, the government contends that pure racial identities do not exist in Sudan. Secondly, it argues that racial discrimination, consequently, does not exist.

To make the first claim, the government described Sudanese identities, beginning with the 'Arabs' in the North, in more fluid and intersecting ways than SANU:

> Historical and anthropological evidence shows that they are a mixture of Caucasians who migrated to the Sudan in ancient Egyptian time, and the negroes who were the original inhabitants. Their claim to be Arab is due in the first place to the infusion of a strain of Arab blood after the infiltration of the Arabs from Egypt into the Sudan after the 7th Century AD and secondly, to the adoption of Islam in the whole region. ...[the Beja are] according to Seligman[,] of the Proto-Egyptian Origin which was more modified in the north by negroid and armenoid influences than the south, and were akin to the riverian peoples of Nubia. Although a strain of Arab blood had been infused into them, they have preserved their racial characteristics and languages which speak of more Hamitic than Arab Origins. ... Central Sudan, with some exceptions in Darfur, the Nuba Mountains and Upper Nile where the inhabitants are predominantly of the old stock known as Sudani, is inhabited by Arab tribes. But even here the people's claim to have pure Arab blood is contested by historians and ethnographists. ... Ethnically the settled population can be classified simply as either Semitized-Hamites or Semitized-Negroes, but more clearly as Semitized-Negroid-Hamites (e.g. Ja'aliyyin) or Semitized-Hamite-Negroid (e.g. Jawama'). ... The degree of diversification in the 3 southern provinces is more pronounced than in the 6 northern provinces from the evidence of a greater number of languages and tribes. Linguistically the inhabitants are divided into three principal groups: The Nilotes, the Nilo-Hamites, and the Sudanic tribes. ... The Nilotic group (Shilluk, Dinka and Nuer) who comprise the largest majority of the population of the South, are generally described as negroes although this is not substantiated by Anthropologists.[5]

Written to correct SANU's characterisations of the nature of ethno-racial diversity in Sudan, this jargon-laden description relied heavily on academic classifications. The text explains that those generally referred to as Northerners self-identify as Arabs, and that identification is more cultural than racial since 'they are a mixture'. By including the Nubians, Beja, Darfuris, Nuba and riverine people, the text sought to emphasise the wide range of ethnic groups that were lumped by SANU's narrative into the Arab identity. It suggested that a clear typology of the diversity of Sudanese people remained contested among scholars ('historians', 'ethnographists' and 'anthropologists'). Accordingly, the text dismissed the racial binary the rebels had constructed as uninformed and lacking the objectivity of racial science and ethnographic research. In keeping with the title, the text presents its narrative as indisputable 'Facts' based on verified and scientific information. This use of academic scholarship is an example of what Christina Boswell terms 'legitimising knowledge'.[6] As a discursive strategy, expert knowledge plays a 'symbolic role' in imparting a sense of believability to the text. By relying on it, the text pursued a form of 'epistemic authority'.[7]

The government's text sought to challenge the Southern exiles' claims to "Black Africa". It specifically aimed to discredit the South's claim to the "Negro" identity by quoting Evans Pritchard's argument that

> [i]t is doubtful whether any peoples in the Sudan can be regarded as true negroes, and their non-negroid characters, their pastoral pursuits, and to a certain degree the structure of their languages, are attributed to Hamite admixture and influence.[8]

Similarly, the text cited the work of the anthropologist John Spencer Trimingham in reference to the racial composition of Sudan, in which he states that

> [i]t is rare to find anything approaching a pure racial type among any of the peoples of the Sudan, for this land has suffered from many vents of racial dispersion. All its people are variations between the pure Caucasian and the pure Negro type.[9]

Dismantling the notion of racial purity reduced the salience of the rebels' argument regarding the racial binary. By framing Sudan as a land of racially 'mixed' peoples, no one region could make a claim to having undiluted 'blood' and thus no region could claim to possess pure loyalty to Africa or elsewhere.

The work of Trimingham, Seligman and Pritchard represented scholarship that reified scientific notions of race. The government's text relied on ethnological anthropology that accepted the biological validity of racial categories. For example, the writings of ethnologist C. G. Seligman, especially the book from which the government's text quotes, the 1913 publication *The Hamitic Problem in the Anglo-Egyptian Sudan*, was at odds with the rapidly changing intellectual landscape. The non-egalitarian racial typologies of the variety that Seligman propounded were contested and becoming discredited.[10] By treating race as a physiological and genealogical descriptor, the government could avoid dealing with the social and political dimensions of racial subjectivities. Hence, the government carefully eschewed any reference to ethno-racial hierarchy.

The biologisation of social identities in this government text served to highlight the government's position that 'a nation is not physically of one "blood." It is a geographical and mental fact, and results from common citizenship.'[11] It suggested that the shared history of "intermingling" in fact united Sudanese people:

> The invalidity of the racial argument has been testified by the anthropologist. It is clear from evidence given earlier that there are no distinct racial or cultural divisions in the Sudan, except in small areas.[12]

By denying the kind of difference embraced by SANU—namely race—the government's account sought to efface all difference and the power relations that produced inequality in Sudan. Ironically, SANU had helped to open the door to this rhetorical move.[13]

It is important to note that this government text strategically deployed jargon and complicated language in a new way. Disproving the existence of racial purity had not been an explicit aim in diplomatic propaganda before. The government had described group differences in less sophisticated language in its official documents apart from the discursive battle it fought against SANU. For example, from the earliest post-independence Sudanese international literature, the Sudanese government maintained a delicate balance of acknowledging group differences but maintaining that they did not suggest that the country should be divided. From 1957 to 1963 the Sudanese Diplomatic Press' annual directory described Sudan's demographic composition in not dissimilar terms from SANU:

> As a broad generalisation, the Sudan is predominantly Arab and entirely Muslim in the north, and predominantly negroid and pagan in the south. However, no definite dividing line exists between the north and the south, whether that line be physical, cultural or ethnical. The differences overlap in a broad zone. Indeed the merging has taken place on so wide a scale that the conclusion can hardly be escaped, and particularly when the economic and administrative considerations are borne in mind, that the country is a single indivisible whole.[14]

In this account, the differences, explained as discrete but fuzzy, were acknowledged but did not constitute a significant challenge to the integrity of the state. By 1964, the annual directory changed its description slightly, adding that:

> Many of the [Southern] tribes have affinities more or less close with tribes to be found in Ethiopia, Kenya, Uganda or the Congo, as the international boundary is nowhere an ethnic one.[15]

This addition suggested that ethnicising Southern nationalism would lead not only to the fragmentation of Sudan, but the reorganisation of the borders of several African countries. Conversely, in *Basic Facts*, the Sudanese government made a radically different argument that Sudan is best understood as a melting pot that had transformed those within its borders into a varied concoction of ethnic 'strains' and that the amalgamation created a coherent and indivisible country.

Further, the text framed Southern nationalists as merely an example of the sub-nationalist causes afoot in many parts of Africa, arguing that 'Kenya, Uganda, Congo, Nigeria, Ghana, Tanganyika and many others would dwindle into splinter groups if the racial argument is applied to them'.[16] The reference to a wide variety of African countries facing secessionist problems was aimed at inciting fear that Southern Sudan's secession would set a harmful precedent on the continent. It also revealed the government's interchangeable use of, and the conceptual slippage of, "race" into "ethnicity".

To make the second argument, that racial discrimination did not exist in Sudan, the authors of *Basic Facts* quoted Southern Sudanese politicians who approved of the government. According to the publication, Santino Deng and Buth Diu 'could see the problem of the South in a clear perspective'.[17] In reference to a newspaper interview Deng gave regarding the 1955 mutiny in the South, the booklet stated that he

> emphasised, 5 days before the disturbances in the *Times* of 13 August 1955 that his people wanted progress first and foremost – more educational, health and communicational facilities; and that they were satisfied that the present administration was doing its 'utmost to provide them.' Consequently they had confidence in the Northern Governor of the Province (i.e. Bahr El Ghazal) and were satisfied that the local administration was acting without bias against Southerners.[18]

Deng was used to give the government credibility and to invalidate SANU's allegations of racism. *Basic Facts* also quoted Buth Diu, a parliamentarian at the time of the mutiny, as preferring a steady, non-revolutionary solution to the "Southern Problem" within the united Sudan's political system. Regarding the mutiny, he is said to have stated that:

> We believe that this action may hamper the social and constitutional developments of our beloved Sudan for years and years and deprive us in the Sudan of all the gains which we have so far achieved.... The Juba Conference of 1947 confirmed that the South and the North should remain as an integral whole, and this has been further confirmed by you Southern people who gave us your votes in membership of the present Sudanese Parliament in which, by presenting our case, we are able gradually to achieve the many developments which we want.[19]

Diu had enjoyed an illustrious career in Sudanese politics. Having served in the lower echelons of the Condominium administration, he stood for parliament in 1947, and was elected to the House of Representatives as a member of the Southern Political Association, and became a founding member and Secretary-General of the Liberal Party.[20] He was the only Southerner on the Constitution Amendment Commission that advised the Governor-General of Sudan during the late colonial period on the steps to self-government. Notably, he was among the Southerners who advocated for a federal constitution, while Northern colleagues on the Commission opposed the proposition.[21] He had subsequently boycotted the Commission in protest.[22] Although indisputably a proponent of the Southern cause, Diu likely criticised the mutiny of 1955, because the military rebellion occurred without the blessing and leadership of the Southern parliamentarians.[23]

Unlike the complicated allegiances of Buth Diu, Santino Deng had long proved his antipathy for Southern exclusivist politics. Having initially stood for parliamentary elections as an independent candidate in 1954, Deng joined the National Unionist Party shortly after. Typically, Southerners joining the mainstream, Northern-based political party actively dissociated themselves from the racial politics of the South. At the time of the booklet's publication, he was the only Southerner to hold a ministerial post when he was appointed Minister of Animal Resources in the Abboud regime. He represents a part of a small group of Khartoum-based Southerners who opposed the Southern cause.

Through usage of academic writings on Sudanese identities and pro-government statements by select Southern politicians, the booklet combated the rebel texts. This very process of the government and the exiles contesting the validity of the other's claims about the nature of racial difference in Sudan was, in effect, shaping the meaning of race in Sudan at that time.[24] The Sudanese government's narrative took an even more interesting turn in writings produced by Southerners who, like Buth Diu and Santino Deng, formed part of the political establishment in Khartoum. In the following section, we will examine a text written by two prominent Southerners.

An Alternative View from the South[25]

By enlisting pro-government Southerners, the government took advantage of the fissures between Southern elites. Santino Deng co-authored a book with Ambrose Wol, titled *Let's Speak the Truth: Presentation of Facts and Views by Two Prominent Sudanese from the South*, through the Publication Section of the Ministry of Information of the Sudan.[26] It was published in 1963, shortly after William Deng and Joseph Oduho's book, with the aim of countering its claims. Like Santino Deng, Ambrose Wol gained prominence in Khartoum. Serving as the editor of the *Sudan Daily* in 1960, Wol became the first Southerner to edit a national newspaper. After an illustrious postgraduate education in India where he presided over the African Students' Union and was even photographed with India's first Prime Minister, Jawaharlal Nehru, he returned to Sudan to serve as an information officer in the Ministry of Information in 1958.[27]

It is difficult to gauge the extent of the circulation of Deng and Wol's book. However, a local newspaper in Vermont, US, *The Bennington Banner*, ran an article about this booklet and quoted it extensively, while also making reference to SANU's Institute of Race Relations (IRR) publication.[28] Another newspaper, *Desert Sun*, in California, US, also cited Deng and Wol's booklet in 1963, suggesting that it had spread through wide networks.[29] Nevertheless, it does not seem to have gained as much traction as William Deng and Joseph Oduho's book, probably because the Sudanese Ministry of Information published and distributed it. Hence, the book's association with the government could be used to dismiss it as government propaganda.

The book featured two prominent Southern politicians in the country at the time, who deliberately identified as 'Sudanese from the South', rather than the qualified, double-barrelled "Southern Sudanese" identity that most Southern exiles espoused. In it, Deng and Wol defended the integrity of the Sudan. Although the authors did not state their objective as providing counter-propaganda, they expressed intense concern for Sudan's declining reputation abroad. In his essay, Deng made frequent references to 'false reports' in the 'foreign press' about Sudan. Ambrose Wol's essay made more explicit pronouncements regarding the purpose of press coverage on Sudan. Directly accusing the Western media, Wol stated that

> [s]everal newspapers and magazines in Western European countries and the United States, have resorted to overt acts of falsification in their reports as a means of waging a relentless anti-Sudan campaign.[30]

He took issue with the initially unnamed group of 'self-exiled' Southerners who 'cry in foreign lands' with their 'hate-campaign' on what has come to be called 'The Southern Sudan Problem'.[31] Deng and Wol felt that 'the barrage of pronouncements these people have made in the foreign press are, to say the least, *destructive*'.[32] They disapproved of the 'malicious campaigning' and the fact that 'this group's activities received more publicity from the unscrupulous foreign press'.[33]

Wol described the negative coverage of Sudan as 'an extreme technique in international news management that clearly betrays the motives of its authors'.[34] Ambrose Wol alleged that the Western press was designed to sabotage 'African unity'.[35] By dismissing the reportage as simply 'the wanton smear campaign against the Sudan ... engineered and managed by foreign elements', Wol and Deng framed the coverage as serving the neocolonial interests of Western states, suggesting that they envisioned anticolonial and African audiences.[36] Wol characterised the reportage as '[t]he nonsense of colonial comeback, cleverly disguised in sugared moralistic expressions'.[37] Their writings echoed the view of press outlets held in Sudan that had framed the SANU-IRR publication as an indication of Britain's intention to conquer Sudan yet again.

The charged rhetoric suggests that Wol and Deng understood themselves to be competing for international legitimacy. Wol, while working as a newspaper editor in Sudan, made several references to 'world opinion', suggesting that he conceived of SANU as attempting to shape it and believed that the government needed to minimise SANU's influence:

> World opinion has shown beyond doubt that it is against separation and neo-colonialism. The United Nations has even used force to bring unity to the Congo. It has used its offices to bring West Irian into Indonesia. World opinion favours the integrity of Laos. These are but a few recent instances in which the world has shown that it prefers a greater coming together of nations to balkanisation. Of course former colonial powers are still interested in Africa. They try to promote their interests through the idiosyncrasies of Tshombes and many other Quislings who lend their short-lived services to them.[38]

Embedded in the statement are analogies used to discredit the Southern Sudanese exile movement. The comparison of SANU to secessionist groups in Katanga, Laos and West Papua served to dismiss SANU as a similarly lost cause. Like 'Quislings', a World War II term for collaborator, Tshombe was, for African liberation movements in the 1960s, an arch sellout. Wol used these loaded terms to demonise and vilify the exile movement.

Wol also alleged that the leaders of SANU incited separatist politics unnecessarily and popularised the idea of becoming a political exile without actually experiencing persecution. Instead of being treated like the illegitimate spokespersons they were, the foreign press had allowed them to carve out a space in international discursive spaces:

> The clandestine moves of the self-styled 'political exiles' became more frequent after the appearance on the scene of the 'trio' (William Deng, Joseph Oduho and Fr. Seterlino [sic]). They began to seek platforms for the spread of their ideas. The foreign press joined in the mounting clamor and lent its columns to the so-called 'Sudanese exiles.'[39]

Wol frequently referred to the leadership of SANU as 'those who have chosen voluntary exile abroad', 'self-exiles', and 'those who call themselves "political exiles"'.[40] By delegitimising their reasons for leaving the country, Ambrose Wol and Santino Deng painted the three leaders as dishonest and opportunistic. The authors also questioned the commitment of SANU's leadership to solving the country's problems, which they maintained 'will not be solved by running away from the country and engaging in subversive activities'.[41] These ways of framing the kind of liberty the leaders of SANU could have enjoyed in Sudan of course eschewed the outburst of war, and the mass incarceration of politically active, anti-government Southerners.

Wol developed his ad hominem attack by providing biographies for all three SANU leaders. Describing their contributions to the Sudanese state, Wol skilfully adopted an air of impartiality by including their positive achievements while they were still in Sudan. He used the biographies as evidence for the absence of discrimination in Sudan given the senior positions that they had all held prior to fleeing the country:

> Both Sayed William Deng Nhial and Sayed Joseph Oduho, in their respective fields held positions of great trust and responsibility which they would not have held if persecution-racial or religious existed in fact.[42]

Wol also described Father Saturnino as a 'brilliant scholar'.[43] This quote is the only reference to race in the booklet, a conspicuous absence given the pre-eminence of the allegations of racial prejudice in SANU's propaganda. Although neither of the authors mentioned race, their photographs clarify that aspect of their identities for the reader. Photographs of both writers decorated the introductions of their respective essays in the booklet, making the reader aware that African (and not Arab) men had written this book.[44] In his essay, Santino Deng focused singularly on religion as a marker of difference in an attempt to disprove the existence of that form of discrimination in Sudan.[45]

The document took an explicitly pro-government stance, evident in Santino Deng's references to the 1958 coup that brought the then incumbent government into power as 'blessed', and regarding its governing track record, he asked, '[w]hat else would a right thinking citizen wish for?'[46] In keeping with the patriotic tone of such statements of allegiance, the authors articulated a striking plea about the meaning of being a Southerner in a united Sudan:

> We feel it is morally wrong to mislead the uneducated masses and the still naïve and immature school children by the fantastic humdrum of the 'promised land'. There is no such 'promised land'. This is our country.[47]

The claim to belonging to Sudan is rare in the textual canon of Southern Sudanese writers at the time, and it intimated the pragmatism inherent in Wol's politics. He portrayed secessionism as unlikely and fanciful. Instead, working within the Sudanese political system seemed to be the best hope for political transformation for Southerners.

It is unclear the extent to which the Southern political elite in exile and in Khartoum knew each other personally, but their publicly scripted criticisms of each other formed an important part of the international discursive disputation about the political destiny of the South. As a result, SANU certainly paid close attention to the writings of these two authors and criticised them heavily. For example, in the SANU publication *Voice of Southern Sudan*, Santino Deng was insultingly described as a 'political prostitute to any Arab government' who was used as 'a showpiece of Southern representation in the government for world consumption'.[48] SANU was aware of the ways in which the government benefited from the optics of having Southerners discredit the exile movement. Likewise, in response to another article Ambrose Wol had published in the magazine *Sudan*, a SANU author in *Voice of Southern Sudan* stated that he could only arrive at one of two conclusions:

> Either [Wol] possesses a conscience which having sold itself out, is devoid of the slightest regard for what is right and humane; or he is an unfortunate journalist locked in a cell of terror ventilated with ignorance.[49]

Let's Speak the Truth introduced the fractures among the Southern elites to the international debate about the South. By showing the lack of consensus among Southerners, the government was able to undermine SANU's presumptive authority to function as the mouthpiece of the South. Wol and Deng's text reframed SANU's writings as malicious disinformation devised by unreliable political entrepreneurs.

Conclusion

The classification of identities that was constructed in the colonial period was reified in the post-colonial context. This may appear to represent Sudan's failure to decolonise as the colonial government's categories continued to 'determine the institutional and discursive parameters' of post-colonial political thinking.[50] These introductory chapters have shown that, in Sudan, political actors maintained colonial logics and categories only when useful to their political agendas. For the rebels, maintaining the rigidity of discrete racial categories made racial nationalism available as a secessionist line of reasoning. In contrast, the Sudanese government made use of the scholarship of Western anthropologists produced during the colonial period to suit their purposes of undermining rebel claims to racial homogeneity. The colonial "Southern Problem" was reinvented, its contents reframed and contested by Sudanese rebels and the state in the early 1960s. The ingenuity of the intellectual footwork of the Sudanese state and the Southern rebels exceeded that of the colonial administration, as they used the old ideas to craft and envision new and radical political possibilities. For the rebels, the possibility was a new state and, for the government, it was the abolishing of Southern racial nationalism.

The discursive techniques both sides employed to elicit support from diverse audiences and amidst the intellectual ferment of Pan-Africanism, the Cold War, decolonisation and Black liberation politics represent a strategic but often overlooked aspect of the battle for legitimacy that the rebels and the state waged in the international public sphere. The interplay of silences and articulations in both the rebels' and the state's texts concealed and complicated certain aspects of the country's political conflict. Both parties were heavily invested in how international audiences understood, imagined and framed the conflict. As a result, the sophisticated rhetorical strategies of both the rebels and the Sudanese state offer crucial insight into Sudanese political thought in the aftermath of decolonisation.

Notes

1. L. Kurr, '"The Problem of the Southern Sudan": Origin of Sudan Government violent attack on Great Britain and the Institute of Race Relations', *Voice of Southern Sudan*, 1/3 (1963), p. 3.
2. Ibid.
3. Government of Sudan, *Basic Facts about the Southern provinces of the Sudan* (Khartoum, 1964), ACR, A/85/2.
4. Sudan, *Basic Facts*, p. 43.
5. Ibid, pp. 1–4.
6. C. Boswell, 'Knowledge, Legitimation and the Politics of Risk: The Function of Research in Public Debates on Migration', *Political Studies*, 57 (2009), pp. 165–186.
7. S. Herbst, 'Political Authority in a Mediated Age', *Theory and Society*, 32/4 (2003), p. 484.
8. Sudan, *Basic Facts*, p. 4.
9. J. S. Trimingham, *Islam in the Sudan* (Oxford, 1949), p. 5.
10. Barkan suggests that as early as the end of World War I, '[a]mong leading scientific circles in the United States and Britain, race typology as an element of causal cultural explanation became largely discredited...One reason for this decline was a lack of epistemological foundations for racial

classification, a lack which led to endless irresolvable inconsistencies and contradictions.' E. Barkan, *The Retreat of Scientific Racism: Changing Concepts of Race in Britain and the United States between the world wars* (Cambridge, 1992), p. 3.

11. Sudan, *Basic Facts*, p. 6.
12. Ibid, p. 91.
13. For example, J. Glassman shows that the pre-revolution Zanzibari government also rhetorically maintained the myth of a multiracial island 'in which most people were "mixtures of mixtures"'. However, despite this rhetoric of assimilative and harmonious identities, in a similar fashion to Sudan, Zanzibar experienced an eruption of racial violence. Glassman, *War of Words*, p. 7.
14. 'The Peoples of the Sudan', *The Directory of the Republic of the Sudan, 1957–58* (London, 1958) p. 15. The directory carried the same excerpt, verbatim in the 1959 version on p. 21; in 1960, on p. 24; in 1961–1962, on p. 22; and in 1963, on p. 16.
15. 'The Peoples of the Sudan', *The Directory of the Republic of the Sudan, 1964* (London, 1964) p. 14.
16. Ibid.
17. Sudan, *Basic Facts*, p. 44.
18. Ibid.
19. *Sudan Weekly News*, No. 53, p. 6, cited in Sudan, *Basic Facts*, pp. 44–5.
20. 'The Peoples of the Sudan', *The Directory of the Republic of the Sudan, 1957/58* (London, 1958) p. 150.
21. A. K. Abdelhay, 'The Politics of Language Planning in the Sudan: The Case of the Naivasha Language Policy' (PhD thesis, University of Edinburgh, 2007), p. 134.
22. S. Poggo, *The First Sudanese Civil War: Africans, Arabs, and Israelis in the Southern Sudan, 1955–1972* (Basingstoke, 2011), p. 32.
23. S. Poggo, *The First Sudanese Civil War*, p. 42.
24. Omi and Winant's work on the meaning-making process of racial identities is instructive here. M. Omi and H. Winant, *Racial Formation in the United States: From the 1960s to the 1980s* (New York, 1989), p. 62.
25. S. Deng and A. Wol, *Let's Speak the Truth: Presentation of Facts and Views by Two Prominent Sudanese from the South* (Khartoum, 1963), p. 7.
26. Deng and Wol, *Let's Speak the Truth.*
27. After William Deng began embracing moderate unionist politics, Ambrose Wol joined SANU-inside. Chapter 6 provides the details.
28. 'Problem in Sudan, Will Test All Africa', *Bennington Banner* (Bennington, Vermont) (7 November 1963), p. 6. https://www.newspapers.com/newspage/63025533/ (accessed on 20 February 2016).
29. W. G. Landrey, 'Sudan Facing Grave Weld Job', *Desert Sun* (California) No. 57, 9 October 1963.

30. Deng and Wol, *Let's Speak*, pp. 7–8.
31. Ibid, p. 15.
32. Ibid. Emphasis in original.
33. Ibid, pp. 15, 12.
34. Ibid, p. 8.
35. Ibid, p. 8.
36. Ibid, p. 15.
37. Ibid, p. 8.
38. Ibid, p. 16.
39. Ibid, p. 12
40. Ibid, pp. 9, 12.
41. Ibid, p. 18.
42. Ibid, p. 10.
43. Ibid, p. 11.
44. The practice of including photographs was not altogether unusual for government documents for public consumption in Sudan. The Nimeiri administration from 1969 included the photographs of the leaders mentioned therein. Southern exiles used images of leaders a great deal in their propaganda as well, and thus it seemed relatively conventional.
45. Santino Deng took particular issue with the allegations of the persecution of Christians. In his essay, he countered them by listing the names of seven Christians from the South who had attaining senior roles in Sudan. Through a brief discussion of the achievements of Southerners in various arenas, ranging from education to health services and agriculture, Deng attempted to argue that Southerners were thriving in Sudan. He argued that all Sudanese people were equal, and that any of the problems the country had were the result of the colonial 'plan to separate the South from the North.' See Deng and Wol, *Let's Speak*, p. 5.
46. Ibid, p. 6.
47. Ibid, p. 17.
48. W. Deng, 'Betray not your people', *Voice of Southern Sudan*, 2/2 (1964), p. 30.
49. 'Editorial Comment', *Voice of Southern Sudan*, 1/2 (1963), p. 1.
50. F. Cooper, 'The Dialectics of Decolonization: Nationalism and labour movements in post-war French Africa', in P. Duara (ed), *Decolonization: Perspectives from Now and Then* (London, 2004) p. 427. Alina Sajed has identified similar discontents in Indonesia, recognising that 'while the anti-colonial nationalist project removes from power the colonial administration and the colonial political rule, it fails to dislodge the colonial logic of modernity by leaving such hierarchies intact or even by instating new hierarchies.' A. Sajed, 'Peripheral modernity and anti-colonial nationalism in Java: economies of race and gender in the constitution of the Indonesian national teleology', *Third World Quarterly*, 38/2 (2016) p. 3.

CHAPTER 5

The Political Afterlives of Rebel Narratives

The Sudan African National Union (SANU)'s discourses aimed to elicit demonstrations of African solidarity, condemnations of the Sudanese government and, ultimately, support for the South's right to self-determination. To this end, SANU spread its propaganda far and wide, ensuring that key international actors heard its version of the events taking place in Southern Sudan. As the first few chapters showed, shaping international opinion about the conflict was a bitterly contested and creative process. However, since scholars have primarily engaged with Southern Sudan's first civil war in military and legal terms, the international reach and diplomatic impact of this battle of narratives has yet to be fully explored.

The failure of Southern politicians to attain a self-determination plebiscite in the 1960s has obscured their gains and the instances in which they were able to influence the perceptions of international audiences. Due to the Organisation of African Unity's (OAU) strong commitment to territorial integrity and non-intervention, it can appear that the Southern Sudanese cause was simply destined to fail.[1] This chapter complicates this deterministic perspective by uncovering the purchase—albeit limited and uneven—that SANU discourses had in the 1960s and the kind of political action they produced. It argues that some of the audiences in Africa and further afield not only consumed but also reproduced these discourses. Moreover, it reveals the various filters and sets of interests through which different audiences decoded and responded to SANU's discursive constructions of the "Southern Problem". It argues that the Southern cause,

S. C. Manoeli, *Sudan's "Southern Problem"*, African Histories and Modernities, https://doi.org/10.1007/978-3-030-28771-9_5

as defined by SANU, remained resilient despite the organisation's inability to achieve the political outcomes for which it advocated.

We begin by mapping the discursive constructions of student-led and other international solidarity efforts in support of the Southern cause.

Student Activism Abroad and International Solidarity

Southern Sudanese students abroad played a crucial role in promoting the Southern cause to international audiences. The following exploration of their activism abroad will offer important insight into the ways in which SANU's discursive constructs spread and were reproduced. For example, in 1964, the National Executive of the Union of Southern Sudan Students and Youth (USSY) based in Leopoldville (now Kinshasa) in Congo published a booklet titled *The Problem of Southern Sudan: The Voice of African Students*, containing a brief statement on the ruinous crisis in the South.[2] Scant evidence exists regarding the political life and activities of this organisation beyond this booklet. A year after SANU published its foundational text, this group of Southern Sudanese students followed suit. The booklet's title and content indicate that these students subscribed to SANU's discursive construction of the Southern cause. Moreover, by using the same title as the seminal book, the students identified themselves as leaders in exile of the same ilk, probably in a bid to accrue reputational benefits.

Addressed to 'all African student organisations', the booklet encouraged the readers to protest against the Sudanese government, to appeal to and lobby their respective national governments and the UN to support Southern Sudanese self-determination.[3] Claiming to represent Southern Sudanese students exiled in the Central African Republic, Ethiopia, Uganda, Kenya and Congo (Leopoldville), the Union lamented the dearth of African solidarity with the South. Commending only the 'youth and people of Uganda' for their unfailing support, the USSY testified that

> [s]o far the African States and Governments have tried to ignore the presence in their midst of the Arab reign of terror in Southern Sudan and of the situation which threatens the very existence of our people. So far [,] no voice has been raised officially to defend us.[4]

The booklet suggested that the lack of official support revealed deliberate neglect. It also detailed the exploitation and marginalisation of Southerners in Sudan. Echoing SANU, they insisted that

> the Southern Sudanese have been subjected to the worst kind of colonialism, racial discrimination, political and economic subjugation and religious persecution. ... The situation is no different to that in Southern Rhodesia, Angola or South Africa, except that the oppressors in this case are Arabs but the oppressed are Africans. In our minds colonialism is associated with the European, but the Arabs in the Southern Sudan have proved a worse type of coloniser.[5]

The booklet's tone, rhetoric and style resembled SANU's propaganda, including the specific repertoire of analogies. The booklet thus reinforced SANU's message, and further demonstrates the authority of SANU discourses among the Southern Sudanese diaspora.

Southern Sudanese students in other parts of the world also took political action. The All African Students' Congress conference held on 6–11 March 1964 in Moscow represented a significant milestone for Southern students exiled in Europe. Hosted by the Federation of African Students in the Soviet Union (FASSS), the biennial conference assembled 147 delegates from 13 countries across Europe.[6] Being the third ever Congress of the Union of All African Students in Europe, the conference aimed at positioning African youth as the 'avant-garde of the struggle for liberation and African unity'.[7] The *Voice of Southern Sudan* reported that the Southern Sudanese representatives at the conference openly disputed the Sudanese government's explanation of the conflict, urging that the "Southern Problem" was in fact a new 'colonial problem'.[8] As a result of their lobbying, the Congress officially condemned the Abboud regime, passing a resolution calling 'on educated and masses in the Sudan to recognise the problem of the Southern Sudan; for an end to racial and religious discrimination'.[9] This phrasing, particularly the reference to Sudan's racial fault line, signified a discursive victory for the Southern exile movement.

By highlighting the cause of Southern Sudan to other African students in Europe, these student representatives broadened the audience that had access to Southern perspectives on the Sudanese conflict. A Pan-African conference was in fact the optimal setting for SANU's message. Not only did the students promote the cause itself, but they also did so in the same charged language. Furthermore, the students communicated the outcomes of their efforts to SANU representatives, who then reported them to their readership through *Voice of Southern Sudan*. A feedback loop of discourse production, dissemination, assimilation, reproduction and further dissemination thus developed.

Another expression of African solidarity for the Southern cause occurred two months later. The East African Students Association of Britain and Ireland, led by three undergraduate students from Kenya, Uganda and Tanganyika (now Tanzania), expressed its displeasure with General Abboud's regime in Sudan at a press conference in London.[10] During the President's portentous first state visit to the UK, which began on 26 May 1964, and lasted ten days, the students had planned a protest march in Victoria, London, but Scotland Yard obstructed them.[11] Their protest action was not unusual as religious networks in Britain also protested General Abboud's visit on account of his anti-missionary policies.[12]

It is likely that the students were prohibited because of the tremendous importance of this visit to the British government, which was indicated by the presence of the Queen, the Prime Minister, the Foreign Minister and the Lord Mayor of London who all waited to receive President Abboud at the Victoria station.[13] Having established a good reputation for himself and his regime abroad, Abboud was honoured in Western (and Eastern) capitals seemingly without reservation.[14] Even President John F. Kennedy welcomed him with exceptionally warm hospitality for a foreign head of state on an 11-day state visit to the US in October 1961.[15] Sudan was an important ally to the UK for geo-political reasons. While Abboud remained the head of state, the UK retained the right to base military forces in Sudan. Further, as a result of this visit, the UK sought to secure rights for its civil and military aircraft to overfly Sudan, in order to access the cheapest route for British aircraft to reach Singapore, Australia, the Gulf and other regions in the East.[16] Thus, the British government turned a blind eye to his 'benign' military dictatorship.[17]

In lieu of a march, the students held up placards along the route of Abboud's procession, some of which read: 'Abboud, you are a threat to African Unity', 'Stop killing Southern Sudanese', 'Equality for all Sudanese' and 'Self-determination for the Sudan'.[18] They also wrote a publicly circulated petition to President Abboud, and submitted it to the Sudanese Embassy in London. The open letter, signed by the three student leaders, noted that many of Sudan's Southern population had fled to Uganda, the Central African Republic, Congo and Ethiopia. This act of solidarity by the students stemmed in part from being exposed to the refugee crisis that spilled into their home countries in East Africa. Thus, they sought to expose the regime's 'diplomatic hypocrisy and double talk', and espoused the racialised discourses of the Southern Sudanese exile leaders.[19] For example, their letter stated:

> The root cause of the troubles that threaten the territorial unity of your Republic today, is not Negro-racial aspirations or secessionist movement of the Southern people, but the racialist and misguided religious ideology of the Afro-Arabs who dominate the country politically and economically. … the Negro has to be civilised to be worthy of citizenship. … These are the things the Negroes hate and will continue to fight against be it in South Africa, Angola or Southern Rhodesia.[20]

By identifying these 'root causes', the group of students employed SANU's diagnostic framing of the "Southern Problem" in the language and logic SANU popularised.[21]

Even though the protests were ultimately ineffective, certain sections of the British press highlighted the disjuncture between these grievances against Abboud and the British government's warm hospitality towards him. The public controversy surrounding the state visit was 'acutely embarrassing for the Foreign Office'.[22] Ultimately, one journalist explicitly noted that '[n]o hint of the threatened demonstrations marred the decorum of the arrival' of Abboud.[23] Such student protests were not formidable enough to undermine Abboud's legitimacy abroad, but they do attest to the strength of the budding network of sympathisers of African origin with SANU and the wide international reach of the Southern Sudanese discourses, as well as the Pan-Africanist appeal these had among non-Sudanese African students. The movement of ideas over time and space show that SANU's discursive networks transcended the purview of the proximate communities of Southern Sudanese refugees in East Africa.

The Southern Sudanese cause increasingly attracted attention across Europe. From 19 to 24 June 1964, SANU was invited to send delegates to the human rights-focused Mediterranean Colloquium in Florence, Italy. Among the distinguished guests, Martin Luther King Jr. was personally invited by the Mayor of Florence to speak at the Colloquium on 'racial segregation in USA'.[24] King did not attend the event, but the invitation suggested that the Colloquium provided a platform for racial justice activism. It served as a sympathetic context for SANU's discursive representation of the "Southern Problem". The organisers of the conference 'expressed their optimism to be able to find a peaceful solution' to the Sudanese conflict.[25] SANU reported that, although invited, the government of Sudan 'refused' to send delegates to the Colloquium.[26] Declining an opportunity to share a platform with Southern rebels was a strategic move on the part of the Sudanese government as such a setting would not allow them to control the narrative or the discursive parameters of discussion. At the event, SANU explicitly framed the conflict as 'a classical case of racial discrimination amounting to a breach of Human Rights'.[27] The Colloquium participants expressed sympathy for the cause, urging the government of Sudan to recognise diversity within the country and allow for the freedom of religious and cultural expression.

As this section has revealed, SANU circulated its rendition of the Southern cause through disparate groups of international students and activists in Africa and Europe. International audiences received, consumed and reproduced the exile political movement's narrative. The following section will uncover more of the gains SANU made specifically in Uganda, the location of SANU's headquarters and a neighbouring country of strategic import.

The Diplomatic Contest over Uganda

Uganda's proximity to Sudan and its accommodation of 70,000–200,000 Sudanese refugees in the 1960s made it a key stakeholder in the conflict.[28] Thus, Milton Obote's first state visit to Sudan in 1963 represented an important diplomatic event for both the government of Sudan and the rebels in exile. If successful, the visit was expected to legitimise the Sudanese government in the eyes of the African head of state, and serve, in the rather hyperbolic words of SANU, 'as the final death blow to the Southern Sudanese aspiration [for] freedom and justice'.[29] In preparation for the state visit, SANU sent Prime Minister Obote a letter cautioning that

> the Arabs will exploit your visit to the maximum extent possible, and construe it publicly to mean a stamp of your personal approval on the policies they are now plotting aimed at absorbing and Arabising the Negro people.[30]

In the high-stakes contestation between the Sudanese state and the Southern rebels, these stamps of personal and governmental approval were coveted commodities. As a result, the rebels sought to introduce

Prime Minister Obote to an alternative perspective. SANU pleaded with him to

> keep in mind that you will be dining and wining with those who are oppressing and despising your fellow Negroes of Southern Sudan now in Arab bondage. The hands that will greet you are full of the blood of your brothers.[31]

In its rhetorical fashion, SANU vied for Obote's sympathy by accentuating the discourse of Sudan's racial binary. By referring to Southerners as 'fellow Negroes' and Obote's 'brothers', SANU alluded to Obote originating in northern Uganda. Moreover, given that the Nilotic northern region bordering Southern Sudan had represented a marginalised part of Uganda, SANU hoped that Obote would sympathise with the political exclusion of the people of Southern Sudan.[32]

Ultimately, Obote's visit to Khartoum did not lead to a strong condemnation of either the Southern rebels or the Sudanese state. Yet, one of Obote's biographers suggests that 'Obote could not help feeling some sympathy for the rebels because he believed that the Sudanese government had no policy for the southern region other than military conquest'.[33] Although the biographer made no mention of SANU's petitions, it is likely that SANU's campaigning played a part. Nonetheless, Obote did little more than tolerate the presence of the exile movement on Ugandan soil.

Although Obote held an ambivalent view of the Sudanese government, on occasion he cooperated with it. Starting with Uganda in March 1964, Sudan sought to sign extradition agreements with its neighbouring countries that were used 'by outlawed persons as centres for anti-Sudan activities'.[34] After General Abboud was toppled in October 1964, Saddiq al-Mahdi rose to the rank of Prime Minister of Sudan in 1966, after a transitional military government which was followed by a civilian one led by Mohammed Mahgoub. Obote established a good rapport with al-Mahdi. On a state visit with the new Sudanese Prime Minister in 1966, Obote decided to cooperate with the government of Sudan to suppress the Southern Sudanese rebellion—armed as well as political—on their shared border. They established a joint Ugandan-Sudanese task force aimed at tracking down Southern rebels in Uganda.[35] Moreover, the Ugandan government officially evicted Southern Sudanese political activists in the country. Since some of the parties in question had decided to relocate into the South prior to the announcement of the expulsion, the exile movement interpreted Uganda's decision as 'window dressing for the OAU, and as an advance gesture before discussions planned for [that] week with the Sudanese Prime Minister in Kampala'.[36] Despite the changes in policy, some of the Southern Sudanese politicians remained in Gulu, northern Uganda.[37]

The Southern Sudanese refugees who entered Uganda came into contact with communities in the country's northern region first, and thus local politicians subsumed the Southern Sudanese refugee crisis into Ugandan regional politics. Northern Ugandan solidarity for Southern Sudan in the 1960s is best understood through the prism of the fragile relationship between the Acholi and Obote. The Acholi constituency had expected Obote, having rallied them under the banner of a shared northern Ugandan identity during his election campaign, to serve their interests once in office.[38] However, Acholi political leaders accused Obote of only serving the interests of his Lango ethnic group. Obote's increasing authoritarianism exacerbated these grievances, and consequently, Acholi ethnonationalism constituted a significant challenge to Obote's government.

Even though Obote backed al-Mahdi's Sudanese government, many members of Uganda's security forces and police—who were relied upon to enforce the cooperation policy—were sympathetic to the cause of Southerners, as many of them originated from ethnicities that overlap Uganda's northern border, including the Acholi. The policy had limited efficacy as 'there were several former southern Sudanese exiles in … senior positions in the Ugandan armed forces and security services'.[39] These Southerners had grown up in Uganda as naturalised citizens, having left Sudan as early as 1955.[40] Obote's newfound camaraderie with al-Mahdi thus affected the Southern Sudanese exile and refugee community in Uganda rather inchoately.[41] After al-Mahdi left office in 1967, and his predecessor, Mahgoub, who was known for his repressive approach to the South, returned to power, the Ugandan forces maintained the partnership only begrudgingly. Prior to his successful coup against Obote, the head of the Ugandan army who also originated from northern Uganda, Commander Idi Amin Dada Oumee, alongside others, assisted Southern rebels surreptitiously as disaffection with the Obote regime 'had permeated the top echelons of the Ugandan army corps'.[42] Upon coming to power in 1971, Amin openly supported the secessionist movement in Southern Sudan.[43]

The sympathies of some of Uganda's government officials towards the South were revealed as early as the OAU Foreign Ministers conference (the Council of Ministers Second Ordinary Session) of March 1964, in Lagos, Nigeria. Uganda's Minister of Planning and Development, Adoko Nekyon, alerted the delegates to the effects the influx of Southern Sudanese refugees had on Uganda, and urged the conference attendees to help solve the problem that had caused the large-scale migration. Nekyon was Obote's cousin, and also originated from northern Uganda.[44] The Sudanese Minister of Foreign Affairs, Mohamed Mahgoub, discouraged the discussion, insisting it was purely an internal matter. Despite the official Sudanese position, the other African ministers passed a resolution calling for the establishment of an OAU committee to investigate the root causes of Africa's refugee crises, including the case of Southern Sudan, and scheduled an investigative commission.[45]

In the run-up to the investigation, Ugandan politicians discussed the "Southern Problem" in ways that reflected SANU's narrative conventions. For instance, in April 1964, a Ugandan Member of Parliament from North-West Acholi, Alexander Latim, expressed his intention as a member of the Opposition to move a motion in the House about the 'genocide' in Sudan in the upcoming parliamentary session.[46] Expressing his sympathy for the Southern Sudanese, Latim told the press that '[w]e want the world to know what is going on'.[47] He told the press that he was

> speaking as a man from the North, not as a member of the Democratic Party. I do not see how diplomatic relations with the Sudan can be tolerated. ... If we explain all the atrocities now being done in the Sudan then no sensible government will tolerate having friendly relations with such a country.[48]

Latim claimed that his sympathy was based on his proximity to Southern Sudan in order to avoid being construed as only criticising the Obote government's relations with Sudan for political gain. By suggesting that Uganda end diplomatic relations with Sudan, Latim reached the exact prognostic framing that SANU discourses aimed to produce. Suggesting that the Sudanese government actively sought to hinder rebel discourses from gaining traction in Uganda, the very next day, the Sudanese Chargé d'Affaires in Kampala, M. H. Abbo told the Ugandan press that his government denied all allegations of 'practicing genocide'.[49] He alleged that 'Mr Latim's story had been one-sided. It seemed he had only heard what the refugees had said, but had he gone to the Sudanese Embassy he would have been given "full information about what is going on."'[50] By phrasing his response to Latim's allegations in this way, Abbo understood the Southern rebels and the Sudanese government as discursive rivals.[51]

Similarly, in a press conference in June 1964, the deputy leader of a Ugandan opposition party accused the Sudanese government of actively preventing a Ugandan delegation from visiting Southern Sudan to investigate the situation.[52] Latim also made the same claim.[53] Abbo denied the allegation that Sudan was stalling by reframing the meaning of the visit: 'the mission was one of good-will, not a commission of inquiry. The idea was for the Ugandans to be shown about the Sudan so they could tell the refugees here that they had nothing to fear in returning home'.[54]

The following month, in July 1964, another Member of Parliament in Uganda, Eric Y. Lakidi, from Prime Minister Obote's political party, the Uganda People's Congress (UPC), also urged his government to intervene on behalf of Southern Sudanese refugees in northern Uganda. He sympathised with them because he believed that 'the Arabs in the North [were] trying to drive out the Southern Sudanese'.[55] Reaching the same conclusion as Latim, Lakidi asked a provocative question of the Ugandan government:

> I don't know how this government is married to the Abboud government and how we can stand on the floor of this House and speak about South Africa and Portugal when people are being slaughtered like cattle next door to us. These are our own African brothers.[56]

By drawing on these specific analogies, it is clear that Lakidi, a representative of Acholi in northern Uganda, had accepted SANU's discursive framing of the conflict. His willingness to take a public stance on the crisis in Southern Sudan may have also stemmed from his own political motives, as he had gained a reputation for being a critic of the Obote administration.[57] Regardless of the varied political interests that animated Ugandan concern for Southern Sudan, these developments suggest that some influential Ugandan political leaders framed the "Southern Problem" precisely in the terms that SANU promoted. As such, SANU's discursive representations of Sudan's conflict shaped the interpretation of Sudan to this strategic neighbouring country.

It also began influencing the OAU. On the recommendation of ministers at the Lagos meeting of 1964, the Organisation established a Commission on Refugees (that later became the Commission of Fifteen on Refugee Problems in Africa, 'then of Twenty and finally of all member states')[58] that initially included Uganda, Burundi, Cameroon, Congo (Leopoldville), Ghana, Nigeria, Rwanda, Senegal, Sudan and Tanzania.[59] Charged with the mandate of handling refugee problems in Africa, the Commission began hearing evidence on 16 November 1964, in Uganda.[60] Milton Obote gave the welcome address at the opening session. He provocatively asked, 'What pride can the Organisation for African Unity have in the achievement of independence... and the unity of Africa when thousands of Africans know life only as a nightmare?'[61] At the time, Uganda housed tens of thousands of Rwandan and Sudanese refugees.[62] Read against the backdrop of SANU's debates at the time about the meaning of African unity in the context of an imposed union between Southern and Northern Sudan, Obote's comments reflect a fledgling sympathy for groups like SANU and a tacit agreement that unity was not necessarily desirable at all costs. The expression of that sentiment at an OAU meeting signified an important step. In effect, a member state's prime minister implicitly challenged the Organisation's policy of non-interference.

Conclusion

The outcomes of the commission, however, were negligible, largely due to the change of government in Sudan a month earlier. In October 1964, a popular revolution toppled the Abboud regime, and a civilian transitional caretaker government took over. By the end of the year, the government had agreed to meet with SANU in a conference dedicated to the "Southern Problem". It is to this landmark event that we now turn. The Round-Table Conference of March 1965 represented the first diplomatic platform designed to enable both Sudan's rebels and the government to make their case to international audiences.

Notes

1. D. Thiam, *The Foreign Policy of African States: Ideological bases, present realities, future prospects* (London, 1965).
2. Union of Southern Sudanese Students and Youth (USSY), 'The Problem of the Southern Sudan: The Voice of the African Students', c. 1964, ARC, A/90, 3/1.
3. While it is unclear how widely it was circulated, I discovered the document in an archive in Rome, Italy. Given the close connections between Catholic missionaries and Southern Sudanese refugees, it is not surprising that the

document made its way there. However, since it was written in English, the intended audience must have been wide.

4. USSY, 'The Problem'. ARC, A/90, 3/1.
5. Ibid.
6. J. Hessler, 'Death of an African Student in Moscow: Race, Politics, and the Cold War', *Cahiers du Monde Russe*, 47/1 (2006), p. 44. The 13 countries included the USSR, Britain, Yugoslavia, Austria, Bulgaria, Hungary, Italy, both Germanys, Poland, France, Romania and Czechoslovakia.
7. I. M. Wallerstein, *Africa: The Politics of Independence and Unity* (Lincoln, 2005), pp. 215–216.
8. 'Students Congress Condemns Abouds [sic] Policy in the South', *Voice of Southern Sudan*, 2/2 (1964), p. 5.
9. Ibid, p. 6.
10. P. Keatley, 'Protest Against "Atrocities"', *The Guardian* (26 May 1964), p. 1.
11. Ibid, p. 7.
12. 'Protest at Sudanese state visit', *The Guardian* (25 May 1964).
13. Keatley, 'Protest', p. 1.
14. Prior to arriving in the UK, Abboud had just concluded a successful five-day state visit to Peking, China, from 16 to 20 May 1964, aimed at solidifying African and Asian solidarity against Western imperialism. The following chapters will delve into the ways in which the Sudanese government circulated its own discourses and how it managed its image and reputation abroad.
15. 'America Welcomes President Abboud of Sudan, October 1961: 4–15', John F. Kennedy Library and Museum, http://www.jfklibrary.org/Asset-Viewer/Archives/USG-01-F.aspx (accessed on 23 July 2015).
16. C. Hollingworth, 'Britain seeks flying rights over Sudan: Cheapest route to Aden and Singapore', *The Guardian* (26 May 1964), p. 1.
17. W. R. Louis and S. R. Ashton, *East of Suez and the Commonwealth, 1964–1971* (London, 2004), p. cxxviii.
18. 'Police Stop Students Demonstration', Voice of Southern Sudan, 2/2 (1964), p. 11.
19. 'A Petition by the East African Students in the United Kingdom and Ireland to President Ibrahim Abboud of the Republic of Sudan During His State Visit to the United Kingdom', 21 May 1964, SAD 944/6/37.
20. 'A Petition by the East African Students in the United Kingdom and Ireland to President Ibrahim Abboud of the Republic of Sudan During His State Visit to the United Kingdom', 21 May 1964, SAD 944/6/39. Emphasis in original.
21. R. D. Benford and D. A. Snow, 'Framing Processes and Social Movements: An Overview and Assessment', *Annual Review of Sociology*, 26 (200), pp. 611–639.

22. Keatley, 'Protest', p. 1.
23. 'Decorous welcome to Sudan President. Pageantry in the sunshine', *The Guardian* (27 May 1964), p. 7.
24. Telegraph from Nicolas Nabokov to Martin Luther King Jr., 29 May 1964, The King Centre, Digital Archive, http://thekingcenter.org/archive/document/telegram-nicolas-nabokov-mlk (accessed on 29 February 2016).
25. 'SANU for Talks on Human Rights', *Voice of Southern Sudan*, 2/2 (1964), p. 12.
26. Ibid.
27. 'Florence Conference Passes Motion on South Sudan', Voice of Southern Sudan, 2/3 (1964), p. 9.
28. By 1969, the US Committee for Refugees estimated that Uganda housed 71,500 Sudanese refugees. Anthony Sylvester argues that the number may have reached 200,000. A. Sylvester, *Sudan under Nimeiri* (London, 1977), p. 171. O. Otunnu, *Crisis of Legitimacy and Political Violence in Uganda, 1890–1979*, p. 219.
29. SANU, 'Letter to Obote', *Voice of Southern Sudan*, 1/2 (1963), p. 16.
30. Ibid.
31. Ibid.
32. For more on the divisions in Uganda, Northern 'Nilotic Military Ethnocracy' and Northern marginalisation in Ugandan politics, see E. Almeida, 'Was the colonial policy of ethnic self-rule responsible for the divided polity in Uganda?' (PhD thesis, University of Western Ontario, 2000).
33. K. Ingham, *Obote: A Political Biography* (London, 1994) p. 117.
34. 'Sudan-Uganda talks on repatriation', *Uganda Argus* (14 March 1964), p. 1.
35. J. Bercovitch and J. Fretter, *Regional Guide to International Conflict and Management from 1945 to 2003* (Washington DC, 2004), p. 67. Heraclides, 'Janus', p. 224.
36. 'Sudan: stalemate in the South?' *Africa Confidential*, No. 5 (4 March 1966), p. 6.
37. Ibid.
38. E. Laruni, 'Regional and ethnic identities the Acholi of Northern Uganda, 1950–1968', *Journal of Eastern African Studies*, 9/2 (2015), pp. 215–225.
39. J. Howell, 'Horn of Africa: Lessons from the Sudan Conflict', *International Affairs*, 54/3 (1978), p. 432.
40. Ibid.
41. Ingham, *Obote*, p. 117.
42. Laruni, 'Regional and ethnic identities', p. 215.

43. Heraclides, 'Janus', p. 224. P. Woodward, 'Uganda and southern Sudan; peripheral politics and neighbour relations', in H. B. Hansen and M. Twaddle (eds), *Uganda Now: Between decay and development* (London, 1988), p. 231. For more on Amin's Southern Sudanese heritage, see M. Leopold, 'Legacies of Slavery in North-West Uganda: The Story of the "One-Elevens"', *Journal of the International African Institute*, 76/2 (2006), pp. 180–199.
44. G. N. Uzoingwe, 'Uganda and Parliamentary Government', *Journal of Modern African Studies*, 21//2 (1983), p. 262.
45. See Organization of African Unity (Council of Ministers), 'Resolution on the Problem of Refugees in Africa' (OAU Lagos 24–29 February 1964) CM/Res 19 (II). Marina Sharpe, 'Engaging with refugee protection? The Organization of African Unity and African Union since 1963', The UN Refugee Agency Policy Development and Evaluation Service: Research Paper No. 226, 2011, p. 7. 'OAU to Examine Southern Sudan's Question', *Voice of Southern Sudan*, 2/2 (1964), p. 9.
46. 'Genocide in South Sudan – MP', *Uganda Argus* (24 April 1964), p. 5.
47. Ibid.
48. Ibid.
49. 'Sudan Denies Genocide Charge', *Uganda Argus* (25 April 1964), p. 5.
50. Ibid.
51. Sudan's government had been placed on the defensive before. For example, as news about the new policies against missionaries were reported in the Ugandan press, Sudan's Minister of Interior Mohammed Ahmed Irwa swiftly addressed the media. He stated in a press conference in Khartoum that the government 'would in no way jeopardise the freedom of the Sudanese to practice their religions without fear and influence'. In a bid to control the narrative, he further suggested that the government was simply punishing 'subversive activities that foreign missionaries were undertaking in Southern Sudan'. '"Sudanese free to practice any religion"', *Uganda Argus* (4 March 1964), p. 2.
52. 'Uganda Parliament Holds Debate on Southern Sudan', *Voice of Southern Sudan*, 2/3 (1964), p. 6.
53. 'Genocide in South Sudan – MP'.
54. 'Sudan Denies Genocide Charge'.
55. 'Call for better houses', *Uganda Argus* (1 July 1964).
56. Ibid. Versions of this also appear in: Mahgoub, *Democracy on Trial*, p. 204. K. D. D. Henderson, *Sudan Republic* (London, 1966), p. 204.
57. Laruni, 'Regional and ethnic', pp. 223–225.
58. The official moniker "Commission of Ten" was first used in February 1973 at the 20th Ordinary Session of the Council of Ministered in Addis Ababa. Sharpe, 'Engaging with refugee protection?' pp. 2, 17.

59. Charles Paulinus Gasarasi, 'The Effect of Africa's Exiles/Refugees Upon Inter-African State Relations: Conflict and Cooperation – 1958–1988' (PhD thesis, Tulane University, 1988), p. 16.
60. 'Refugee Commission of the OAU Hears Evidence', *Voice of Southern Sudan*, 2/4 (1965), p. 3.
61. Ibid.
62. Yosa Wawa suggests that 50,000 had entered Uganda by 1964. Y. Wawa, *Refugee Aid and Development: A Case of Sudanese Refugees in West Nile, Uganda* (Kampala, 2008).

CHAPTER 6

Discourse, Diplomacy and Disintegration at the Round Table Conference

The fall of the Abboud administration in October 1964 signified the start of a new political dispensation. Ostensibly centred on the Abboud government's failure to settle the war in the South, the October Revolution of 1964, as it came to be known, was sparked when the police murdered a student activist in a clash between the Khartoum University Student Union and the police.[1] A network of Khartoum University-educated professionals banded together to mount a strike against the government that led to its overthrow.[2] In its wake, the Revolution brought about the restoration of parliamentary democracy under the leadership of a transitional government until elections could be held in 1965. A group of Southerners in Khartoum swiftly formed the Southern Front two days after the Revolution in order to mobilise Southerners and 'lead the South through the political vacuum that the overthrow of Ibrahim Abboud regime had created'.[3]

In its publications, the Sudan African National Union (SANU) portrayed the Southern Front as a legitimate 'body representing and safeguarding the interests of the Africans of Southern Sudan'.[4] SANU even went so far as to endorse the Front as possessing the 'authority to prevent the creation of any political parties in the South'.[5] It was careful to debunk the rumours that the formation of the Front represented 'a move by Southerners within the Sudan to take over leadership from SANU'.[6] SANU described the relationship with the Southern Front as one of solidarity and saw itself as the leader in the partnership.

S. C. Manoeli, *Sudan's "Southern Problem"*, African Histories and Modernities, https://doi.org/10.1007/978-3-030-28771-9_6

A month after the October Revolution of 1964, founding member of SANU William Deng wrote a letter that ultimately led to a schism in SANU.[7] While in Geneva, he composed an unusual letter to the new prime minister of Sudan's transitional government, unbeknownst to the other SANU leaders.[8] The letter called for a round table conference with foreign observers and listed other demands, including the official recognition of SANU as a political party in Sudan, and amnesty for returning refugees. It is unclear whether there had been conflict within the SANU leadership that would have led Deng to reject the party line. It is likely that Deng wrote the letter due to being slighted at the SANU Convention of 1964. Taking place between 7 and 16 November in Kampala, Uganda, SANU's first party convention was significant as elections for senior leadership positions were held. After having served as Secretary General and the Secretary for International and African Affairs, William Deng's conspicuous absence from the convention was striking. As a result, he did not attain a new position within SANU.[9] The reasons for his absence remain unclear. The inability of the former Southern parliamentarian and rebel leader Dominic Muorwel to attend the conference, due to being confined to the Central African Republic, did not prevent him being elected to serve as SANU's National Chairman.[10]

Deng undermined SANU's Black Nationalist discourse in the letter. Initially, the language he used corresponded with SANU's established discourse, noting the reified differences between the 'two distinct personalities, cultures and temperament' of 'Negroid and Arab' people.[11] However, in contradiction to the binary view of Sudan that SANU had painstakingly constructed, Deng alleged that 'we are not racialists because we are aware that races have been mixing over the centuries with the result that few can really trace their original blood'.[12] This resembled the Sudanese government's discourses which emphasised the Sudanese population's genetic and social complexity, as we have seen. Deng posited that rather than racial homogeneity, 'it is mainly Constitutional justice that can create nations'.[13] Deng also alleged that SANU supported federalism, an assertion that had not featured in any of SANU's reviewed international publications. Having recanted SANU's commitment to racial distinction and incompatibility, Deng could proffer federalism as a possible political solution to the "Southern Problem". He argued that 'unity in diversity is the answer to the Southern problem and this can be forged in a federal Constitution'.[14]

The letter caused monumental damage to SANU's political unity. William Deng publicised his new political position under the auspices of SANU far and wide, and thus sabotaged the organisation's bargaining power. He sent copies of the letter to all the governments in Africa, the Secretary General of the Organisation of African Unity (OAU), all the political parties in Sudan and the Vice-Chancellor of the University of Khartoum.[15] Given that SANU only published *Voice of Southern Sudan* on a quarterly basis, it is unclear the immediate steps that the leadership took against William Deng for straying away from the official line. However, in the next edition of *Voice of Southern Sudan*, published in February 1965, SANU claimed that William Deng's 'subsequent disagreement with other members of the Executive, for leading a policy not in accordance with SANU's objectives, has now ended'.[16] However, in the following edition of May 1965, after the Round Table Conference (RTC), the President of SANU, Aggrey Jaden, declared Deng officially expelled for violating the party's constitution. Jaden reported that Deng had sought to 'confuse Southerners and mislead the world about SANU policy'.[17]

Deng subsequently returned to Sudan. He explained in another letter to the new prime minister of Sudan that the goodwill he perceived from the transitional government, which had acted on some of his demands, triggered his decision to return to Sudan.[18] These demands included the Sudanese government making a statement to the OAU guaranteeing the safety of any refugee or rebel who wished to return to Sudan, and signing a repatriation agreement with the Ugandan government that guaranteed refugees the freedom of political association.[19] Thereafter, he established a political party dubbed "SANU-Inside". SANU-In-Exile, as it came to be colloquially known, reported that Deng had 'virtually created a new party although he still calls it SANU'.[20] Emphasising Deng's position as a pariah to the liberation movement in exile, SANU's leadership informed its readers through *Voice of Southern Sudan* that none of Deng's former colleagues had joined him in the new faction, suggesting that he acted alone.

The new Prime Minister of Sudan, Khatim Khalifa, responded positively to Deng's aberrant letter and agreed to the conference. Despite the Round Table Conference occurring as a result of Deng's betrayal, SANU-In-Exile as well as the Southern Front agreed to participate. Their participation, however, was conditional upon the Conference being held 'anywhere in the world except Northern Sudan' in order to ensure the participation of the armed rebels from the South who required neutral ground for their safety.[21] Since Northern Sudanese political leaders expressed their preference for hosting it in Khartoum, the Southern bloc suggested Juba as a compromise location. However, a few days before the Conference was scheduled to begin, Sudanese soldiers opened fire on civilians in Juba.[22] As a result of the subsequent instability, the Conference was moved to Khartoum. The Southern Front, like other Southern organisations, agreed to the venue change because 'the end game was very clear: the goal had always been to articulate the political agenda of Southern Sudan in an international forum, no matter where that forum was held'.[23] Ultimately, the Northern political establishment outmanoeuvred SANU and its allies, as they attended the Conference on what they perceived to be Northern terms.

The Round Table Conference: A Discursive and Performative Moment

A group of 27 representatives from the Southern region and 18 from the Northern region gathered in Khartoum from 16 to 30 March 1965, for the Round Table Conference (RTC). Four political parties represented the South, namely SANU-In-Exile (under the leadership of Aggrey Jaden), its ally the Southern Front, the breakaway faction SANU-Inside (led by William Deng) and the broad coalition dubbed 'Other Shades of Opinions' representing pro-government views including parties such as the Sudan Unity Party. As I will elucidate below, the latter were included later in the proceedings at the behest of the Northern political parties. Six political parties represented the North, including the Islamic Charter Front (ICF), the Umma Party, the People's Democratic Party (PDP), the Sudanese Communist Party (SCP), the National Union Party (NUP) and the Professionals Front.[24] Envoys from seven African countries (Kenya, Ghana, Algeria, Nigeria, Tanzania, Egypt and Uganda) gathered alongside the participants to witness and contribute to the proceedings.[25] In their advisory capacity, the international observers represented not only their national governments but also the OAU. After years of seeking a hearing from the OAU in order to air the Southern cause, the Southern leaders finally gained Africa's attention. I reconstruct the narrative contest here from the speeches given, documents circulated and media reporting during the RTC mainly from the Sudan Informazioni News Agency, as it contained the most comprehensive compilation of newspaper cuttings from both the local and the foreign press, speeches and proposals circulated at the RTC.[26]

The Conference offered an international discursive platform to the proponents of the Southern cause. For SANU-Inside, the RTC marked 'the first time, the Southern Problem has come to the notice of International Organisations'.[27] The Southern Front saw it as an opportunity 'for Southern Sudan to put its political agenda on the map of the world stage'.[28] The Secretary General of the Southern Front at the time, Bona Malwal, launched the Front's periodical *The Vigilant* in March 1965, during the Conference, signifying the importance of the RTC as a discursive moment.[29] The RTC gained significant media coverage nationally and internationally.[30] Although most Northern political parties did not object to the presence of foreign observers, one of the parties, the Umma Party, stated that it feared the 'internationalisation of a domestic problem'.[31] The Sudanese political elites in the North had laboured to obscure and minimise the "Southern Problem" in international eyes, especially those of African states.

The RTC represents a critical moment for the competing conceptions of the "Southern Problem", as both sets of actors sought legitimation from international audiences. Although it failed to produce a peace accord to end the first civil war, SANU-In-Exile maintained that 'this historic conference can be regarded as an important achievement'.[32] The Conference created a context for discussing the *meaning* of the "Southern Problem" and to communicate its contested interpretations to the world. A delegate from the Southern Front remembered feeling that the Southern delegates 'needed to show not only flexibility but some political sophistication too' to the African observers.[33] Regarding the seven African states at the conference, representatives of SANU-In-Exile also expressed the party's plan 'to enlist their sympathy and support'.[34] These reflections suggest that the Southern delegates treated the Conference as a setting in which they would have to articulate a deliberate narrative and offer a political performance to rival the Sudanese government. Similarly, the RTC offered an opportunity for the Northern political elite to offer a counter-narrative and publicly discredit the Southern cause for self-determination.

The Southern Narrative

The politicians from SANU-In-Exile, the Southern Front and William Deng's SANU-Inside all shared the established narrative of the "Southern Problem's" genesis and development, but Deng's faction differed on its solution. Maintaining the mainstream perspective, the Southern Front, echoing earlier renditions, blamed Britain for the "Southern Problem" as it 'imposes unity where it is not wanted and divides where unity is demanded as it suits her imperial interests'.[35] As in earlier narratives, placing the blame on the British colonisers allowed the Southern politicians to seek sympathy from the African observers who were also subjected to European colonialism and Western imperialism. If the formation of Sudan only served British interests, it was assumed to be inimical to the indigenous population's interests and to be mistrusted.

At the RTC, the narrative would then typically focus on a well-rehearsed list of grievances that appeared frequently in articles and speeches given by the secessionist Southern representatives. It included the 1947 Juba Conference as the Southern delegates there had 'no mandate from the people, and they could not commit the Southern Sudan to anything',[36] the 1953 Anglo-Egyptian Agreement when 'the South was denied representation',[37] the 1954 Sudanisation process, disdainfully called 'Northernisation', as it largely excluded Southerners from posts,[38] and parliamentarians from Northern-based parties during the 1950s who in response to Southern politicians' calls for federalism 'adopted a delaying tactic to give them sufficient time to dominate the South and to assimilate the Southerners into the Northern way of life'.[39] The Southern representatives heavily criticised Abboud's policies in the South, which they viewed as processes of forced Islamisation and Arabisation. According to SANU-In-Exile leader Aggrey Jaden, the policies were not only oppressive; they also 'meant that 1/3 of the country has been left without an active or constructive part in nation-building'.[40] The combination of all these events created a perception that Sudan's Independence in 1956 meant 'the substitution of one foreign colonialism with another savage Arab colonialism'.[41] The Southern Front held that the North had put on 'the shoes of his British predecessor and stepped further to abuse',[42] and effectively established 'Northern colonialism'.[43] These incidents formed a critical part of the Southern narrative of political dispossession and systematic exclusion, which built on and elaborated earlier discursive constructs, and served to cast a shadow on the legitimacy of the Northern-based government.

As in earlier iterations, Jaden argued that a 'real division' in Sudan existed, in a fundamental, primordial and unchangeable way.[44] He maintained that

> there are in fact two Sudans and the most important thing is that there can never be a basis of unity between the two. There is nothing in common between the two. ... no body of shared beliefs, no identity of interests, no local signs of unity and above all, the Sudan has failed to compose a single community.[45]

He maintained that unity was only a 'historical accident', not to be honoured because of its specious origins and harmful consequences.[46] According to this narrative, it was too late to call for reconciliation. The Southern Front held that '[t]he South has tried all types of Governments of the North and each of them quickly proves how impossible it is to live with the South in peace and understanding'.[47] Aggrey Jaden concluded that the solution lay in the North ceasing to 'dominate the Southern Sudan' and the recognition of the South's right to self-determination.[48]

Based on SANU-Inside's official position paper circulated during the RTC, it appeared to share its external namesake's foundational narrative of the "Southern Problem". The paper's introduction refers the reader to the SANU-Institute of Race Relations publication, *The Problem of the Southern Sudan*, as the 'general back-ground are better discussed' therein.[49] Building on Deng's letter, his faction promoted federalism as the only viable solution, reasoning that Sudan was one of many countries grappling with ethno-racial conflict: 'The Americas, the Swiss, the Canadians, some countries in the Eastern world, Nigeria and the Cameroons have had to find systems to bring about national harmony.'[50] Mentioning Nigeria in the list of countries that found a federal solution, in the presence of a representative of that country, had strategic value. Given the vast difference between federation and secession, the proponents of the former could easily be characterised as more reasonable. SANU-Inside presented the external audience with a less costly political alternative, compared to the seismic change of secession for which SANU-In-Exile and the Southern Front advocated. Thus, on the whole, both groups retained a commitment to aspects of an established historical narrative but came to different political conclusions that diluted the potency of the secessionist position.

The Northern Counter-Narrative

The Northern political elite, despite its internal disagreements, articulated a united opinion on the "Southern Problem".[51] Southern Front representative Bona Malwal held that Northern politicians agreed in advance 'to speak as a bloc' because with elections looming, '[n]o leader from Northern Sudan wanted to be accused of being soft on the South'.[52] Thus, at the RTC, they generally highlighted the undesirable implications of secession, focused on the imperial origins of secessionism in the South, and aimed to discredit the Southern Front and SANU-In-Exile.

Building on its earlier narrative, the government emphasised the prospect of setting a dangerous example internationally. In his opening address, Prime Minister Sayed Sirr El Khatim El Khalifa emphasised that 'the conclusions which this conference will reach, will form important precedents, not only in the history of Sudan, but in the evolution of all newly independent States, especially African States'.[53] As in earlier government publications, Prime Minister Khalifa highlighted the complexity of the "Problem" and Sudan, referring not only to North and South, but also to East and West. The inclusion of other regions served to cast doubt over the rebels' understanding of the country. The Prime Minister argued that reductionist understandings of the "Problem" would hinder progress. As in the government narrative explained in Chap. 4, he urged that 'the differences between the two parts of the country have been conventionally portrayed in simple terms to the effect that [the] North [is] Muslim and Arab while the South is Pagan and African'.[54] By portraying these interpretations as simplistic, the Prime Minister urged that they were 'based on certain misleading generalisations and assumptions which could not be accepted in any serious discussion of the situation such as the discussion which will take place in this Conference'.[55] He claimed that this perspective, which was the standard Southern exile politician's narrative, gave external audiences 'a distorted picture of the situation in the Sudan'.[56]

Explaining the government's relationship with the Arab world, Prime Minister Khalifa asserted that Arabism represented 'not a racial concept which unites the members of a certain racial group' but instead 'it is a linguistic, cultural and non-racial link that binds together numerous races, black, white and brown'.[57] By framing it as a non-racial ideology, Sudan's leader divorced the country's Arab linkages from allegations of racial supremacy. He equally conceptualised Africanism as a non-racial, thus inclusive, ideology for all (including Arab people) on the continent of Africa.[58] For him the two were not incompatible in the ways the secessionist politicians suggested. Thus, he called for 'the close association, indeed the complete unity between African nationalism and Arab nationalism … for the common cause of emancipation from the shackles of imperialism, backwardness and disunity'.[59] It was unity that Sudan needed, in his view, rather than fragmentation. The Prime Minister emphasised that the Arab and African worlds have a shared enemy—Western imperialism—and thus implied it was not in their shared interests for the proponents of Africanism to be seen to be at odds with those of Arabism, and vice versa.

All the Northern representatives acknowledged the excesses of the previous military regime within limits. The new government framed itself as diametrically opposed to the policies of its predecessor. Prime Minister Khalifa characterised the preceding regime's error as the folly of responding 'to the Southern question [as] a security matter'.[60] His narrative hinged on the critical moment of the coup of October 1964, which he characterised as the people's revolution that led to 'a new era in which the interest of all the Sudanese people without exception or preference will be safeguarded and promoted'.[61] In order to distinguish their military action from that of their predecessors, the incumbent government developed a new discourse of "law and order" at the RTC. The government conveyed its 'dismay' that the armed rebels did not heed the call to a ceasefire and participate in the talks.[62] As a result 'the Government was therefore obliged to carry out its duties to maintain law and order and safeguard national interests'.[63] The 'outlaws' left the government no option. Other members of Northern political parties also defended the ongoing war, by suggesting that the Sudan Armed Forces 'were not only maintaining order, but defending the country from Tshombe's aggression' in Zaire.[64] Tshombe, who most African leaders at the time deemed illegitimate for his close relations with Western powers, signalled an enemy Sudan shared with the observer countries.

Like their Southern counterparts, Northern politicians constructed a discourse of blame regarding 'imperialistic' Britain and its 'evil colonial policies', but with a different purpose.[65] The People's Democratic Party representative, Ali Abdel Rahman, held that the "Southern Problem" was 'inherited from the imperialist regime', and concocted to 'undermine the unity and the independence of the Sudan.'[66] According to the Prime Minister, the Condominium government's bifurcated administration of Sudan was a 'grotesquely unjust campaign which enormously exaggerated the role of our ancestors both Northerners and Southerners in the slave trade'.[67] He argued that the only reason the history of slavery loomed large in the memories of Southerners was due to missionaries who exclusively managed the education of Sudan during the Condominium. Khalifa blamed

> imperialists and hypocritical European missionaries who played down the enormous role of their own ancestors in this shameful trade, turned a blind eye to the trading in slaves which went on amongst the Southern tribes themselves and put the onus for these activities on the shoulders of the Northern Sudanese alone.[68]

The missionaries allegedly exploited these histories of enslavement 'in order to create a barrier of animosity' between 'compatriots' from the North and South who equally 'suffered under the yoke of imperialism'.[69] This mis-education, he maintained, made it 'impossible for the people of this one country to realise their own common interest in forgetting the past' and working together towards a united future.[70]

According to the Northern politicians, the war was a consequence of the pernicious impact of 'prejudiced imperialist propaganda' caused by 'the monopoly of the missionary societies' who 'worked for the perversion of education to suit their own ends'.[71] Employing a familiar demonisation discourse, the Prime Minister insisted that

> efforts at the deliberate distortion of the picture of historical relations between the peoples of the Northern and the Southern Sudan, were not an isolated phenomena, but an organised part of an evil policy which was evolved by the imperialists for the purpose of destroying all human, cultural and economic links between the Northern and Southern Sudanese. This policy had its final objective the separation of the Southern Provinces of the Sudan…

According to this line of reasoning, to allow the South to federate or to secede would be to buckle to Britain's machinations. The Prime Minister construed all pleas for federalism as deriving from missionary indoctrination. The leader of the Sudanese Communist Party (SCP), Abdel Khaliq Mahgoub, similarly stated that 'separation means the surrender of the south to imperialism'.[72]

The rhetoric of missionaries having 'poisoned the minds' of all the Southern political leaders not only served to allot blame, but also to discredit the intellectual independence of the exiles.[73] The representative of the Islamic Charter Front at the historic Conference phrased it as follows: '[f]acts are mixed up in their minds and history was taught to them in such a way that made them stand for a certain point of view'.[74] These allegations portrayed Southerners as gullible victims. Prime Minister Khatim also accused the British of severing the pre-existing 'cultural' and 'human, economic and political links' between the regions.[75] However, he and other Northern politicians did not elaborate on the nature of these pre-existing connections, and they did not offer an alternative historical account of relations between the two regions besides slave raiding.

Northern politicians rejected the accusation that in post-independence Sudan, the Northerners held colonial attitudes towards Southerners. The representative of the PDP, Ali Abdel Rahman, considered Southern self-determination an option only made possible by this harmful mischaracterisation of the country. He contended that since some Southerners (such as Santino Deng and Buth Diu, as discussed in Chap. 4) 'took active part in the country's administration', the situation in the country could not be likened to colonialism.[76] He upheld the view that Sudan followed a legitimate path to state formation. Similarly, the PDP leader, Sayed Ali Abdel Rahman, 'could see no differences between the Sudanese to justify the undermining of the country's unity, and that unity should not be based on racial factors'.[77] Thus, as in previous years, the Northern politicians generally adopted what might be seen as a colour-blind stance on the accusations of racial discrimination in Sudan.[78]

Rahman also called the authority of secessionist Southern leaders into question. He asked if SANU-In-Exile and the Southern Front could claim to be the true representatives of the South, and urged for the inclusion of groups advocating for unity.[79] He was not alone. Many Northern politicians repeatedly requested the representation of pro-government Southern groups. The Sudan Communist Party's Khaliq Mahgoub claimed that there were politicians of Southern origin who opposed self-determination but were excluded from the RTC proceedings.[80] Similarly, the National Unionist Party's Ismail El Azhari demanded the representation of 'all the sections of southern public opinion', suggesting the exclusion of more moderate voices.[81] On the second day of the proceedings, the Islamic Charter Front's delegate, Mohamed Yousef Mohamed, even threatened to withdraw from and boycott the conference if 'the other southern political groups' apart from the two SANU factions and the Southern Front were not included.[82] In response, the leader of SANU-In-Exile, Aggrey Jaden, threatened to protest the inclusion of Southerners who he did not consider legitimate representatives of the South.[83] Ultimately, the chairperson of the Conference, Vice-Chancellor of the University of Khartoum Professor El Nazeer Dafalla, conceded to the request for the addition of "other views" from the South.[84] Having been called upon by the Northern parties, Ambrose Wol was one of the individuals under the canopy of "Other Shades of Opinion". He was to join Santino Deng in the fragile coalition of "alternative" Southern voices.[85] However, Wol withdrew from the proceedings 'as he found out that his own opinions on the southern problem coincided with those of SANU party'.[86] Shortly after the Conference, Wol joined William Deng's SANU-Inside. This switch undermined the Northern case, albeit only marginally.

In a second attack on the legitimacy of the secessionists, the PDP's Rahman questioned their authority on the ground in Southern Sudan. He highlighted the absence of the armed Southern Sudanese liberation group, Anya-Nya, from the RTC. In so doing, he asserted that while the SANU factions and the Southern Front had condemned the violence in the South, they were unable to enforce a ceasefire. This inability led him to believe that 'this meant one of two things: either the southern leaders sitting at the conference did not represent the south or they lacked good faith'.[87] (The fraught and complicated relationship between SANU and Anya-Nya will be addressed in the next chapter.)

Besides the range of the arguments that the Northern political parties made, several factors worked in their favour at the Conference. The immediate aftermath of the October Revolution of 1964 was an unfavourable time for the Southern secessionist politicians. The transitional government had no track record with which to engage and the new, hopeful post-Revolution political establishment manipulated the fears of the observer countries in the room. Moreover, the government's resources gave it advantages at the Conference. For example, the Secretariat of the Round Table Conference hosted a reception party on the second day, 17 March 1965, under the patronage of the government, for the 'Heads of the African, Arab and Foreign Diplomatic Corp… in honour of the observers and conferees'.[88] By treating the foreign representatives and the wider diplomatic community in Khartoum to a sumptuous soirée, the government was able to create unofficial spaces to influence the observers and reinforced its narrative. It also astutely invited diplomats from Arab states to the same dinner as the African observers at a Conference that, in part, debated the compatibility of Arabism with Africanism in the case of Sudan.

The Northern politicians organised themselves and collectively remained on-message while their Southern counterparts appeared divided. Ultimately, fragmentation in SANU weakened the Southern position at the Conference. Southern politicians had expected the RTC to serve as a vital event through which they could obtain legitimacy, but instead it caused confusion. The proponents of self-determination appeared unrealistically radical in their demands and their representativeness was called into question, while the Northern position remained cohesive.

Conclusion

The international observers veiled their pro-government stance in platitudinous rhetoric. In a joint statement, they credited the Round Table Conference as having 'been convened on the inspiration of the Government of the Sudan', making no reference to William Deng or SANU's initiative.[89] After acknowledging the importance of gathering all the political actors in the conflict for the first time, they tellingly framed the Conference as a discussion on 'the question of the Southern Sudan in the context of *one* Sudan'.[90] The joint statement included other pleasantries without a single reference to Southern politicians, the possibility of self-determination or the ongoing war in the South. They also thanked the Government of Sudan for its hospitality and the Secretariat for the supplementary arrangements it made in conjunction with the Conference, thus indicating a measure of patronage, which may have skewed the objectivity of the observers.

Two observers addressed the Conference at the end of the proceedings. Firstly, Nathaniel Welbeck, the Ghanaian delegate who served as the Propaganda Secretary of the Convention People's Party and the Minister of Information, spoke as head of his country's delegation. He highlighted the importance of gatherings where differences can be discussed in 'a tolerant spirit' and 'the spirit of African Unity'.[91] Welbeck referenced a proverb: 'in my country they say, even though the tongue and the teeth are together in this mouth, there are times when they bite'.[92] The saying implied that as teeth and a tongue belong to one mouth, Sudan was similarly inseparable. In a subtle rhetorical move, he also suggested that the conflict was akin to mere teething problems.

The Chairperson's response to Welbeck's comments suggests that he perceived that the reputation of the Government of Sudan had remained intact throughout the Conference. He asked Welbeck to extend Sudan's gratitude to Kwame Nkrumah 'for the attention which he is giving to our cause and we have no doubt, we never had doubts that we are friends in arms; so let us proceed to defeat oppression'.[93] By affirming the friendship between the people of Ghana and those of Sudan and the camaraderie in the anti-imperial struggle, the chairperson asserted that Khartoum did not represent an imperial capital, that it was aligned with the African nationalism of Nkrumah, and that the political establishment in Sudan received his support. A country fighting oppression could not, the logic suggested, itself enact oppression.

The head of the Nigerian delegation, Yousif Maitama Sule, who served as the Minister of Mines and Power, gave the second speech. His address suggested that his sympathies also lay with the Sudanese government. Contrary to the claims of the exiled and other secessionist politicians, Sule asserted that Sudan's problem was 'in no way, peculiar to the Sudan' and stated that he was 'not aware of any country in the world that has not got some internal problems in one form or another'.[94] He characterised the conflict as a 'family difference', and he maintained that such difficulties 'almost inevitably confront any country of your size and diversity'.[95] Sule removed secession as the only solution and opened the possibility of drawing from the experiences of other countries as examples. In particular, he drew on Nigeria, claiming that '[t]he people of the Sudan and Nigeria have a lot in common'.[96] He highlighted the religious diversity and the shared experience of British colonialism. In light of these commonalities, he felt compelled 'to give [the Sudan] the benefit of our huble [sic] experience in a country which is very similar to yours'.[97] The comparison to Nigeria was slanted towards a unionist, pro-government solution. With calls for self-determination afoot in Eastern Nigeria (what came to be known as Biafra two years later) by 1965, the Nigerian government was a natural ally to the Sudanese government. Sule urged the participants to 'forgive and forget the past' and set an example of 'harmony and national unity within their own borders'.[98]

While they could not vote or enforce a solution as their role was only to observe, the African delegates' interpretation of the "Southern Problem" mattered. The Conference represented a significant discursive moment that not only brought Southern and Northern elites and exiles together, but it also convened narratives of contested histories in an international forum.

Notes

1. Y. F. Hasan, 'The Sudanese Revolution of October 1964', *Journal of Modern African Studies*, 5/4 (1967), pp. 491–509.
2. Berridge, *Civil Uprisings in Modern Sudan.*
3. Malwal, *Sudan and South Sudan*, p. 88.
4. 'Report from SANU Central Office', *Voice of Southern Sudan*, 2/4 (1965), p. 10.

5. Ibid.
6. Ibid.
7. Letter from SANU to the Prime Minister of the Sudan, Khatim Khalifa, November 1964, Yosa Wawa draft, p. 154, DHJ PP.
8. M. M. Vambheim, 'Making Peace While Waging War: A Peacemaking Effort in the Sudanese Civil War, 1965–1966' (MA thesis, University of Bergen, 2007), pp. 62–63.
9. Sulton, 'Regional Autonomy in the Southern Sudan', pp. 131, 137.
10. 'Report from SANU Central Office', *Voice of Southern Sudan*, 2/4 (1965), p. 11. Kuyok, South Sudan, p. 281.
11. Letter from SANU to the Prime Minister of the Sudan, Khatim Khalifa, November 1964.
12. Ibid.
13. Ibid.
14. Ibid.
15. Ibid.
16. 'Change in SANU leadership', *Voice of Southern Sudan*, 2/4 (1965), p. 11.
17. 'Report from SANU General Office', *Voice of Southern Sudan*, 2/4 (1965), p. 8.
18. Letter from William Deng to Prime Minister of Sudan, January 1965, Yosa Wawa draft, pp. 171–175, DHJ PP.
19. Ibid, pp. 171–172.
20. 'Report from SANU General Office', *Voice of Southern Sudan*, 2/4 (1965), p. 8.
21. Malwal, *Sudan*, p. 2. The relationship between SANU and the armed rebels will be explored in the next chapter.
22. Ibid, p. 5.
23. Ibid, p. 95.
24. Although this group does not constitute an exhaustive list of Sudanese political parties at the time, it does generally represent the spectrum of political persuasions in Khartoum.
25. M. O. Beshir discusses the political reasons behind the selection of this particular group of countries, and the reasons for the exclusion of certain key neighbouring countries, in his book *The Southern Sudan: From Conflict to Peace* (London, 1975), p. 7.
26. I located the Sudan Informazioni publication at the Comboni Archives in Rome.
27. No. 52, 'SANU's position paper during the Round Table Conference', 18 March 1965, p. 194, Yosa Wawa Draft, DHJ PP.
28. Malwal, *Sudan*, p. 5.
29. Ibid, p. 105.
30. Sudan Informazioni, 'The Round-Table Conference in the Foreign Press', *Round-Table Conference on the Southern Sudan*, pp. 224–226.

31. Malwal, *Sudan*, p. 93.
32. *Voice of Southern Sudan*, 3, 1 (1965), p. 1.
33. Malwal, *Sudan*, p. 97.
34. *Voice of Southern Sudan*, 3, 1 (1965), p. 1.
35. Sudan News Agency (SNA), 'English Daily Bulletin', Service No. 2 (18 March 1965), p. 5, ACR A/85/23/2.
36. Ibid, p. 188.
37. No. 52, 'SANU's position paper during the Round Table Conference' (18 March 1965), p. 193, Yosa Wawa Draft, DHJ PP.
38. Ibid.
39. Ibid.
40. No. 51, Jaden, 'The Problem' (16 March 1965), p. 189, Yosa Wawa Draft, DHJ PP.
41. Ibid, p. 190.
42. SNA, *English Daily Bulletin*, Service No. 2 (18 March 1965), p. 7, ACR A/85/23/2.
43. Ibid.
44. Jaden, 'The Problem'.
45. Ibid, p. 190.
46. Ibid.
47. ACR A/85/23/2.
48. Jaden, 'The Problem', p. 187.
49. No. 52, 'SANU's position paper during the Round Table Conference', 18 March 1965, p. 192, Yosa Wawa Draft, DHJ PP.
50. Ibid, p. 194.
51. P. K. Bechtold, *Politics in the Sudan: Parliamentary and military rule in an emerging African nation* (New York, 1976).
52. Malwal, *Sudan*, pp. 94, 98.
53. SNA, 'Supplement: Inaugural Address by Prime Minister Sayed Sir El Khatim El Khalifa at the North-South Round Table Conference', 17 March 1965, p. 1, ACR A/85/23/1.
54. SNA, 'Supplement', 17 March 1965, p. 2, ACR A/85/23/1.
55. Ibid.
56. Ibid.
57. Ibid.
58. This is a view that Kwame Nkrumah held that was deemed controversial in Pan-Africanist circles. Negritude's relationship to Pan-Africanism was contested among prominent African thinkers, including Tanzania's Julius Nyerere. See A. Mazrui, *Towards a Pax Africana*, especially chapter 4. A. Mohiddin, 'Nyerere and Nkrumah on African Unity' (unpublished paper, delivered December 1968, Social Sciences Conference, University of East Africa, Makerere, Kampala).

59. Ibid, pp. 2–3.
60. Ibid. 6.
61. Ibid, p. 5.
62. Ibid.
63. Ibid.
64. SNA, 'English Daily Bulletin', 18 March 1965, p. 3, ACR A/85/23/2.
65. SNA, 'Supplement: Inaugural Address by Prime Minister Sayed Sir El Khatim El Khalifa at the North-South Round Table Conference', 17 March 1965, pp. 1, 3, ACR A/85/23/1.
66. SNA, 18 March 1965, p. 2, ACR A/85/23/2.
67. Ibid, p. 3.
68. Ibid.
69. Ibid.
70. Ibid.
71. Ibid.
72. SNA, 'English Daily Bulletin', 18 March 1965, p. 3, ACR A/85/23/2.
73. Ibid, p. 5.
74. D. D. A. Ruay, *The Politics of Two Sudans: The South and the North, 1821–1969* (Uppsala, 1994), p. 113.
75. Ibid, pp. 4–5.
76. SNA, 18 March 1965, p. 2. ACR A/85/23/2.
77. Ibid.
78. The growing literature on colour-blind and post-racial politics, especially in the US, tends to frame the notion of race-blindness as a myth that prevents states from addressing actual social inequality. It further holds that lacking racial awareness is a privilege of those belonging to identity groups at the centre of power. See O. Obasogie, *Blinded by Sight: The Racial Body and the Origins of the Social Construction of Race* (Stanford, CA, 2013); M. K. C. Brown, et al., *Whitewashing Race: The Myth of a Color-Blind Society* (Berkeley, 2003).
79. Ibid.
80. Ibid, p. 3.
81. Ibid, p. 4.
82. Ibid.
83. Ibid.
84. Ibid, p. 5. D. Wai, *The Southern Sudan: The Problem of National Integration* (London, 1973) p. 151. The Northern academic Professor Dafalla served in the crucial capacity of chairman. As Vice-Chancellor of the University of Khartoum, he was expected to be politically neutral. However, it is unclear to what extent this was possible given that politicians based in Khartoum could have access to him by virtue of their proximity, and that the university's relationship with the government precluded it from being indepen-

dent. Moreover, the Secretary General of the RTC was also an academic from the North, Mohamed Omer Beshir.

85. The Southern Sudanese generally opposed unity. The founding member of the Southern Front, Bona Malwal, reflected on the popular sentiment at the time as favourable to radical political solutions. 'At that point, given the atrocities committed by the North against the South since the so-called independence of Sudan in 1956, every South Sudanese, not just the delegates at the convention but the whole of the South Sudanese population, wanted extreme measures. Everybody wanted the Southern Front to table separation at the Khartoum Round-Table Conference, nothing else. Any South Sudanese in favour of anything short of separation was considered at best a coward and at worst a Northern stooge.' In light of this admittedly partisan reflection, it appears that it was improbable that a significant group of Southerners would find unity with the North desirable at the time. Hence the "Other Shades of Opinion" canopy was generally unrepresentative at the time. Malwal, *Sudan*, pp. 96–97.
86. SNA, 'English Daily Bulletin', 18 March 1965, p. 7, ACR A/85/23/2.
87. SNA, 18 March 1965, p. 3, ACR A/85/23/2.
88. SNA, 'English Daily Bulletin', Service No. 2, 18 March 1965, p. 2, ACR A/85/23/2.
89. Sudan Informazioni, 'A Statement made by the Observers on 25 March 65 at the Round Table Conference Evening Session, Read by Mr. FK Onama, Minister of Interior, Uganda', *Round-Table Conference on the Southern Sudan*, p. 197, ACR A/85/17.
90. Ibid. Emphasis added.
91. Sudan Informazioni, 'Speech of Mr. Welbeck Minister of Information and Head of the Ghanaian observers delegation to the Conference of the Round Table on Wednesday', *Round-Table Conference on the Southern Sudan*, pp. 194–195.
92. Ibid, p. 195.
93. Sudan Informazioni, 'Comment on the Chairman of the Round Table Conference on Mr. Welbeck's Speech', *Round-Table Conference on the Southern Sudan*, p. 196.
94. Sudan Informazioni, 'Speech delivered by the Hon. Yousif Maitama Sule, Nigeria's Federal Minister of Mines and Power to the Round Table Conference on the Southern Sudan', *Round-Table Conference on the Southern Sudan* pp. 199, 198.
95. Ibid, p. 200.
96. Ibid, p. 199.
97. Ibid.
98. Ibid, p. 200.

CHAPTER 7

SANU's Discursive Legacies

Beyond convincing their putative constituency, the Sudan African National Union (SANU) intended for its discourses to attain taken-for-granted hegemonic status internationally in order to shape diplomatic outcomes. This chapter will focus on the demise of SANU and the protracted fragmentation that occurred within the wider Southern Sudanese rebel movement, as well as the continuing influence of SANU's discursive framings on Southern politics. It maintains that the fact that the liberation movements that replaced SANU in the post-1965 political landscape employed its narratives without attribution demonstrates the moribund movement's discursive power. SANU's failure to survive and its discourses' failure to persuade international audiences in the anticipated ways can conceal the resilience of their rhetoric and ideas. Regarding the durability of discourses, Roxanne Doty reminds us

> [t]o suggest that the identities constructed by… practices of representation were fragile is not, however, to deny their power and durability. On the contrary, it is repetition and dissemination that gives representations their power, not an inherent stability and closure.[1]

Rooted in a grievance of the "Southern Problem", Southern political identities have since sprang from the intellectual traditions that SANU developed and popularised. This chapter will show that as relics, these discourses could very well be SANU's most enduring legacy.

S. C. Manoeli, *Sudan's "Southern Problem"*, African Histories and Modernities, https://doi.org/10.1007/978-3-030-28771-9_7

SANU's Post-RTC Crisis

The Round Table Conference (RTC) began to expose the strained relationship between the exile political movement, led by SANU, and the armed struggle, led by Anya-Nya. At the beginning of the organised armed struggle in 1963, SANU denounced Anya-Nya as a '"terrorist movement" likely to harm rather than help the cause of self-determination' to the Western press.[2] It is unclear whether this statement reflected actual antagonism or a strategic distancing from Anya-Nya's violence as it risked jeopardising SANU's political lobbying. Less than a year later, in response to the excesses of the Sudan Armed Forces in the South, SANU issued a statement to the press stating that 'our patience is exhausted. We have been driven to arms'.[3] This was the first time SANU publicly associated itself with Anya-Nya. The representations of Anya-Nya in *Voice of Southern Sudan* subsequently reflected SANU's sympathy with the armed struggle, and a loose association between the two emerged. It appears that relations remained civil as long as the soldiers did not seek to usurp the political leadership of the exile leaders.

Founding SANU member Father Saturnino established military training camps for Anya-Nya soldiers,[4] and he covertly smuggled weapons from Uganda into Southern Sudan to the under-resourced armed movement in 1964, when their supplies ran low.[5] Later, however, John Howell observed that

> [i]nevitably, those ex-soldiers and policemen in the bush came to disregard the politicians in exile in East Africa, and when Father Saturnino, still the most influential of the Southerners in exile, gave his support directly to the Anya Nya, it was only a matter of time before the armed insurgents took over the political leadership.[6]

Father Saturnino's assassination in 1967 ended a period of a measure of cooperation and led to further fragmentation.[7]

Meanwhile, shortly after the RTC, SANU-In-Exile collapsed. Aggrey Jaden and Joseph Oduho split up and led different factions. A successful reconciliation committee was established to reunite them, and by December 1965, the two leaders had established the Azania Liberation Front (ALF). The reconstituted remnants of SANU decided that exile was no longer an appropriate location from which to lead the struggle for self-determination. Thus, the ALF established its headquarters in Equatoria,

Southern Sudan, and from April 1966, the Southern political movement ceased to be led in exile, even though it continued to have representatives who lobbied foreign governments in exile.[8] But by the end of 1967 the ALF had lost its prominence and finally dissolved.[9] The Southern Sudan Provisional Government (SSPG) replaced it. Contemporaneously, the guerrilla forces also faced fragmentation as the two main commanders, Emilio Tafeng and Joseph Lagu, fell out with each other.[10] Led initially by Jaden, the SSPG enjoyed the support of Tafeng's guerrilla faction. By 1969, the SSPG had changed its name to the Nile Provisional Government. Meanwhile, Joseph Lagu formed a political organisation for his branch of the guerrilla movement dubbed the Anyanya National Organisation (ANO). Other groups established rival governments and declared the independence of various parts of the South, including the Anyidi Revolutionary Government. These groups were rarely coordinated and frequently declared coups against each other.

By 1971, Joseph Lagu led a united military and political movement under the banner of the Southern Sudan Liberation Movement (SSLM) that became the sole leader of the rebel movement in the South. Monetary and military support from Uganda and Israel enabled the SSLM to capture and consolidate power by mounting coups on provincial armed groups within the South.[11] The SSLM eventually reached a settlement with the Sudanese Government in 1972 through the Addis Ababa Peace Accord.[12]

Part of the tensions between the military and political wings of the liberation groups in the first half of the 1960s stemmed from the exilic, and thereby remote, nature of the political groups. The politicians lived in foreign capitals, travelled extensively and had a thin presence in the South. In contrast, even when training in neighbouring countries, by necessity the military groups maintained a strong presence in the theatre of war in Southern Sudan. Therefore, not unlike the Northern politicians at the RTC, some of the leaders of the armed wing called into question the authenticity and authority of the exile politicians on account of their absence from Southern Sudan.

The new Southern rebel groups of the late 1960s shared this anti-exile sentiment. For example, at its founding, the Southern Sudan Provisional Government (SSPG) declared that 'never again shall we leave our fatherland. Never again shall our politics be timidly conducted in Foreign Capitals'.[13] Later, the Nile Provisional Government (NPG) similarly 'denounced all political groups outside and appealed to them to return home because one's country can only be liberated from within by rendering useful services'.[14] They declared their 'deep concern about some foreign organisations who had always intended to control the Movement' from 'foreign capitals'.[15] The Anyidi Government likewise asserted that '[t]hose who went outside, acquired large sums of donations but stored them in foreign banks under their own names'.[16] Not only did they characterise the politicians as corrupt, they depicted them as cowards:

> The freedom fighters initiated this liberation struggle in 1963... armed only with machetes, knives, spears ... and arrows. The politicians had already *given up* and were living outside ...as refugees. Some had sought employment with neighbouring countries.[17]

It is important to note that these movements also held Southerners in Khartoum who were moderates and unionists in utter contempt.[18]

Even though the guerrilla forces and the political movement were chronically fratricidal, these new groups relied on the discourses developed by SANU, as the first major political movement in exile. Albeit far more advanced and effective than SANU, SSLM built upon the foundation of SANU's discourses. The record suggests that none of the secessionist political movements invented new discourses in the 1960s. SANU had defined the parameters of secessionist thought in Southern Sudan. While each group engaged in practices of imagining the Southern Sudanese nation, with distinctive symbols, flags and styles of projecting power, they all subscribed to SANU's conceptions of a bifurcated Sudanese state, with two discrete and incompatible races, that was oppressive to Southerners. A brief exposition of the content of the propaganda material produced by these groups offers insight into the legacy of SANU's discursive influence.

The NPG's propaganda material reveals that it reproduced these discourses wholesale. For instance, it maintained the racial binary and held that the two regions were incompatible, declaring that '[n]o basis of unity had ever existed or will exist between the Arab Sudan and the African Nile'.[19] It developed the narrative of unbearable oppression that SANU had popularised, as its claim suggested 'that the Nile Provisional Government and the Nilean people are engaged in a war of survival engendered and perpetuated by Arab policy of genocide and racial subjugation'.[20] It showed deep concern for press coverage suggesting that it too was invested in the propaganda war, as it accused the government of Sudan of attempting to 'mislead world public opinion'.[21]

Despite the similarly low regard in which it held exiled politicians, the Anyidi Government also depended on SANU's discourses. Representatives of Anyidi claimed that 'the politicians were unable to explain the Anyidi Africans case to Black African states and governments in particular and the world in general'.[22] The very fact that it conceived of 'Black Africa' as uniquely positioned to sympathise with the Southern cause is a result of the pre-existing discursive framework. Moreover, the ways in which the secessionist group distinguished themselves from one another reflected SANU's discursive influence. For instance, in the following attempt to distinguish itself from the NPG, Anyidi representatives followed logics within the discursive terrain delimited by SANU. They contended that

> [t]he name Southern Sudan is meaningless and is associated with the Arab North Sudan. The new name Anyidi is unique and associated with wars fought by our tribesmen in unity against the Arabs. The place Anyidi is historic for its wars and it is African in origin. The name Nile is associated with Arabs, particularly of Egypt, it passes through several countries and it is a foreign name. Be African please and be original.[23]

The need to be distinct from the 'Arabs' and to assert affiliation with Africa derives from values that become important within the framework developed by politicians in exile.

ALF representatives insisted to international audiences that the 'policies of Sudan Arabs towards the black man can only earn the name of imperialists because imperialism is not a white man's monopoly'.[24] Exasperated, the rebel organisation submitted a memorandum to the 1967 Organisation of African Unity (OAU) Summit in which it asked 'whether the OAU should stand by and watch the Arabs clear away the people of Southern Sudan in the name of African Unity and domestic affairs'.[25] It claimed that the silence of African leaders on the "Southern Problem" 'leads every reasonable man to conclude that the OAU is nothing more than an association of the fortunate and strong to keep the unfortunate and the weak in subjection[, it is] not a Union of African peoples'.[26] Through these kinds of memoranda and disruptions of African diplomatic meetings, the Southern rebels continued to bring Sudan's battle of narratives into the international domain.

Equally, Joseph Lagu's Anyanya National Organisation (ANO) in 1969 described the war for liberation in precisely the terms that SANU scripted at the beginning of the decade. The Organisation believed that the

Sudanese government sought to turn 'the South into an Arab colony of settlement and reduced its populace into a class of slaves hewing wood and drawing water'.[27] It reproduced SANU's phrasing almost verbatim.[28] The ANO also employed the racial prism, maintaining that Northern soldiers 'have orders to shoot at [the] sight [of] any black man'.[29] Unlike their contemporaries, the ANO described SANU in more favourable terms as 'spokesmen' for the Southern Sudanese people, whose task 'consisted mainly in petitioning world organizations such as the UNO, the OAU and publicising the cause and events in Southern Sudan to the outside world'.[30] Moreover, it described SANU's operations in exile not as cowardice but as a matter of political necessity, and included the parallel rise of the 'freedom fighters' as complementary.[31]

In addressing the fragmentation of the Southern movement, Lagu's ANO claimed that 'an ideological dispute has not so far arisen among Southern leaders'.[32] This coherence of thought is reflected in the consistency of the messages in the propaganda material produced by the disparate groups. As such, the splits among secessionists did not signal a change in the narrativisation of the "Southern Problem", even though they did reflect a change in strategy. Unlike SANU at the dawn of the decade, whose main task was to lobby international institutions and governments to gain sympathy for the Southern cause, these new groups aimed at performing "state-ness" in Southern Sudan by establishing governments-in-waiting.

Perhaps the very fact that none of the groups acknowledged their intellectual ancestry demonstrates the efficacy of SANU's discursive power. Whether they absorbed the discourses unwittingly, having accepted it as the true framing of the "Southern Problem", or political pragmatism warranted that they do not credit another organisation for this construction, SANU's discourses prevailed. It is especially telling that despite the ineffectiveness of SANU's ideas among international observers at the RTC, these Southern secessionist groups continued to use SANU's discourses. Given that it was inexpedient to continue using them, the fact that these groups continued suggests that they themselves were persuaded by SANU's articulation. Their ideas had attained "taken-for-granted" status as accepted truths, and were not seen as the handiwork of politicians in a specific historical context. The influence of these discourses reached beyond the boundaries of expected audiences, as the next section reveals.

Unintended Audiences and 'Unfortunate Friends'

Unintended audiences became sympathetic to the Southern cause, in part due to the wide reach of media coverage employing the discursive constructions of exiled Southerners. Ironically, white settlers in southern Africa formed one such group. A South African right-wing analyst, F. R. Metrowich, expressed concern over Southern Sudan in the following terms:

> Much of the news on the genocide never reaches the outside world, and, in any case, even if it does both Western and Black African news media prefer to ignore this embarrassing situation as it could upset anti-South African and anti-Rhodesian strategy. The latter attitude, naturally, fits in nicely with Communist plans… if the world refuses to take notice of what is happening in the Sudan, Communist campaigns will be that much easier. Where the world has ventured forth to express an opinion on the Sudan, it has, surprisingly, been largely a favourable one.[33]

The existence of the robust Sudanese Communist Party (which Chap. 9 will discuss) as well as Sudan's opposition to the Apartheid regime made the country a natural enemy for South Africa. Thus, it is plausible that despite the irony that Southern Sudanese rebels condemned the racism of the South African government, this South Africa apologist saw an opportunity to tarnish the Sudanese government's reputation as a way of criticising communism in Africa.

Sudan's failure to avoid civil war fed into white supremacist notions of the inability of Africans to self-govern.[34] It was in the best interests of white settler states to undermine sovereign African states, and hence supporting groups lobbying for self-determination within Africa served the purpose. Both South Africa and Rhodesia were rumoured to have supported Biafra in the war against Nigeria.[35] In fact, in a debate among Rhodesian parliamentarians on a motion about constitutional proposals on 17 October 1968, Lord Graham, a Rhodesian Front representative, remarked

> I would like to say, furthermore, that on the evidence we have had from those countries, which have in recent years been given independence, that it is when there is African majority rule that appeal to the Privy Council is most necessary. I believe the southern Sudanese or the Biafrans or the Indians in Kenya would very much like to be able to appeal to the Privy Council, but there is no appeal for them.[36]

This statement of concern for the Southern Sudanese among others is directly connected to the problems that ensue from 'African majority rule', which require European intervention through the British-led Privy Council.[37]

Southern Sudan remained a byword for abject oppression among Rhodesian parliamentarians. On 23 April 1969, Rhodesian Front member for Greenwood, Mr T. M. Ellison made a sympathetic reference to the Southern cause in an attempt to make Rhodesia look better in comparison:

> Possibly they would like to use the Sudan as an example and consider the Arabs with their policy of killing anybody with a black skin who is not prepared – and I use the word "killing" deliberately – who is not prepared to kowtow to them, to bow down to them in the streets. If they are unfortunate enough to come from the south of the Sudan, they are fair game for all the Arabs of the northern Sudan. ... I believe that we in Rhodesia have nothing to be ashamed of. We can hold our heads high because we have treated everybody in this country, everybody, fairly.[38]

Sudan, listed among other states in which minorities are treated unfairly including Canada (Native Americans), Kenya (Asians) and the US (African-Americans), was used as a contrast to Rhodesian civility.

Malawi represented another unintended ally. On 28 June 1968, President Hastings Banda was the first African head of state to publicly condemn the Sudanese government for 'literally obliterating African villages', as 'Arabs are butchering Africans in the south'.[39] The President's articulation of the crisis mirrors SANU's descriptions. Still, Malawi, long seen as a collaborator with Apartheid South Africa, served as yet another 'unfortunate friend'.[40] The accepted liberation movements that SANU sought to be equated with, such as the South West Africa People's Organization (SWAPO), referred to Malawi as an example of a 'Black client' state to South Africa, as the country had 'policies of subservience to white racist mentors'.[41]

Southern politicians in exile thus failed to convince the OAU, and particularly the group of states that conferred legitimacy to liberation movements—generally the Committee of Nine that coordinated the African Liberation Committee.[42] These gatekeepers of legitimacy on the continent, including a fairly nebulous group of influential African states, certainly did not include Malawi or Rhodesia. By and large, only these illegitimate political actors in Africa publicly reproduced SANU's discourses in the latter half of the 1960s. For them, SANU's discourses accidentally 'gave them publicity to counter anti-Apartheid propaganda' and as such, their support 'did little to win the southern Sudan more friends on the continent'.[43]

Conclusion

Analysis of the spread of SANU's discursive constructs reveals the long-standing and wide-ranging impact of this political movement. While SANU can be dismissed as a political failure due to its inability to present a united front at the Round Table Conference and to survive past 1965 in its original form, its discourses influenced every major Southern Sudanese liberation movement of the 1960s, and produced sympathisers in Africa and the West (as we saw in Chap. 5). Although the RTC revealed the limits of discourse alone in the context of diplomatic and realpolitik concerns, the power inherent in SANU's discursive contribution can easily be overlooked. It acquired not only the power of knowledge production, as shown in Chap. 3, but it also established what became a regime of truth among Southerners—both in the South and in the diaspora. This attainment of commonsensical status, revealed in this chapter, attests to SANU's discursive authority in the 1960s.

However, this authority was not without its problems too. When 'the terrain of dominant discourse is the only plausible arena of struggle', the political actors fall hostage to the structures of the discourse.[44] Discourses create 'rhetorical universes' with their own logics that determine political strategy.[45] For SANU, the fixed racial binary represented a significant building block of the argument for self-determination. Yet, it ensnared Southern Sudanese political imagination, and inadvertently gave the Northern Sudanese political establishment at the RTC convincing ammunition as it had the advantage of appearing to stand for inclusive, multicultural statehood. Moreover, it opened the South up to obtaining 'unfortunate friends'. In the final analysis, SANU's reductive representations effectively made the "Southern Problem" legible to international audiences in negative ways. Thus, SANU's undisputable and underappreciated influence among Southern movements came at an unforeseen cost.

Next, we turn to a discussion of the ways in which the Sudanese governments of the 1960s competed diplomatically and discursively to protect the country's reputation from the attempts of rebels to tarnish it. This examination of the Sudanese state's diplomatic self-representation to

Africa and socialist networks abroad, particularly as it relates to the "Southern Problem" and the subsequent allegations the Southern political exiles levelled against the state, reveals the deliberate and coordinated effort by successive Sudanese governments to garner international approval.

Notes

1. R. Doty, *Imperial Encounters: the politics of representation in North-South relations* (Minneapolis, 1996), p. 72.
2. Special Correspondent, '"Death to Arabs" call in south Sudan', *The Observer* (6 October 1963), p. 14.
3. P. Seale, 'Sudan Drive on Rebels in South', *The Observer* (15 March 1964).
4. 'The Southern Sudan's leaders', *Africa Confidential*, No. 14 (12 July 1968), p. 7.
5. His efforts were eclipsed in 1965 when Anya-Nya received a windfall of weapons at the end of the Simba rebellion in the Congo. S. McCall, 'The Rise of a Provisional Government in Southern Sudan' (unpublished paper, delivered 8–12 December 1969, University Social Sciences Council Conference, the University of East Africa, Nairobi, University College), SAD 803/4/26-34.
6. J. Howell, 'Political Leaders in the Southern Sudan', 1972, SAD 803/5/19-35.
7. Johnson, *Root Causes*, pp. 32–33.
8. SAD 803/5/19-35.
9. 'Southern Sudan: The Decline of the ALF', *Africa Confidential*, no. 8 (12 April 1968), p. 2.
10. 'S. Sudan: Who controls what?', Africa Confidential, no. 12 (17 June 1966), pp. 4–5. Joseph Lagu resigned as Second-Lieutenant in the Sudan Armed Forces in 1962, when he left to join the Southern rebellion from Gulu, Uganda. He played an instrumental role in managing the logistics of supplying arms to the rebel movement from Congo through the Ugandan towns of Kitgum and Arua close to Gulu. Tafeng el Lodongi had also previously served in the Sudanese Army. He functioned as the commander of Anya-Nya in Eastern Equatoria in the South.
11. Johnson, *Root Causes*, pp. 36–37.
12. R. P. Stevens, 'The 1972 Addis Ababa Agreement and the Sudan's Afro-Arab Policy', *Journal of Modern African Studies*, 14/2 (1976), pp. 247–274.
13. L. Wol Wol, *Voice of Southern Sudan*, no. 1 (New Series) (15 January 1969), p. 2.

14. A. Wanji, 'The Attitude of Successive Sudanese Arab Governments Towards the Nile Problem Since 1954 (Former Southern Sudan)', Minister of Foreign Affairs & Government Economic Advisor, 4 April 1969, p. 5.
15. Ibid.
16. E. Tafeng Longodi 'Declaration to the Anyanya Armed Forces' (11 June 1969), p. 2. DHJ-PP.
17. Wanji, 'The Attitude of Successive Sudanese', p. 5. Emphasis added.
18. Howell, 'Political leadership and organisation in the southern Sudan', p. 7.
19. Wanji, 'The Attitude of Successive Sudanese', p. 7.
20. Ibid, p. 9.
21. Ibid, p. 11.
22. E. L. Surur, 'Statement on the Military Takeover of Government in the State of Anyidi (The Former Southern Sudan)', Anyidi Revolutionary Government (11 July 1969), p. 1.
23. Ibid.
24. Mr Agolong Col Agolong and Mr James Amou de Arok, Memorandum submitted by the Azania Liberation Front (ALF)—Congo Branch to the 4th Summit Conference of the Organization of African Unity Meeting in Kinshasa, Congo, 1967, p. 7.
25. Ibid, p. 8.
26. Ibid.
27. Anyanya National Organization, *Resistance: The Story of Southern Sudan* (London, 1969), p. 10.
28. See Chap. 2.
29. Ibid, p. 18.
30. Ibid, p. 12.
31. Ibid, p. 12–13.
32. Anyanya National Organization, *Resistance*, p. 20.
33. F. R. Metrowich, *Africa and Communism: A study of successes, set-backs, and stooge states* (Johannesburg, 1967), p. 77.
34. Brownell, 'Diplomatic Lepers', p. 209.
35. See J. H. Polhemus, 'Nigeria and Southern Africa: Interest, Policy and Means', *Canadian Journal of African Studies*, 11/1 (1977), p. 49.
36. *Southern Rhodesian Hansard*, 'Constitutional Proposals', 17 October 1968, Column 139.
37. This is especially telling in a context in which Rhodesians tenaciously rejected Privy Council provision as an abrogation of their own sovereignty, accepting it only because it became the only way for Rhodesian independence to be obtained from Britain in the absence of majority rule.
38. 'Referendum Bill' (23 April 1969), *Rhodesia Parliamentary Debates Vol. 73 1968–69* (Salisbury, 1969), p. 1375.

39. D. O'Grady, 'The Forgotten War', *The Tablet* (26 October 1968), http://archive.thetablet.co.uk/article/26th-october-1968/3/the-forgotten-war (accessed on 23 November 2014).
40. Douglas Johnson coined the phrase "unfortunate friends" in reference to Malawian sympathy for Southern Sudan. In person conversation, 2014.
41. 'International Conference in Support of the Peoples of Portuguese Colonies and Southern Africa in Khartoum, Jan 1969', 'Background Paper Submitted by SWAPO', p. 9, Weston Library, University of Oxford, MMS, Anti-Apartheid Movement Archive (AAM), 1393.
42. The Coordinating Committee for the Liberation of Africa (previously called the Committee of Nine) consisted of Tanganyika (where it was headquartered), Uganda, Algeria, Congo (Leopoldville), Nigeria, Senegal, Ethiopia, Guinea and United Arab Republic (Egypt).
43. Johnson, *Root Causes*, pp. 31–32.
44. J. Scott, *Domination and the Arts of Resistance: Hidden Transcripts* (New Haven, CT, 1990), p. 102.
45. Krebs and Jackson, 'Twisting tongues and twisting arms', p. 45.

CHAPTER 8

'We Have No Harlem in Sudan': Sudan's Deflective Diplomacy

In December 1964, the then incumbent Minister of Foreign Affairs, Mohamed Mahgoub, arrived in New York City to a barrage of questions from reporters. They asked: 'What is behind the news that the African section in Khartoum is rioting against the Arab section?'[1] The day before Mahgoub arrived in the US, an uprising broke out between "Africans" and "Arabs" in Khartoum as Southerners waited for the Minister of Interior, Clement Mboro, to return from a trip to his native South. Mboro occupied 'the highest position held by a southerner up to that time' and was one of two Southerners in a ministerial position in the recently established transitional government in the aftermath of the October Revolution of 1964.[2] Upon hearing rumours that he had been assassinated, the crowd began to chant secessionist slogans and to protest violently across the city. Mboro also served as the president of the newly minted Southern Front, the main political home for Southerners in Khartoum.[3] To his followers, an assassination only two months after the Front's founding symbolised an attack on Southern enfranchisement. At the time, a British fortnightly newsletter, *Africa Confidential*, posited that the Southern crowds in Khartoum had compared the rumour of Mboro's murder to Patrice Lumumba's assassination three years prior, a killing that had also sparked rioting across the Congo as well as in several major cities across the world.[4] In response to the demonstrations, some residents of Khartoum attacked the crowd. Scores of people were killed and approximately 400

S. C. Manoeli, *Sudan's "Southern Problem"*, African Histories and Modernities, https://doi.org/10.1007/978-3-030-28771-9_8

injured.[5] It later transpired that Mboro had not been assassinated, but that his trip had simply been delayed.

Not having heard news of the riots because they had started while he was en route to the US, Mahgoub vociferously denied the existence of racial conflict in Sudan, retorting: 'We have no Harlem in Sudan and no segregation of any kind.'[6] In the US to attend his first General Assembly as Foreign Minister, Mahgoub's first address to the world was not in the halls of the UN Headquarters in lower Manhattan. Instead, this ad hoc press conference was his first diplomatic act on this trip. Mahgoub's response captures the Sudanese government's adamant denial of the country's racial tensions that were especially apparent in the country's urban nodes. Memorialised as 'Black Sunday',[7] the riots drew international attention and were characterised as 'racial rioting' or 'racial fighting' in the international press.[8] In addition to Willow Berridge's observation that '[t]he Black Sunday riots demonstrated that conflict in the peripheries [i.e. the war in the South] could have resonances in Khartoum', Mahgoub's inquisition in New York equally demonstrated that the crisis in Sudan could reverberate in foreign cities.[9] Hence, Mahgoub experienced the expanding influence of the narratives of Southern Sudanese rebels, and specifically their insistence on framing the conflict in racial terms. In his incisive turn of phrase, Mahgoub rejected a comparison between the riots in Khartoum and those in Harlem a few months earlier. The riot of 18 July 1964, in the New York borough, exposed America's racial tension afresh to a watching world.[10] The Sudanese government at the time and thereafter worked hard to cloak the country's crisis of identity from the world's gaze, and claimed that whatever troubles may have existed fell solely under the remit of internal affairs and ought not to be subjected to international scrutiny. Mahgoub sought to shield Sudan from acquiring a reputation for racial discrimination, knowing that efforts to brand Sudan as such were afoot.

Reflecting on the Sudanese government's diplomatic veneer, another one of Sudan's former Ministers of Foreign Affairs opined, in an interview I conducted in his home in Khartoum, that 'this is the problem with Sudanese politicians… because they are Northerners, they say the right things in the right place – [the Organization of] African Unity and UN. But they do the very wrong things inside Sudan'.[11] A Northern politician himself, the former Minister believed that Sudanese politicians lacked authenticity abroad, and described the consequent discrepancies between Sudan's international rhetoric and its national conduct as the

Sudanese government 'playing a game against the whole world. The world knows what's happening. South Sudanese know what is happening'.[12]

This chapter investigates the means through which Sudanese governments outmanoeuvred rebels internationally throughout the 1960s by analysing the intertwining of Sudan's discursive and diplomatic strategies for protecting its reputation in Pan-Africanist and anti-imperialist circles. The chapter argues that Sudan employed a strategy of deflective diplomacy that drew international attention away from the "Southern Problem" while addressing the pertinent areas of reputational damage. This deflection paradoxically placed Sudan in the international limelight as a paragon of Pan-Africanism, while concealing the "Problem" in plain sight. It explores Sudan's relations with African networks and organisations after the fall of the Abboud regime, specifically in the tenures of the most significant prime minister of the 1960s: Mohamed Mahgoub. It addresses neither the premiership of Khatim al-Khalifa that lasted eight months nor that of Saddiq al-Mahdi that spanned ten months, as they were too brief. The chapter will begin by examining Mahgoub's approach to international affairs and to the "Southern Problem", and then chart his connections in Black internationalist and anti-imperialist networks. This will reveal how Mahgoub constructed an image of Sudan as a supporter of African liberation movements.

'The Eyes of the World Were Focused on Us': Sudan's Quest for International Legitimacy

In their work on status-seeking in the international system, Benjamin de Carvalho and Iver B. Neumann contend that status is an important driver of everyday policies of small states. By examining the routine aspects of international life, the authors hold that small states seek status more than great states due to the insecurities associated with smallness. They aver that '[g]reat power status is about being a state to be reckoned with; small-power status is about being noticed or seen'.[13] The Sudanese government in the 1960s held a commitment to attaining status and building a reputation for the country abroad. In particular, Mohamed Mahgoub played an indispensable role in shaping Sudan's image abroad. He became Prime Minister of Sudan in 1965 until 1966, and again from 1967 until 1969 when Ja'afer Nimeiri mounted a successful coup against his administration. As the longest serving Prime Minister in the 1960s after the fall of Abboud, Mahgoub's approach to diplomacy is worth noting. In his memoir, he reflected

> I believe that nowadays, and particularly for a developing country, devotion to international affairs is a necessity. I have always believed that developing countries can only hope to obtain foreign aid and development assistance if they take a keen interest in international and foreign affairs. They must place themselves conspicuously on the map of the world; otherwise they will be *too small to be noticed.* This theory was proved beyond any reasonable doubt during our involvement in the Six-Day War, in convening the Fourth Arab Summit in Khartoum after the conflict, and in bringing about the Yemen Peace Agreement. During this time, news of and from the Sudan made headlines in all the major newspapers and was continually reported on the world's radio and television stations. I remember one journalist said to me in Khartoum that the publicity that the Sudan received through the Khartoum Arab Summit could not have been bought for £10 millions [sic]. The eyes of the world were focused on us.[14]

As a result of his government's involvement in the Middle East, Mahgoub gained a reputation as a skilful diplomat.[15] Before becoming prime minister, Mahgoub served as Sudan's Minister of Foreign Affairs between 1956 and 1958, and again in 1964 to 1965.[16] As Sudan's Commander-in-Chief and Chief Diplomat, Mahgoub gave primacy to Sudan's international image to the extent that he says citizens criticised him for what they perceived to be an excessive focus on foreign affairs.[17] For example, in 1968, an *Africa Confidential* international journalist noted that there had been dissatisfaction in Sudan, 'part of it arising from the feeling that the Government had been ignoring internal affairs and concentrating on Arab and international affairs'.[18]

Despite its shortcomings among the Sudanese electorate, Mahgoub's 'theory' of 'devotion to international affairs' could be understood partially as a small state's attempt at status-seeking. Even though he couched his imperatives in monetary terms (i.e. obtaining access to development assistance), Mahgoub also sought the world's attention in order to have Sudan recognised as a relevant player in its region. Given that 'small states achieve status through making themselves *useful*', Sudan's attempt to craft an image as a responsible and valuable actor in the international community was a bid to attain prestige.[19] The resultant credibility functions as diplomatic currency.[20] Further, Mahgoub's keen awareness of 'news of and from Sudan' in the international press also suggests that he also noticed the poor publicity Sudan garnered as a result of Southern rebel discourses of the "Southern Problem".

Mahgoub began accruing diplomatic capital in the pre-independence era, between 1946 and 1947, in London while serving as the secretary of Sudan's delegation in the UK. He arrived a year after the historic Pan-African Congress hosted in Manchester, UK, which is credited with building momentum for the decolonisation of Africa as well as the British West Indies, and for fomenting African nationalist sentiment.[21] Mahgoub struck up a friendship with men who organised the Congress and who later became Pan-Africanist icons, namely Kwame Nkrumah and Jomo Kenyatta, as well as the Trinidadian writer George Padmore. Other Pan-Africanist leaders with whom he developed a rapport included Jamaican statesman Norman Manley, Guyanese-born activist T. Ras Makonnen and South African novelist Peter Abrahams. As a group, they were involved in the League of Coloured Peoples, an organisation modelled after the National Association for the Advancement of Colored People (NAACP) in the US, and it became the largest Pan-Africanist organisation in Britain in the 1930s and 1940s.[22] As a member of this group of activists, Mahgoub participated in the activities of the Congress of People against Imperialism.[23] He became well known in London's Black anti-imperialist networks. For instance, in the summer of 1947, Cedric Dover, who served as the president of the Coloured Writers Association in London, hosted an exclusive dinner for critically acclaimed African-American writer Richard Wright to which he invited Mahgoub, along with a select group of Pan-Africanists. Other dinner guests included George Padmore, Peter Abrahams and the West Indian poet Peter Blackman.[24]

These contacts arose in the context of the Umma Party—Mahgoub's political party—lobbying anti-imperial groups in Britain to support Sudan's efforts to attain independence from Egypt.[25] As we saw, Sudan was governed by the British-led Condominium with Egypt. In the post-World War II period, tensions emerged among Sudan's political elites who sought self-determination and complete independence, such as the Umma Party, and those who sought to uphold the unity of the Nile Valley under Egyptian governance, such as the National Unionist Party. In this context, the Umma Party established an alliance with members of the British government.[26] Nationalist efforts succeeded in November 1950 when Egypt agreed to annul its claims to Sudan.[27] Besides Mahgoub, other Northern politicians from the Umma Party such as Yosuf Osman and Yacoub Osman were involved in the anti-imperial efforts in London that Padmore convened.[28]

Through the efforts of Northern politicians like Mahgoub, Sudan came on to the radar of Pan-Africanist activists. Padmore, who was also a journalist for the *West African Pilot* and the *Ashanti Pioneer*, covered Sudan's journey to independence extensively.[29] His work was exceptionally influential, holding the headline spot almost daily.[30] Padmore formed meaningful personal bonds with Sudanese political leaders from the North and he remained engaged in Sudanese independence politics for most of his life. He and his wife, Dorothy Padmore, often hosted Sudanese activists and politicians, mainly members of the Umma Party and the Independence Front, in their home.[31] After independence, the representatives of Sudan at the embassy in Paris hosted Padmore in exclusive hotels as their honoured guest.[32] Upon Padmore's sudden death in September 1959, the Sudanese embassies in the UK and the US sent delegates to his funeral and the memorial services hosted in London and Chicago respectively. Exemplifying the close association of Padmore and the post-independence Sudanese government, Ghana (where Padmore spent his final years) and Sudan were the only two countries that sent diplomatic representatives to both services.[33] The endorsement of anti-colonial leaders like Padmore granted the Sudanese government some legitimacy in the Third World and anti-colonial networks.

Beyond his own personal networks within Pan-African circles, Mahgoub built upon the diplomatic strategies of his predecessor Ibrahim Abboud in Africa, their domestic political differences notwithstanding. When Mahgoub came to power, he inherited a state that had garnered a reputation for supporting African liberation causes, as defined by the Organisation of African Unity (OAU). At its founding in 1963, the OAU institutionalised the 'severance of diplomatic relations' and the use of 'diplomatic action against colonial powers in Africa', including white settler states.[34] A year before, in 1962, Sudan's Prime Minister, Ibrahim Abboud, enabled Nelson Mandela to meet a small group of African National Congress (ANC) youths in Sudan who were en route to Tanganyika and Cuba for military and academic training.[35] Soon after Mandela left Sudan, he was arrested in South Africa.[36] In his historic Rivonia Trial speech of 20 April 1964 in which he and nine other ANC members were tried for committing acts of sabotage against the Apartheid government, Mandela made special mention of Abboud alongside bona fide African Nationalist figureheads Julius Nyerere, Haile Selassie and Leopold Senghor in recognition of his exceptional support to the ANC.[37]

In his memoir, Mahgoub boasted that 'Sudan offered her territory for the training of freedom fighters'.[38] Indeed, in 1963, Abboud's Sudan was one of the first three countries in Africa to close its air and seaports to South Africa and Portugal in protest of those regimes.[39] It was also one of the first to pass a comprehensive Boycott Bill for South Africa in 1963. Continuing in the tradition of progressive, Pan-Africanist legislation, three years later in al-Mahdi's administration, Sudan passed the comprehensive Southern Rhodesia Boycott Act.[40] Moreover, Sudan became one of five members of the Zambia Solidarity Committee established in 1966 to assist the country as its economy had suffered due to its support of the liberation movements south of it, and due to its strong financial links with Southern Rhodesia.[41] Sudan's record of fulfilling the OAU mandate in these ways built on a longer Pan-Africanist history and afforded the country a kind of diplomatic surplus, which Mahgoub capitalised on in a way that ultimately helped to deflect the attention of African political leaders from the "Southern Problem". Further, by condemning the racist white settler states in southern Africa, Sudan could distance itself from being painted with the same brush by Southerners who alleged that the Sudanese government was also racially prejudiced.

In light of Sudan's significant investment in these liberation efforts, Mahgoub's memoir suggests that he occasionally found the pace of the anti-Rhodesian activities of African governments discouraging. In his account, he recalled feeling particularly disappointed that only eight African countries (of which Sudan was one) had severed all ties with the UK as a means of ending 'British procrastination' in condemning Ian Smith's regime in Southern Rhodesia.[42] Sudan did in fact sever ties with Britain in 1965 in protest of Rhodesian independence, only to restore relations in 1966.[43] In 1967, they were severed again after the Six-Day War, but they were restored a year later. In reality, the stakes of severing ties to the UK and the Commonwealth were different for Sudan as it had access to Gulf petro-dollars as a member of the Arab League. According to Mahgoub's memoir, at the time he felt that African heads of state 'were paying only lip service to the African cause if, having severed relations with Britain, they remained within the Commonwealth'.[44] According to his account, he wrote personal letters to the heads of state of Nigeria, Uganda, Ghana, Kenya and Tanzania in which he urged them to leave the Commonwealth. But he allegedly only received one response in the form of 'a most evasive and baffling' letter from Kwame Nkrumah that did not lead to Ghana exiting the Commonwealth as per his advice.[45]

While other countries on the African continent delayed, Sudan went even further. Its representatives at the OAU proposed that Zimbabwean rebels establish a government-in-exile in Khartoum. The OAU rejected the proposal on account of the divisions in the Zimbabwean nationalist movement.[46] Mahgoub's radical position nevertheless served to draw attention to Sudan's unwavering commitment to anti-colonialism, and it portrayed Sudan as the true torchbearer of OAU causes. Before we turn to a detailed discussion of the first OAU conference dedicated to African liberation movements that Sudan hosted, we briefly highlight an attempt Mahgoub made to delegitimise the Southern rebellion both domestically and through its international activities.

As a result of the importance he attached to Sudan's reputation, Mahgoub approached the "Southern Problem" as a scourge that, if not dealt with decisively, could negatively affect Sudan's standing internationally. In early 1965, while serving as the Foreign Minister in the period leading up to the Round Table Conference where he represented the Umma Party, Mahgoub openly admitted that he believed that 'strength rather than compromise' was the best approach to the Southern rebels.[47] Upon coming to power as Prime Minister in May 1965, Mahgoub intensified the civil war in the South. In his memoir, he recalled that 'one of the first things I did was announce our policy on the South. I also called for an increase in arms and equipment for the Army to combat the continuing rebellion there'.[48]

His government also supported African governments facing secessionist threats. The Biafran cause for secession presented the Sudanese government such an opportunity. In Mahgoub's view, Biafra's success had the potential of torpedoing the efforts to stigmatise separatism in Sudan. He recounted:

> I considered that, if the breakaway of Biafra had been tolerated, it would have meant not just the disintegration of Nigeria, but also the disintegration of the Sudan, and almost all the other independent African states throughout the continent. It was an example that could not be permitted to succeed.[49]

He viewed his international involvement as having direct bearing on the war in Southern Sudan, and the military solution he supported in Nigeria mirrored the military solution he implemented in Southern Sudan. The rising sympathy for the Biafran cause among African leaders alarmed

Mahgoub. Within the first year of the Biafran war, the heads of four African states (Zambia, Tanzania, the Ivory Coast and Gabon) officially recognised Biafra and others, including the Cameroonian President, were vocally sympathetic.[50] As a result, Mahgoub strengthened his support to Nigeria.

Both the Sudanese government and the Southern rebels shared a sense of the significance of Biafra to the civil war in Southern Sudan. For the rebels, Biafra represented hope. In their propaganda vehicle, Anyanya National Organization (ANO) coveted the international community's response to Biafra, stating that '[b]ut of all contemporary tragedies, this one is unique in that while the world has woken up over the Biafran tragedy, it has not done so in Southern Sudan'. Thus, ANO held that 'the world has turned a deaf ear to the human suffering of the Southern Sudanese people'.[51] Mahgoub's approach to the Nigerian-Biafran war and his exceptional involvement in African liberation causes highlight that he used both offensive and defensive strategies to combat the Southern rebel campaign to bring Sudan into disrepute.

The Khartoum Conference of 1969

Sudan sought to gain a reputation for being at the forefront of the fight against white settler rule in southern Africa and colonialism in other African countries. From 18 to 20 January 1969, while Mahgoub served as prime minister, the government of Sudan hosted the momentous International Conference in Support of the Peoples of the Portuguese Colonies and Southern Africa in Khartoum, also known as the Khartoum Conference. To a broad international audience, Sudan showed itself to be essential to liberation efforts across the continent. Hosted at the Grand Hotel, the Republican Palace and the University of Khartoum, the Conference attracted the continent's heads of state and government. Delegates from over 50 countries in Africa, Latin America, the Eastern Bloc, Asia, Western Europe and North America attended.[52] Senior representatives of organisations such as the World Council of Peace, the Afro-Asian People's Solidarity Organisation (AAPSO) and the OAU's African Liberation Committee (ALC), as well as other solidarity groups,[53] and a select group of liberation movements attended the Conference.[54] The representatives of the latter included Sam Nujoma of South West Africa People's Organisation (SWAPO); Stephen Nkomo and Samuel Parirenyatwa of Zimbabwe African People's Union (ZAPU); Dr Eduardo

Mondlane who represented Frente de Libertação de Moçambique (FRELIMO) and Thabo Mbeki, Ambrose Makiwane, Tennyson Makiwane and Joe Matthews of the ANC.[55] For the Sudanese government, it was invaluable to have these luminaries of the legitimate movements in Khartoum as they could personally witness Sudan's public performance of Pan-Africanist solidarity.

The Sudanese government was concerned to establish the legitimacy of the liberation movements that were invited as a means of associating itself with only those endorsed by the OAU. The selection process of the members of the committees reveals this point. At the conference, the diplomats and heads of state present formed five committees, namely the Steering Committee, the Mobilisation Committee and the three Political Committees devoted to various tasks. These included mobilising material support and analysing the political situations in each liberation movement. A representative of each of the six "authentic" African liberation movements (the Movimento Popular de Libertação de Angola [MPLA], Partido Africano da Independência da Guiné e Cabo Verde [PAIGC], FRELIMO, SWAPO, ANC and ZAPU) that received support from the ALC was invited to join each committee. Other committee members included two representatives of AAPSO, two members of the World Council of Peace (WCP) and a representative of the Sudanese government. The Steering Committee also served as the Credential Committee and it was expected to be 'competent to ascertain the authenticity of every representative in accordance with the list of invitation to the Conference'.[56] The Mobilisation Committee made a number of recommendations that aimed at ensuring that only legitimate liberation movements would receive recognition and assistance. It specifically requested that 'all governments of the world' recognise the six liberation movements invited to the conferences as 'the sole official and legitimate authorities of the respective countries'.[57] In addition, they were to 'assure the peoples and the authentic liberation movements of [their] support and of [their] militant and concrete solidarity'.[58]

Moreover, the Conference delineated between legitimate and illegitimate countries. In a document circulated at the event, the imperialist countries were listed as Great Britain, France, Italy, West Germany, Japan, the US and Israel.[59] African heads of state publicly shamed states on the continent that maintained relations with these "pariah" governments and the white settler states they upheld. For instance, a representative of the DRC openly condemned Malawi, Botswana, Lesotho, Kenya, Libya and

Cameroon for their 'open treason to the African cause' for their relations with the South African government at the time.[60]

By leading the efforts to combat racism in other African states, Sudan was safeguarding its own legitimacy among the states that participated in this Conference, which had been threatened by Southern rebel propaganda. To further affirm the authority of the liberation movements, and similarly discredit the states they opposed, the Conference encouraged

> governments to recognise the liberation movements as the alternative and future governments of the territories concerned; to break off all relations with the illegal and despotic regimes, to give every facility and aid to the representatives and supporters of the liberation movements and remove every let or hindrance to their noble missions.[61]

The Conference insisted that maintaining diplomatic relations with the states in question allowed them to 'gain respectability in the rest of the world when they should be condemned, isolated and cast out of the ranks of the international comity of nations'.[62]

Sudan's representatives at the Conference strategically included influential Southerners based in Khartoum, who had refused to boycott the government. These included Philip Obang Ojway, Joseph U. Garang, Abel Alier and Bona Malwal.[63] Ojway had served in the executive committee of the then deceased William Deng's Sudan African National Union (SANU) from 1965 to 1969, and he was the deputy secretary general of the party. At the time, he had close relations with the Umma Party, serving as a member of the editorial staff of that party's publication, the *Nile Pilot*.[64] The first Southern Sudanese law graduate from Khartoum University, Joseph U. Garang had been a member of the Sudan Communist Party (SCP) from the 1950s, and from 1965 he served as the editor of the Party's daily paper, *Advance*. Yale Law graduate Abel Alier was a founding member of the Southern Front in 1964, and served as an MP for Bor District between 1968 and 1969.[65] Fellow Southern Front founding member and a renowned journalist, Bona Malwal founded the Khartoum-based *Vigilant* newspaper, having received a diploma in journalism from Indiana University and a Master's degree in journalism and international relations from Columbia University.[66]

The presence of Southern Sudanese officials at this occasion helped to undercut allegations that the Sudanese government was anti-Black and anti-Southerner. The Southern Sudanese rebels in the South and in exile portrayed this group of Khartoum-based intellectuals as compromised. Lawrence Wol Wol, in the edition of *Voice of Southern Sudan* immediately following the conference, portrayed the government's use of this group, particularly the Southern Front, as an 'Arab diplomatic tactic'.[67] Wol Wol argued that while the Southern Front had aimed at being a 'watch-dog' in Khartoum, 'in pursuance of this role it has allowed itself to be used by the Arab demagogues to contradict all concern about the Southern problem'.[68] From this point of view, the government paraded these figures internationally because they served the government's narrative that Southerners did not experience racial discrimination in Sudan. Wol Wol took issue with an article in the *Vigilant* in which a Southern Front journalist denounced Malawian President Hastings Banda for 'calling world attention to Arab persecution of the Africans of Southern Sudan'.[69] The *Vigilant* article insisted 'that the situation has returned to normal in the South', despite the ongoing war.[70] Further, it displeased Wol Wol that the Southern Front's Secretary General, Hilary Paul Logali, who also served as the Minister of Co-operation and Labour, led the Sudanese delegation to the East and Central African Ministers' Meeting in Dar es Salaam in February 1969. As a result, the Southern rebel movement distanced itself from Southern politicians based in Khartoum, claiming that 'the diplomatic game played on the Southern Front was for them to deny before African leaders assembled, the existence of the Southern problem'.[71] At the Khartoum Conference of 1969, this Southern group was seen to be playing a similar role.

The Sudanese government thus portrayed itself as progressive by both showcasing co-opted Southern politicians in Khartoum and associating with leaders in the fight against oppression elsewhere. Because it hosted a conference that opposed 'anti-African regimes',[72] Sudan signalled that it could not simultaneously be anti-African on the domestic front in the ways the Southern rebels posited. Sudan's strategy worked to a significant extent. The international delegates present recognised Sudan for the exceptional role it played in the liberation efforts on the continent, as the following excerpt in the declaration written to mark the occasion reveals:

> We have decided with unanimity that Africa and the world must take action to give more effective help to the African Liberation Movements fighting for the freedom of their peoples. Coming to Khartoum from all over Europe, from Asia, from America, North and South, we solemnly resolve that this

> Khartoum Conference shall prove a historic new stage of advance in Africa's march to freedom, independence and unity.[73]

One of the ANC's representatives, Robert M. Resha, made a special statement of gratitude to 'the Government and people of the Sudan' for their expressions of solidarity, their hospitality, and for 'making it possible to hold this august conference in Khartoum'.[74] Nujoma similarly expressed gratitude to the Sudanese government. Others included R. Khadilkar, leader of the Indian Delegation and the Deputy Speaker of the Indian Parliament, who commended Sudan for its continued role of providing 'a bridge of understanding between the peoples of Africa and the Arab world'.[75] The Chief Representative of the ANC, Alfred Nzo, gave a speech in which he commended 'the noble ideals of the Afro-Asian solidarity', noting with admiration 'the tremendous demonstration of solidarity by our Asian brothers'.[76]

No commendation exceeded the one read by a FRELIMO representative on behalf of all six liberation movements:

> The liberation movements in Africa attach particular importance to this Conference for many and obvious reasons. In the first place, in the last few years, there have been many conferences in support of liberation struggles in other parts of the world. But not until the present Conference has ever been a serious thought on organising one in support of liberation movements in Africa. In the last three years, we have been looking for a place in Africa where we could voice our cause to the world in search of support. But this had not materialised until the present Conference.[77]

FRELIMO further stressed the close linkages between the anti-imperialist struggles across the world. It notably linked the liberation of African states to the 'fight of the fraternal Arab people against imperialist-backed Zionist aggression'.[78] Likewise, the Conference delegates stood in solidarity with the second International Conference in Support of Arab Peoples, to be held in Cairo a week later.[79] In a resolution, the delegates declared that '[t]he Khartoum and Cairo Conferences are closely connected with each other', and regarding the struggles against imperialism in Africa and in the Arab world, the group affirmed that '[t]he two struggles are inextricably linked'.[80] In so doing, with the strong presence of the Cairo-based Afro-Asian Peoples Solidarity Organisation, the Khartoum Conference aimed at fighting 'imperialist domination, exploitation of man by man and race bigotry'.[81]

These statements reflected a growing euphoria surrounding the solidarity between Africa and the Middle East. The Arab world, under the leadership of the Pan-Africanist figure Gamal Nasser, had been lobbying African governments to support the Palestinian cause from the 1950s.[82] Due to a confluence of factors, it was only in 1973 that a wave of African countries severed ties with the Israeli government on account of the Palestinian cause. This powerful rhetoric of Afro-Arab solidarity at the Khartoum Conference preceded its concrete demonstration.

The Khartoum Conference was a success for the Sudanese government. It allowed the Sudanese government to align itself with Africa's leading liberation movements, and deflect attention away from the war in the South. The Conference brought the international community physically to Khartoum, but did not enable the participants to engage with the "Southern Problem". The only reference to Sudan's domestic politics and history in the written documents from the Conference is a brief mention of the October Revolution of 1964 that toppled President Ibrahim Abboud, in the context of a larger conversation about military coups in Africa.[83] The statements of gratitude from the liberation movements at the Conference implicitly diminished the salience of the Southern Sudanese allegations of Arab racial domination in Sudan. The Sudanese government went beyond its narrative of colonial blame, and the denial of racial and religious discrimination it had established in its propaganda in the early 1960s. Mahgoub's government used a combination of tactics, including performing its commitment to African liberation causes, mobilising material resources for them, convening both Pan-Africanist and Pan-Arabist networks, and exhibiting its inclusivity by involving non-secessionist Southern politicians based in Khartoum in the Conference. It rebutted SANU discourses of racial oppression, specifically SANU's claims that Sudan's membership in the Arab League signalled the government's lack of commitment to Africa, and that the Southern cause for self-determination ought to be compared to the legitimate liberation movements in southern Africa. Moreover, it mirrored SANU's rhetoric of a 'noble' struggle against what the Khartoum Conference termed 'race bigotry' and applied it to the authentic six.[84] Further, it firmly associated itself with the Pan-Africanist audiences that SANU sought to influence. Thus, the Khartoum Conference of 1969 exemplifies Sudan's deflective diplomacy. Once in the international spotlight, the Sudanese government performed the sleight of hand that cast shadows on the "Southern Problem".

Conclusion

Mahgoub's regimes usurped the attention of the audiences and networks the Southern rebels sought to influence and associate with, in a bid to garner legitimacy internationally, especially in Africa. For Sudan, publicly supporting OAU-endorsed liberation movements served as currency in the African political landscape. Sudan thus neutralised the international criticism the Southern rebels fomented abroad by adeptly harnessing the intersection between race and reputation, diversity and diplomacy. Through personal networks, solidarity efforts and conference diplomacy, the government proved a formidable diplomatic opponent to the secessionist Southern rebels. Mahgoub's efforts made it difficult for Pan-Africanist and anti-imperialist audiences to condemn and ostracise Sudan as an illegitimate state. His government diverted international attention away from Sudan's internal crisis by characterising itself as the consummate supporter of African liberation.

Notes

1. M. Mahgoub, *Democracy on Trial: Reflections on Arab and African politics* (London, 1974), p. 193.
2. R. S. Kramer, R. A. Lobban Jr., C. Fluehr-Lobban (eds), *Historical Dictionary of the Sudan* (Metuchen, NJ, 1992), p. 388. Ezboni Mondiri Gwonzi, the other Southerner, served as the Minister of Communications in the post-October Revolution, caretaker government.
3. It is important to note that some estimates approximate that by 1964, the Southern population in Khartoum reached a million people. E. O' Ballance, *Sudan: Civil War and Terrorism, 1956–99* (Basingstoke, 2000), p. 28.
4. 'The Sudan: A red-hot winner?', *Africa Confidential*, no. 25 (18 December 1964), p. 5.
5. R. O. Collins, *Civil Wars and Revolution in the Sudan: Essays on the Sudan, Southern Sudan and Darfur, 1962–2004* (Hollywood, 2005), p. 213. R. O. Collins, *A History of Modern Sudan* (Cambridge, 2008), p. 82.
6. Mahgoub, *Democracy on Trial*, 193.
7. It is unclear how the day came to acquire this name. It may have stemmed from the visual attire donned since '[r]ioting Southerners had black mourning ribbons on their chests and their banners had paintings of hangings and military planes attacking citizens.' See '6 Die in Sudan Clashes', *Uganda Argus* (8 December 1964), p. 1.
8. For example: H. Smith, '10 Dead, 400 Hurt in Sudan Rioting: Hundreds reported Jailed in African-Arab Strife', *New York Times* (8 December

1964), p. 4; 'Sudan Torn by Violent Race Riots', *Northwest Arkansas Time* (Fayetteville, Arkansas) (7 December 1964), p. 1; 'Sudan Race Riot – 10 Die, 250 Hurt', *Evening Standard* (7 December 1964); 'Negro Mob Wrecks Cars in Sudan', *Evening Standard* (7 December 1964); '10 Killed in Sudan Race Riots', *Evening Standard* (7 December 1964); 'Southerners "Spark Riot" – 6 Die in Sudan Clashes – Plane's Delay Blamed', *Uganda Argus* (8 December 1964); 'Arab-Negro Riots Kill 14 in Sudan', *Daily American* (8 December 1964); 'Sudan Negroes Herded in Camp for Safety', *New York Herald Tribune* (8 December 1964); D. Wilson, 'Mboro's Difficult Task', *The Guardian* (8 December 1964), p. 1; 'Probe Sudan – A Land Torn by Anger and Hate', *Sun* (8 December 1964); 'Racial Tensions High in Sudan', *Daily American* (24 December 1964).

9. W. J. Berridge, *Civil Uprisings in Modern Sudan: The 'Khartoum Springs' of 1964 and 1985* (London, 2015), p. 219.
10. On 16 July 1964, Thomas Gilligan, a New York Police Department Lieutenant, killed Jason Powell, an African-American teenager in a confrontation in a predominantly white neighbourhood in New York City. The incident sparked outrage in the predominantly African-American borough of Harlem, thus leading to six days of rioting. The crowds had violent confrontations with the police who fired thousands of bullets to disperse the angered citizens. In the aftermath, Gilligan was acquitted of all charges.
11. Interview with Malik, conducted by Sebabatso Manoeli, Khartoum, 20 November 2015.
12. Ibid.
13. B. de Carvalho and I. B. Neumann (eds.), *Small State Status Seeking: Norway's quest for international standing* (London, 2015), p. 2.
14. Mahgoub, *Democracy on Trial*, p. 203. Emphasis added.
15. 'Yemini Faction is Extended an Ultimatum', News, *The Times* (9 December 1967), p. 8. Sudan played an active role in the Middle East's confrontation of Israel, even prior to the Six-Day War. At the start of the war, Mahgoub announced that Sudanese soldiers would join Arab troops on the battlefield; however, they arrived after the war had ended. Nevertheless, Sudanese soldiers were involved in the 1000-day war of attrition that occurred from 1967 to 1970 along the Suez Canal. S. Carol, *From Jerusalem to the Lion of Judah and Beyond: Israel's Foreign Policy in East Africa* (Bloomington, IN, 2012), p. 186.
16. Mohamed Mahgoub gained a reputation as a renowned nationalist during the period leading up to independence while he was a radical member of the Graduate's Congress in Sudan, a political organisation that represented Northern intellectuals. He had an illustrious career as a lawyer, advocate, judge and parliamentarian. T. Niblock, *Class and Power in Sudan: The Dynamics of Sudanese Politics, 1898–1985* (Basingstoke, 1987), p. 66;

P. Woodward, *Condominium and Sudanese Nationalism* (London, 1979), p. 83; C. Fluehr-Lobban, 'Islamization in Sudan: A Critical Assessment', in J. Voll (ed), *Sudan: State and Society in Crisis* (Bloomington, IN, 1991), pp. 78–79.

17. Mahgoub, *Democracy on Trial*, p. 203.
18. 'Sudan Faces its Elections', *Africa Confidential*, no. 4 (16 February 1968), p. 7.
19. Carvalho and Neumann, *Small State*, p. 2. Emphasis in original. For an example of the diplomatic dividends of image-crafting, see D. Scott, 'China's Public Diplomacy Rhetoric, 1990–2012: Pragmatic Image-Crafting', *Diplomacy and Statecraft*, 26/2 (2015), pp. 249–265.
20. For more on credibility in international relations, see F. Harvey, 'Fighting for Credibility: US Reputation Building in Asymmetric Conflicts from the Gulf War to Syria, 1991–2013', *Canadian Journal of Political Science*, 48/3 (2015), pp. 503–530.
21. H. Adi, M. Sherwood, G. Padmore, *The 1945 Manchester Pan-African Congress revisited* (London, 1995).
22. 'League of Coloured Peoples', in R. M. Juang, ed. *Africa and the Americas: Culture, Politics, and History* (Santa Barbara, 2008), p. 682; A. S. Rush, *Bonds of Empire: West Indians and Britishness from Victoria to Decolonization* (Oxford, 2011), p. 108.
23. Mahgoub, *Democracy on Trial*, p. 248.
24. N. Slate, *The Prism of Race: WEB Du Bois, Langston Hughes, Paul Robeson, and The Colored World of Cedric Dover* (New York, 2014), p. 108; 'Richard Wright and the Coloured Wrighters', *Pan-Africa*, 1 (August 1947), pp. 35–36.
25. Ahmed Abushouk captures the intricacies of Egypt and Britain's troubled relationship, and their impact on the Umma Party and others in: A. I. Abushouk, 'The Anglo-Egyptian Sudan: From Collaboration Mechanism to Party Politics, 1898–1956', *Journal of Imperial and Commonwealth History*, 38/2 (2010), pp. 207–236.
26. D. H. Johnson, 'Document 223', *Sudan: British Documents on the End of Empire*, Pt. 2 (London, 1998), pp. 56–58.
27. Daly, *Imperial Sudan*, pp. 285–287.
28. J. Hooker, *Black Revolutionary: George Padmore's Path From Communism to Pan-Africanism* (New York, 1970), pp. 104, 108, 113.
29. For example, see G. Padmore, 'British Expatriates Given Notice To Quit Sudan By 1955: African Civil Servants To Head All Government Departments', *Accra Evening News (AEN)* (5 June 1953); 'Sudan Government Plan Complete Africanisation By 1956: Money Voted To Compensate Officials', *AEN* (16 September 1954); 'Sudanese Nationalists Want Complete Independence', *West African Pilot* (6 December 1946);

and 'Strikes in Rhodesia and Sudan', *Ashanti Pioneer* (19 May 1948); 'The Sudanese Nationalists', *Public Opinion* (7 June 1952).

30. L. E. James, "What we put in black and white": George Padmore and the Practice of anti-imperial politics' (PhD thesis, London School of Economics, 2012), p. 164.
31. James, "What we put in black and white", p. 161.
32. Ibid, p. 188.
33. Ibid, pp. 235–240.
34. G. Binaisa, 'Organization of African Unity and Decolonization: Present and Future Trends', *The Annals of the American Academy of Political and Social Sciences*, 432 (1977), p. 58.
35. POV, Season 19, Discussion Guide: Twelve Disciples of Nelson Mandela, A film by Thomas Allen Harris, www.pbs.org/pov, p. 15. http://pov-tc.pbs.org/pov/downloads/2006/pov-twelvedisciples-discussion-guide-color.pdf accessed on 9 September 2014.
36. M. Uvarona, "On the Chemistry of Social Change", *The Moscow Times* (20 July 2001), http://www.themoscowtimes.com/arts_n_ideas/article/on-the-chemistry-of-social-change/360038.html Accessed on 9 September 2014.
37. 'Nelson Mandela's statement from the dock at the opening of the defence case in the Rivonia Trial', South African History Online, http://www.sahistory.org.za/archive/nelson-mandelas-statement-dock-opening-defence-case-rivonia-trial
38. Mahgoub, *Democracy on Trial*, p. 259.
39. 'Sudan closes her sea and airports to South Africa and Portugal', South African History Online, http://www.sahistory.org.za/dated-event/sudan-closes-her-sea-and-airports-south-africa-and-portugal 10 August 2012.
40. 'Report on the Activities', January 1977, p. 5, Folder 72, Box 218, UK/Ireland Mission, ANC Liberation Archives (henceforth ANC Archives).
41. Ibid, 264. 'Organization of African Unity', *International Organization*, 22/4 (1968), p. 1016.
42. In November 1965, Rhodesia issued the Unilateral Declaration of Independence (UDI), in which it stated that, although it was a self-governing British territory from 1923, it regarded itself a sovereign independent state. It precipitated a crisis in which the breakaway colony lacked international recognition as it did not allow for majority rule. Despite the global antipathy towards the minority rule in the country, British government did not act swiftly and some British politicians (especially from the Conservative Party) openly supported Rhodesia. Ibid, 1017. See Carl Peter Watts, 'The Rhodesian Crisis in British and International Politics, 1964–1965' (PhD, University of Birmingham, 2006). J. Barber, 'The

Impact of the Rhodesian Crisis on the Commonwealth', *Journal of Commonwealth Political Studies*, 7/2 (July 1969), pp. 83–95. G. Barclay, 'Friends in Salisbury: Australia and the Rhodesian Unilateral Declaration of Independence, 1965–72', *Australian Journal of Politics and History*, 20/1 (1983), pp. 38–49.
43. Kramer, Lobban, Fluer-Lobban, *Historical Dictionary of the Sudan*, pp. 159–160.
44. Mahgoub, *Democracy on Trial*, p. 262.
45. Ibid.
46. 'Organization of African Unity', pp. 1017, 1023.
47. 'The Sudan's party politics', *Africa Confidential*, no. 4 (19 February 1965), p. 5.
48. Mahgoub, *Democracy on Trial*, p. 212.
49. Ibid, p. 267.
50. Ibid, p. 268. 'Biafran war (1967–70)', in D. Townson (ed), *A Dictionary of Contemporary History*. http://www.blackwellreference.com/subscriber/tocnode.html?id=g9780631209379_chunk_g97806312093793_ss1-22 10 April 2017.
51. ANO, *Resistance*, pp. 17, 26.
52. 'International Conference in Support of the Peoples of Portuguese Colonies and Southern Africa in Khartoum, Jan 1969', 'Declaration of the International Conference in Support of the Peoples of the Portuguese Colonies and Southern Africa', p. 1, 1393, MMS, Anti-Apartheid Movement Archive, Bodleian Library, Oxford (AAM).
53. Other organisations in attendance include the Executive Secretariat of Tri-Continental, the World Federation of Democratic Youth and the International Democratic Women's Federation. 'First List of Arrivals', 16 January 1969, 1393, MSS, AAM.
54. Doc. No. 27/4, 'Draft Agenda', 1393, MSS, AAM.
55. 'Second List of Participants', 18 January 1969, 1393, MSS, AAM.
56. Doc. No. 34/1/b, 'Rules of Procedure', 1393, MSS, AAM.
57. 'Mobilization Committee', p. 3, 1393, MSS, AAM.
58. 'RS No (2) Political Committee, 1st Sub-Committee', p. 2, 1393, MSS, AAM.
59. 'Report on Apartheid – The World Must Act', p. 8, 1393, MSS, AAM.
60. 'Report presented by the Organization of the Solidarity of the Peoples of Africa, Asia and Latin America', p. 2, 1393, MSS, AAM.
61. 'Declaration' p. 3, 1393, MSS, AAM.
62. 'Political Committee, 2nd Sub-Committee', p. 4, 1393, MSS, AAM.
63. Ibid.
64. Kuyok, *South Sudan*, p. 570. He also later served in Nimeiri's Ministry of Foreign Affairs as a diplomat.

65. Ibid, p. 448.
66. Ibid, p. 481.
67. L. Wol Wol, "National Unity is sacrosanct", *Voice of Southern Sudan*, 3 (15 March 1969), p. 2.
68. Ibid.
69. Ibid.
70. Ibid.
71. Ibid.
72. 'Declaration of the International Conference in Support of the Peoples of the Portuguese Colonies and Southern Africa', p. 1, 1393, MSS, AAM.
73. Ibid.
74. 'Report on Apartheid – The World Must Act', p. 1, 1393, MSS, AAM.
75. 'Address by Honorable Mr R. K. Khadilkar', p. 1, 1393, MSS, AAM.
76. 'Stay the Hands of the Murderers', p. 2, 1393, MSS, AAM.
77. 'Joint Statement of the Liberation Movements of Portuguese colonies and Southern Africa', p. 1, 1393, MSS, AAM.
78. 'Declaration', p. 1, 1393, MSS, AAM. They also stood in solidarity with the Vietnamese struggle against American forces.
79. 'General Declaration', 1393, MSS, AAM.
80. 'Resolution on the Second International Conference in Support of the Arab Peoples', 1393, MSS, AAM.
81. 'Report on Apartheid – The World Must Act', p. 8, 1393, MSS, AAM.
82. D. M. Wai, 'African-Arab Relations: Interdependence or Misplaced Optimism?' *Journal of Modern African Studies*, 21/2 (1983), p. 195.
83. 'Background Paper on "Neo-Colonialism, Military Coups and African Liberation"' by Jack Waddis, p. 2, 1393, MSS, AAM.
84. In Lawrence Wol Wol's letter to Milton Obote, written on behalf of SACD NU, in 1963, he suggested that secessionism in the South was a 'noble cause'. He stated that 'It is indeed of the noble task of the already liberated Africa[n] countries to help in the liberation of other African peoples who are still under the yoke of the foreigner who had until a few years ago trodden on us and compared us to animals. We are everywhere dedicated to the noble cause of lifting the African back to his dignity and human status.' 'Letter from Sudan African Closed Districts National Union to Milton Obote', *Voice of Southern Sudan*, 1, 1, 1963, p. 3.

CHAPTER 9

'The Cuba of Africa': Sudan's Socialist Networks and Narratives

Upon coming to power in 1969, Ja'afer Nimeiri established the Revolutionary Command Council (RCC) as the national governing body and vowed to 'turn Sudan into the Cuba of Africa'.[1] His government established strong trade relations with Arab and leftist countries, and it immediately declared Sudan a socialist and Arabist state. This chapter details the discursive strategies the Sudanese government employed to consolidate international political legitimacy in the eyes of African and socialist audiences during the first three years of Nimeiri's premiership from 1969 to 1971. Sudan's diplomatic gains in this period are often obscured by the diplomatic respect that Sudan garnered due to the Addis Ababa Agreement of 1972 that halted Sudan's first civil war. The chapter posits that, while war raged in the South during this period, Nimeiri's government used Joseph U. Garang, a Southern Sudanese socialist thinker, to shift the government's international "Southern Problem" discourse away from questions of racial difference to those focused on class. Distilling Garang's materialist interpretation of the "Southern Problem", the chapter will show how this discursive shift was used to sanitise and bolster Sudan's image abroad, and to undermine the objectives of the secessionist Southern rebels.

Garang was the first Southern Sudanese student to graduate from the University of Khartoum's law faculty in 1957 where he was the first Southerner to be elected to the Students Union. While in University, he joined the Socialist Students' Group, and in June 1955, he organised an

S. C. Manoeli, *Sudan's "Southern Problem"*, African Histories and Modernities, https://doi.org/10.1007/978-3-030-28771-9_9

anti-imperialism conference for Southern Sudanese students in Wau (Bahr el Ghazal State) as a student leader.[2] Despite being the only Southern member of the Sudanese Communist Party (SCP), Garang held a prominent place within the organisation. In the immediate aftermath of the coup of 1969, Garang was selected to serve as the Minister of Supply, and thereafter he headed the newly minted Ministry of State for Southern Affairs. In that capacity, Garang participated in the government efforts that eventually resulted in the 1972 Addis Ababa Peace Agreement. During the period in which the May regime (as Nimeiri's government came to be known) established the Sudanese Socialist Union (SSU), Joseph U. Garang briefly helped form the Southern branch named the Sudan African Socialist Union (SASU) in May 1971.[3] Despite his prominence, Garang lost every election he contested in the South and thus lacked a constituency.[4] The contributors of *Africa Confidential* labelled him and the other pro-unity Southerners based in Khartoum as 'men so much committed to the North that they are in effect Northerners'.[5]

Two weeks after the coup, Nimeiri issued the historic 9 June 1969 'Declaration on the Southern Question', which Garang drafted.[6] Through this act, Nimeiri signalled that his new regime would prioritise solving the "Southern Problem". The declaration resonated with the SCP's previously existing approach towards the South that Garang had developed. It recognised the cultural distinctiveness of the region and its right to regional autonomy within a united Sudan. This federal arrangement would commence only after the government had established 'a broad socialist-oriented democratic movement in the South, forming part of the revolutionary structure in the North and capable of assuming the reigns of power in that region and rebuffing imperialist penetration and infiltration'.[7] It identified the North and South's 'common enemy' as 'imperialism and neo-colonialism, which is oppressing and exploiting the African and Arab people, and standing in the way of their advance'.[8] In the Declaration, Nimeiri's government, under Joseph U. Garang's intellectual leadership, upheld the "Arab"-"African" binary. In so doing, it deviated from the established discursive tradition of previous governments (as we saw in Chap. 4) of referring to the 'the Southern provinces'[9] and 'Sudanese from the South',[10] and of obfuscating the existence of racial difference in order to eschew the racial dualism. For example, Mahgoub's memoir reveals that he had held the established view, as he described the binary as 'ridiculously simplistic and distorted' and that 'the much abused newspaper cliché of a war "between North and South" was nonsense'.[11]

Although it rejected the discourse that described Sudan as a melting pot in which 'there is no distinct racial or cultural divisions', the May regime portrayed Sudan as a country in which the discrete "African" and "Arab" populations were united under its socialist banner.[12] The recognition of unity in diversity conformed to what Quinn Slobodian calls the socialist 'racial rainbow', an idea (often visualised) that relies on the existence of discrete phenotypical differences of racial groupings in order to construct a 'vision of politically unified humanity'.[13] In Sudan's English-language diplomatic magazine *Sudan News*, Nimeiri's government performed racial harmony by publicising its activities in the South to international audiences. For example, on 9 June 1970, the government launched the First Youth Festival in the South. A delegation of members of the RCC and ministers of government went to Juba to join the festivities where the government had invited 'many representatives of African States, journalists from Britain and America, radio and television authorities, British Trade Unionists and Parliamentary groups who witnessed the occasion'.[14] It is unclear how the event participants navigated the war, or how the invited groups responded to the invitation. In the same publication, Garang embraced a pro-government stance and referred to the May regime as 'working for [the] good' of Southerners, as it was 'determined to rebuild anything destroyed by the outlaws'.[15] Having joined the government, Garang took a public stance 'condemning anti-Sudanese propaganda in European capitals' and assured the readers that '[a] programme would be planned to counter such activities'.[16] Garang maintained that the new regime had 'created at an international level [,] a serious split and rifts between dissident leaders'.[17] The government wielded his writings as a weapon to achieve that outcome.

A document Garang produced in 1961 titled *The Dilemma of the Southern Intellectual* sheds light on his solitary political vision among Southern leaders. Given the life the text had beyond its creation, it represents a seminal statement of Garang's perspective. The pamphlet was first published in 1961 in the *Southerner*, a communist underground newspaper, and it reappeared in *Advance* in 1965, the SCP English-language daily newspaper of which Garang became editor. Through the Ministry of Southern Affairs, in 1971, the document was disseminated and circulated yet again. In his later preface, Garang stated that the document 'presents the development of the views of the author up to that time'.[18] It is important to note that during the period between the document's creation and its widest circulation, dramatic changes occurred in Sudanese politics, and yet Garang insisted on his essay being 'published as a historical document without any alterations', thus revealing his commitment to his views.[19]

Garang held that 'the southern movement against the Arab nationality' which regarded the latter 'as being the principal adversary of the southern people' was misguided, dangerous and antithetical to a progressive stance.[20] In the introductory chapter of the 1971 edition, sharing Garang's opinion, a Northern intellectual, Mutasim El Beshir, characterised Southern calls for secession as being based wholly on 'uncompromising racial prejudice'.[21] In Garang's view, the conflicts across Africa (such as the contemporaneous ones in Nigeria, Ghana, Uganda, Liberia and Egypt) and further afield (Iraq) were not sparked by racial prejudice. Soviet multiculturalism exemplified by the USSR (where he believed Russians, Armenians, Tartars, Georgians, Uzbeks, Kazakhs and Mongols co-existed in harmony) proved that racial difference in itself could not have been the decisive factor in stirring conflict. He went on to write that 'even in South Africa the essence of the question is not racial. ... Racial prejudice is a result, a manifestation of a more hidden factor'.[22] This comment on South Africa, an important conceptual motif in Sudanese debates about the "Southern Problem", offers a striking indicator on Garang's commitment to the class struggle narrative.

Garang considered imperialism the greatest threat to post-independence Sudan. He held the 'exploiting classes' of the North, 'namely the feudal landlords and the bourgeoisie (middle-class) and their intellectual and bureaucratic representatives in the state apparatus', responsible for the inequalities between the North and South.[23] However, this local exploitation, in his view, was secondary to the global exploitation the whole of Sudan experienced:

> If the northern exploiting classes are the chief enemy of the southern people, then it follows that imperialism takes only second place; it therefore follows that the northerners are greater imperialists than the British imperialists – an absurdity.[24]

He continued by stating that due to the limited nature of capitalism in Khartoum, the 'northern propertied classes'[25] could not pose the most significant threat to the South as these classes were subservient to global imperialists, and could only ever be 'picking up crumbs' from international capitalists' tables.[26]

In his view, the imposition of Arabic and Islam on the South was odious simply because they represented 'bourgeois culture'.[27] He argued that the 'Abboud dictatorship', the government with the most aggressive linguistic and religious policy at the time, pursued 'a policy of ***national*** oppression in earnest, aimed, in the main, at the assimilation of those nationalities into the Arab nation'.[28] A staunch communist, Garang described the presence of oppression in Sudan as 'national' rather than racial or religious. This was because he generally ascribed the violent excesses of Abboud and his successors to the Northern elite's quest for economic domination. He urged Southerners to note that 'the struggle against imperialism is at the same time the struggle against the bourgeoisie'.[29] Garang aspired towards a revolutionary government 'led by the Communist Party and in co-operation with the minority peoples'.[30] In his vision, an alliance of Sudan's minorities could remove imperialism from Sudan.

Garang criticised the Southern rebel movement for 'it has been dominated by rightists' concepts' and ignoring imperialism or 'subordinating it' to the North-South issue.[31] Reproducing established Northern political narratives, he alleged that they 'could not strip themselves of the British and missionary cultural influences'.[32] In his view, the Southern rebellion was a 'Tshombe type of programme', suggesting that it symbolised the most visceral form of disloyalty.[33] Like Santino Deng and Ambrose Wol, Joseph U. Garang viewed the exodus into exile as a ploy to 'quit the country'.[34] He did not believe that the South could gain independence, and as the Southern movement was only based on 'suspicion' of Northerners, he concluded that '[m]ere suspicions have never given rise to a national liberation movement'.[35] Moreover, he blamed the British for the emergence of anti-North sentiments, for the Southern Policy that ensured that 'the South was cut off from the civilized world', and for 'instilling an inferiority complex into the people, preaching anti-Arabism to divert attention from colonialism'.[36]

Adopting the government's earlier tactic, Nimeiri exploited the antagonism between the Southern political elites by popularising Joseph U. Garang's unrepresentative view. In this text, Garang depicted the pro-unity Southerners who remained in the North as a visionary group, applauding them for identifying their generation's challenge as imperialism. He acknowledged their only failing as the lack of an ideology for the social reconstruction of the country. He plotted them in a proud tradition of Southern liberators '[o]riginating from the Nuer-Zande-Dinka armed struggle against British colonialism', and those who supported uniting

Northern and Southern Sudan at the Juba Conference.[37] This inversion, in which Garang commended the group the secessionists depicted as traitors, indicates the degree to which competing Southern elites variously narrativised Sudanese history.

The leftist rhetoric that suffused Joseph U. Garang's early writings continued into his later works. The second seminal piece of writing that contributed to the discursive shift of the period as one of the most circulated of Garang's works was an essay titled 'On Economics and Regional Autonomy'.[38] Initially written as a public address for the Sudan Erkowit Seminar held in Juba in 1970, it was first published as the sixth edition of the *Revolution in Action* series, a journal produced by the Public Relations Bureau of the Ministry of Southern Affairs. It also was re-circulated beyond Garang's lifetime. For example, Dunstan M. Wai published it in 1973 as a chapter in an edited volume, *The Southern Sudan and the Problem of National Integration*. Wai's book included, inter alia, the pro-unity perspective of Garang's protégé Abel Alier, alongside those of Canadian visiting scholars at the Makerere University, Storrs McCall and Peter Russell, whose chapter focused on the legal merits of secessionism, and a chapter by prominent scholar of Islam and Africa Ali Mazrui. The *Review of African Political Economy* (RoAPE) also published the essay in 1983.

This section relies on the version of the essay that appeared in RoAPE, a journal dedicated to providing a radical analysis of the social processes and change in African countries. The RoAPE editorial team lauded Garang's essay as a work that 'treats the South within the broader context of the national question and has an enduring theoretical relevance not just for Sudan but for the African continent as a whole'.[39] Curiously, a photograph of Garang adjoined his essay in the RoAPE journal, revealing his identity as a Black, Southern man. In contrast, it also described the statement by the Student Union of Southern Sudanese in the UK, included in the same edition but written in the year of publication, as a view 'couched in the language of regionalism rather than that of solidarity among all those disadvantaged under the current regime'.[40] Another essay in the compilation aimed to provide a unionist, left-leaning analysis of the question of the South, which 'affirms that the problem of the South can be solved only in the context of a programme giving full rights of the democratic participation to the whole of the population and priority to the development of those areas "left behind"'.[41]

The arguments in Joseph U. Garang's essay were consistent with his earlier work, but it deviates slightly by providing a striking view of the South. Exhibiting no special regard for the region in his writings, Garang believed that it was the duty of progressives to bring 'the Southern masses out of centuries old backwardness and superstition'.[42] It was the 'primitive', 'pre-capitalist' nature of the South that led him to believe that it was in the region's best interests to form alliances with Northern workers.[43] He held that

> at the time of the European scramble for Africa in the second half of the last century most African peoples lived in conditions of natural economy which could not give rise to a political system higher than tribalism. They have not developed into nationalities because of their primitive economic conditions which do not provide for a social division of labour and development of the language and culture. In such pre-capitalist conditions a national movement proper cannot arise.[44]

In contrast,

> [a] real Sudanese Arab nationality has appeared with its distinct traditions, culture and sentiments. It has left tribalism behind in view of the clear appearance of its social classes and division of labour.[45]

Although he was referring to Marxist stages of development that are based on modes of production and social organisation, in view of the Black pride and affirmation of African cultures among his anti-government Southern contemporaries, Garang's statements could be read as the veiled subscription to Arab supremacy. Along the same lines, he peppered his writings with slightly disparaging statements about the South. Garang referred to 'the low cultural standard of her people' in reference to the South, while in the North he noticed that 'the cultural standard of the people was higher'.[46] Garang averred that in order for the Southerners to evolve and progress, '[i]t will not be profitable for them to cling to their languages, traditions or other peculiarities'.[47]

In keeping with the precedent set by Santino Deng and Ambrose Wol, Garang's essay discredited secessionist Southern leaders. He maintained that 'right-wing leaders' had dominated the Southern movement.[48] Motivated by 'the interests of the small intellectual elite' and 'aspirations for power and prestige', these leaders, Garang opined, did not have a plan for 'social change'.[49] They were wrong to insist that racial differences warranted the pursuit for independence, because, in his view, racism did not cause the inequalities between the two regions. Instead, Britain's uneven capitalist exploitation of the North at the expense of the South led to the "Southern Problem". Deviating from the established government narrative, Garang also held all the previous Sudanese governments in contempt, describing them as 'corrupt', 'incompetent and unconcerned leaders who did not take interest in problems of progress or the redress of the uneven development'.[50] He maintained that both the Northern politicians and the secessionists of the South had approached the "Problem" in an 'unscientific' manner.[51] For Garang, 'the problem appears in its true light as a class struggle'.[52] As a result, he asserted that allegations of 'racism' were the reason 'the real issue of social progress is lost sight of'.[53] Garang's commitment to the class struggle and the communist vision for social transformation is conspicuous in an era in which Black Nationalism shaped the political vision of his fellow Southern elites.

Despite Garang's lack of a political constituency, Nimeiri's government used his publications to promote an alternative Southern narrative that was grounded in leftist interpretations. However, between February and July 1971, Nimeiri purged communists from government posts. A number of the senior members of the May regime were members of the SCP, including the former Chief Justice and prominent politician Babiker Awadalla who served as Sudan's Prime Minister for five months (between May and October 1969) and as Foreign Minister (from 1969 until 1971). Although long-time allies,[54] the SCP and Nimeiri's RCC had strained relations by 1971 on account of attempted coups by some members of the SCP.[55] Due to Joseph U. Garang's value to the RCC, he was not permitted to resign or to be dismissed during this period. But when the SCP attempted another coup on 19 July 1971, which succeeded for three days, upon returning to power, Nimeiri swiftly executed Garang along with the remaining communist leaders working in his government.[56] Despite the brevity of his involvement in Nimeiri's government, Joseph U. Garang played a crucial role in the government's strategy for attaining legitimacy in international leftist circles through his booklets published by the Ministry of Southern Sudan.

Peace and Sudan's Rising Status

The Addis Ababa Agreement of 27 March 1972 that ended the first civil war in Sudan defused the Southern Sudanese rebellion. It enshrined the autonomy of the South through the Southern Sudan Provinces Regional Self-Government Act among other constitutional arrangements. The following year, elections were held for the Southern regional assembly in which former members of the then disbanded Southern Sudan Liberation Movement (SSLM), the Southern Front and others contested. Thereafter, many of the previously opposed Southern Sudanese elites such as Lawrence Wol Wol, Bona Malwal and Joseph Lagu served in the Assembly, Abel Alier replaced the deceased Joseph U. Garang as Minister of Southern Affairs, and Ambrose Wol joined Sudan's Foreign Service.[57] In the wake of the 1972 Addis Ababa Peace Agreement, Nimeiri's government portrayed itself to international audiences as reformed. In a Ministry of Foreign Affairs publication in 1973, it claimed that

> [t]hrough this conflict, the Northerner has come to realize that the Southerner bitterly resented his lower status and was willing to fight and die for recognition. This made the Northerner feel that there must be something vitally important, worthy of respect, and probably justifiable in the Southern demands. The Southerner on his part must have realized that national unity was of paramount value to the Northerner and that he was willing to fight and die for it.[58]

This was the first Sudanese government document to recognise the 'lower status' of Southerners in Sudan and to describe their cause as 'justifiable'. It was politic of the Nimeiri administration to make this seemingly remorseful admission of guilt once the main Southern rebel movement agreed to abandon its pursuit of secession.

Sudan subsequently framed itself as an Afro-Arab country and thus a 'microcosm of the continent' to African leaders.[59] Testifying to the influential nature of this framing, Leopold Senghor, President of Senegal, publicly applauded Nimeiri for being 'a hero among other heroes in Africa' for securing the Peace Agreement.[60] Likewise, Amilcar Cabral, the Guinea-Bissauan and Cape Verdean anti-colonial icon, moved for Sudan to be relieved of its financial obligations to the African liberation movements, and instead to focus its attention on attaining national cohesion because he believed that 'Africa needs a strong united Sudan'.[61] To this suggestion,

Sudan respectfully declined having its financial burden lightened, further demonstrating its commitment to the African cause.[62] Due to Sudan's continued support of the southern African liberation movements, G. S. Magombe,[63] a Tanzanian official who served as the Executive Secretary of the OAU's African Liberation Committee, singled out Sudan in August 1973 as the only member of the OAU that had fulfilled all its financial obligations to the Organization.[64] Moreover, Sudan had begun fulfilling its promise 'to arm and train two companies of freedom fighters every year'.[65] This suggests that Sudan's deflective diplomacy continued to serve its broader aims of status-seeking beyond the first civil war.

Sudan maintained its Africa strategy in the 1970s through an organisation Nimeiri founded, the Sudan Socialist Union (SSU). He launched it in January 1972, in order 'to lay down a stronger basis of legitimacy for the regime' both within and outside Sudan.[66] It became an important vehicle through which the government conducted its international relations and through which it could demonstrate its 'fidelity to international responsibilities'.[67] It became a significant public relations tool for Nimeiri's government. Modelled to resemble the mass-based socialist political parties in Tanzania, Guinea, Egypt, North Korea and Yugoslavia, the SSU functioned as an 'arm of the regime'.[68] It encouraged self-help projects, developing village facilities at the local level, and promoted women's and youth empowerment.[69] It was recognised as a legitimate socialist organisation by African Nationalists such as Julius Nyerere who demonstrated his endorsement by delivering a congratulatory speech to the SSU on 2 January 1973.[70]

The SSU's widely circulated publications detailing the extent of Sudan's internationalism and its commitment to socialist ideals provide the basis of the following brief analysis. I discovered these documents at the African National Congress (ANC) Liberation Archives in South Africa's Eastern Cape, which indicates that the Sudanese government distributed the SSU's activities to the liberation movements it supported and possibly through wider Pan-Africanist networks. The SSU established The National Council for Friendship, Solidarity and Peace (NCFSP), which published annual reports in English detailing the ways it observed, for example, Africa Day, and the Week of the Solidarity with the Peoples of Zimbabwe and Namibia called for by the UN. It was an instrument through which the Sudanese government could demonstrate its support for African causes.

The SSU publications catalogued a litany of instances of solidarity and visually signalled Sudan's support for African liberation movements in particular. The SSU often celebrated occasions of national significance in a way that drew attention to its support of internationalist causes, and in so doing, the regime branded itself as an ally of revolutionary causes abroad. For instance, in a speech President Nimeiri gave in 1974, which was published in an SSU pamphlet on the occasion of the fifth anniversary of the May revolution that ushered in his regime, he reiterated his support for Zimbabwe's impending liberation and called for all the people of Zimbabwe to be treated equally and be freed from segregation due to 'origin, colour or race'.[71] Some of the events the SSU publicised include the Seminar for Liberation and Development that the Council hosted in Khartoum in 1976 where it reiterated its support for Zimbabwe's fight against racism and the armed struggle against white minority rule. Similarly in 1977, Nimeiri hosted Sam Nujoma in Khartoum, in an expression of Sudan's support of the cause of the South West Africa People's Organisation (SWAPO).[72]

SSU members energetically participated in international activist networks. Its representatives attended the International Conference against Apartheid in Lisbon from 16 to 19 June 1977, held in honour of the first anniversary of the Soweto Uprising. The Council reported that, in partnership with the UN Information Office, it gave talks on national television and radio, published articles in newspapers on the aims of the Lisbon Conference and circulated posters condemning the policies of the Apartheid government in South Africa. Similarly, from 22 to 26 August 1977, a delegation from Sudan attended the International Conference for the Struggle Against Racism, held in Lagos, Nigeria.

A year later, the UN called for 1978–1979 to be celebrated as 'The International Year for Combating Apartheid'. Sudan's National Council observed the call by hosting a major conference titled the 'National Congress for the Popular Organization' in the Sudan 'in support of the fighting peoples of South Africa and everywhere – for Freedom and Justice'.[73] This gathering took place in preparation for the OAU summit held in Khartoum from 18 to 21 July 1978, celebrating the Organisation's 15th anniversary, with 30 countries in attendance. Representatives of Zimbabwean liberation movements (Zimbabwe African People's Union [ZAPU] and Zimbabwe African National Union [ZANU]), SWAPO, ANC and the Pan Africanist Congress (PAC) attended, including key figures like Robert Mugabe, Joshua Nkomo and Alfred Nzo, as well as Gamal El Sawrany (representative of the Palestine Liberation Organization [PLO]). Akin to the Khartoum Conference of 1969, this was yet another example of Sudan's use of "conference diplomacy" that allowed it to harness international media attention to portray itself as a country that stood for African liberation.[74] The SSU thus provided a means by which the Sudanese government could project its commitment to Africa liberation causes to international audiences. These activities cemented its standing among Pan-Africanist institutions such as the OAU and the African Liberation Committee (ALC), and the countries that shared the ideology. These status-seeking exercises continued to be important throughout the 1970s as some Southern rebels who rejected the 1972 Addis Ababa Peace Agreement continued protesting in exile, albeit to a lesser extent initially (as Chap. 10 will show), and the peace in the South remained fragile.

Conclusion

Sudan's reputational gains did not last. The government's relations with the Eastern Bloc suffered after Nimeiri ordered the execution of the Sudanese Communist Party leaders in 1971. However, it was only after the 1976 Libyan-sponsored coup attempt that he completely severed ties with the USSR as the Soviet Union supported his aborted overthrow.[75] Free from the communist influences domestically, the Sudanese government reached a rapprochement with the US in 1972, and had further strengthened ties by 1977. Renewed relations facilitated the reinstatement of the World Bank Consultative Group for Sudan, which had ceased to meet after Sudan severed diplomatic ties with the US in 1967, on account of the superpower's involvement in the Six-Day War.[76] American aid helped to finance a wide range of large-scale development projects in Sudan from 1973 onwards. The US encouraged American companies to explore business opportunities in Sudan, leading to Chevron's discovery of oil in the Southern provinces in 1978.[77] Nimeiri's administration became dependent on American aid such that 'Sudan was at the time [the early 1980s] the 6th or 7th largest recipient of American economic and military aid'.[78] It also increasingly relied on development aid from Western European countries, including France, Norway, Italy, Denmark, Austria, Western Germany and the UK.[79]

Close relations with Western countries led Nimeiri's government to take conflicting positions in international institutions, and damaged Sudan's foreign policy towards African liberation movements. In the late 1970s, Nimeiri began instructing the diplomats at the Sudan mission to the UN in New York to offer 'no condemnation of the USA at any cost' and to abstain from voting on paragraphs that included the US in the UN Apartheid initiatives.[80] The African bloc in the UN considered the US's policy of abstention unjust as it, for all intents and purposes, propped up the Apartheid regime.[81] In a divergence from prior Sudanese support for the OAU position on these matters, Sudan increasingly voted on pro-US lines at the UN General Assembly. By the end of the 1970s, Nimeiri's Foreign Minister, Mansour Khalid, described socialist internationalism and Pan-Africanist solidarity as matters for 'only lip-service'[82] in sharp contrast to the earlier period when 'support for liberation movements and African causes was made into a revolutionary dogma'.[83] Nimeiri's contemporaneous support for the anti-Apartheid struggle through the SSU, as shown above, may have functioned as compensation for Sudan's dwindling support of African liberation efforts at the UN and its burgeoning relations with "imperialist countries" that upheld white minority governments in southern Africa. Despite the roaring success of the Nimeiri administration in the early years, its inability to remain consistent abroad ultimately undermined Sudan's international political capital.

Notes

1. M. Khalid, *Nimeiri and the Revolution of Dis-May* (London, 1985), p. 298.
2. Kuyok, *South Sudan: Notable Firsts*, p. 520.
3. Fluehr-Lobban and Voll, *Dictionary of the Sudan*, p. xli.
4. R. L. Bidwell, *Dictionary of Modern Arab History* (London, 2012), p. 155.
5. 'Sudan's last chance in the South?', Africa Confidential, No. 3, February 5, 1965, p. 2.
6. Fluehr-Lobban and Voll, *Historical Dictionary of the Sudan*, pp. 173, 406.
7. Government of Sudan, 'Declaration on the Southern Question', 9 June 1969, in D. M. Wai, *The Southern Sudan and the Question of National Integration* (London, 1973), p. 220
8. Ibid.
9. See: Sudan, *Basic Facts.*
10. See: Deng and Wol, *Let's Speak the Truth.*
11. Mahgoub, *Democracy on Trial*, pp. 206, 215.
12. Sudan, *Basic Facts*, p. 91.
13. Q. Slobodian, 'Socialist Chromatism: Race, Racism, and the Racial Rainbow in East Germany', in Q. Slobodian (ed), *Comrades of Color: East Germany in the Cold War World* (New York, 2015), 24.

14. Sudan Embassy, *Sudan News* [London] (June 1970), p. 15.
15. Sudan Embassy, 'Five Year Plan', *Sudan News* [London] (June 1970), p. 22.
16. *Sudan News*, p. 12.
17. Ibid, p. 16.
18. J. U Garang, *The Dilemma of the Southern Intellectual: Is it Justified?* (Khartoum, 1971), p. 1.
19. Ibid, p. 1.
20. Ibid, p. 25.
21. Ibid, p. 2.
22. Ibid, p. 10.
23. Ibid, p. 12.
24. Ibid, p. 26.
25. Ibid, p. 19.
26. Ibid, p. 13.
27. Ibid, p. 12.
28. Ibid, p. 24.
29. Ibid, p. 14.
30. Ibid.
31. Ibid.
32. Ibid, p. 20.
33. Ibid, p. 23.
34. Ibid, p. 24.
35. Ibid, p. 27.
36. Ibid, p. 15.
37. Ibid.
38. J. U. Garang, 'On Economics and Regional Autonomy', *Review of African Political Economy (RoAPE)*, 10/26 (1983).
39. 'Introduction', *Review of African Political Economy (RoAPE)*, 10/26 (1983), p. 82.
40. Ibid.
41. Ibid.
42. Ibid.
43. Ibid, 83.
44. Ibid.
45. Ibid, 87.
46. Ibid, 85.
47. Ibid, 86.
48. Ibid, 87.
49. Ibid, 82, 84.
50. Ibid, 86.
51. Ibid, 83.

52. Ibid, 84.
53. Ibid, 85.
54. T. Y. Ismael, *The Sudanese Communist Party: Ideology and Party Politics* (London, 2013); T. Nimblock, *Class and Power in Sudan: The Dynamics of Sudanese Politics, 1898–1985* (Basingstoke, 1987), p. 237.
55. A. Gresh, 'The Free Officers and the Comrades: The Sudanese Communist Party and Nimeiri Face-to-face, 1969–1971', *International Journal of Middle East Studies*, 21/3 (1989), pp. 393–409.
56. Ismael, *The Sudanese Communist Party*, p. 256.
57. Stevens, 'Sudan's Afro-Arab Policy', pp. 249–250. Kuyok, *South Sudan*, p. 464.
58. Ministry of Foreign Affairs, *Peace and Unity in the Sudan: an African achievement* (Khartoum, 1973), p. 6. Cited in Stevens, 'Sudan's Afro-Arab Policy', p. 249.
59. Khalid, *Nimeiri and the Revolution*, p. 327.
60. Ibid, 328.
61. Ibid, 327.
62. Interview with Foreign Minister, 22 November 2015.
63. SADET, *The Road to Democracy in South Africa: 1970–1980* (Cape Town, 2004), p. 652.
64. C. Legum (ed), *Africa Contemporary Record: Annual Survey and Documents, 1973–1974* (London, 1974), p. B110.
65. Ibid.
66. T. Niblock, 'The Role of the Sudanese Socialist Union in Sudan's System of Government', in Centre of African Studies, *Post-Independence Sudan* (Edinburg, 1981), p. 13.
67. Sudanese Socialist Union, 1st National Conference, 1974, 'Draft Comprehensive Resolution on Foreign Policy and External Relations', Oxford, Bodleian Library, 750.13 s. 17.
68. 'Draft Resolution Concerning External Co-operation with Political Organisations', pp. 264, 272, Oxford, Bodleian Library, 750.13 s. 17.
69. 'Sudanese Socialist Union. Workers Secretariat Report. Summary', p. 2. Oxford, Bodleian Library, 750.13 s. 17.
70. The speech focused on the benefits of socialism, independence and development. J. Nyerere, *The rational choice: address delivered at Sudanese Socialist Union headquarters, Khartoum, 2nd January 1973* (Dar es Salaam, 1972).
71. 'Draft Comprehensive Resolution on Foreign Policy and External Relations', Oxford, Bodleian Library, 750.13 s. 17.
72. 'Khartoum Declaration on the Eradication of Racial Discrimination in Southern Africa, 21 July 1978', Khartoum, 1978, The Sudanese National Council for Friendship, Solidarity and Peace (NCFSP), Correspondence

between ICSA and Sudan, 1963–1979, p. 12. Folder 72, UK/Ireland Mission, ANC Archives.

73. 'Khartoum Declaration', p. 1. ANC Archives.
74. J. Kaufmann, *Conference Diplomacy: An Introductory Analysis* (New York, 1988). Normally, "conference diplomacy" refers to diplomacy that takes place through large multilateral or bi-lateral conferences focused on peace negotiations. Here, the concept denotes the diplomatic influence the host country exerts during international conferences, which are by nature media events.
75. J. A. Lefebvre, 'Globalism and Regionalism: US Arms Transfers to Sudan', *Armed Forces & Society*, 17/2 (1991) p. 217.
76. The Committee comprised the US, Japan and Western European countries, and after the resumption of relations, Sudan invited Yugoslavia, Romania, Kuwait and the UAE to join. For more on Sudan's relationship with the World Bank during this period, see J. Prendergast, 'Blood Money for Sudan: World Bank and IMF to the "Rescue"', *Africa Today*, 36/3–4 (1989), pp. 43–53. J. Faaland, 'Economic Disarray and Dependence: The Case of the Sudan', in K. J. Havnevik (ed.), *The IMF and the World Bank in Africa: Conditionality, Impact and Alternatives* (Uppsala, 1987).
77. L. Patey, *The New Kings of Crude: China, India, and the Global Struggle for Oil in Sudan and South Sudan* (London, 2014) pp. 11–30. Woodward, *US Foreign Policy*, pp. 113–114.
78. 'The Dangers of Numeiry's Islamic Politics', Sudan Colin Legum's Third World Reports, 21 October 1983, No. C.E/2, MEDU 17/1/GEN, SAD.
79. Khalid, *Revolution*, 331.
80. Ibid, 355.
81. V. D. Johnson and E. Dickinson, 'International Norms and the End of Apartheid in South Africa', *Journal of South African and American Studies*, 16/4 (2015), pp. 355–377.
82. Ibid, 347.
83. Ibid, 355.

CHAPTER 10

Narrative Jiu-Jitsu

From 1978, Nimeiri's Sudan was in disarray at home and abroad. On the domestic front he had allied his government with Islamist political forces and effectively abandoned secular statehood.[1] Shortly afterwards, he introduced Islamist legislation that antagonised non-Muslim constituencies, including those in the South. Moreover, Nimeiri abrogated the 1972 Addis Ababa Peace Agreement by moving the border between the North and the South in order to have the newfound oilfields fall under the North's jurisdiction.[2] He further divided the South, undermining its regional autonomy.[3] These infractions, in the context of a suffering national economy, led to severe internal discontent, precipitating the most significant wave of dissidence since the signing of the 1972 Addis Ababa Peace Agreement.

Beyond the borders of Sudan, neighbouring Ethiopia played a crucial role in the re-emergence of the rebellion in the South. In addition to ending the first civil war of Sudan, the 1972 Addis Ababa Peace Agreement symbolised the diplomatic goodwill between the governments of Sudan and Ethiopia.[4] However, the harmony did not survive the 1974 Revolution in Ethiopia in which the socialist Derg replaced Haile Selassie's government. In the early 1970s, Sudan, under pressure from Arab states, increasingly supported Eritrean dissidents and thus antagonised the regime in Addis.[5] In one of many warnings, the Ethiopian Minister of Foreign Affairs in 1976 alerted the Sudanese Minister of Information that unless the Sudanese state ceased supporting Eritrean rebels, Ethiopia would support

S. C. Manoeli, *Sudan's "Southern Problem"*, African Histories and Modernities, https://doi.org/10.1007/978-3-030-28771-9_10

the remnants of Anya-Nya (the armed wing of the Southern Sudan Liberation Movement [SSLM]) that had fled to Ethiopia when the first civil war ended.[6] Although the majority of Anya-Nya forces accepted the 1972 Addis Ababa Peace Agreement, a minority rejected it and fled into exile. From the mid-1970s, as groups of Southern mutineers defected from the Sudanese army and joined the rebel efforts on the Ethiopian frontier, the Ethiopian government provided arms to a variety of Sudanese dissidents.[7]

Increasing political disaffection made the South susceptible to insurgency. Southern guerrillas based in Ethiopia conducted various minor acts of sabotage in the South against the Sudanese state, but they posed only a negligible threat to the Sudanese government until the early 1980s.[8] The proliferation of small arms, smuggled in from Ethiopia, had led to an increase in insecurity in the rural areas of the South by the early 1980s.[9] The Ugandan border also became a substantial arms trading zone in the aftermath of the overthrow of Idi Amin in 1979. In addition to anti-government forces gaining access to guns, informal militia increasingly used firearms to raid cattle, which prompted the communities subjected to raids to solicit weapons for self-defence. The droughts in the Southern region in the 1970s and 1980s exacerbated these feuds as competition for scarce resources increased tensions.[10] Intensified insecurity and violence fomented by anti-government forces and militia led to heightened volatility in the South.

As the groups defecting from the Sudan Armed Forces (SAF) steadily increased and established camps in Ethiopia, the loosely associated guerrilla forces were jointly informally called Anya-Nya II. By 1982, as Nimeiri's central government increasingly undermined the 1972 Addis Ababa Peace Agreement, disaffected ex-guerrillas in the SAF made contact with the Anya-Nya II forces. By the middle of 1983, several Southern garrisons had mutinied and escaped to Ethiopia.[11] By July of the same year, these defectors, having absorbed some of the Anya-Nya II forces, established the Sudan People's Liberation Movement and Army (SPLM/SPLA; henceforth SPLM), and war erupted in Southern Sudan.

The SPLM, as this chapter will argue, gained a measure of international legitimacy in the 1980s, mainly among African liberation and international socialist networks, due to a confluence of three factors: Sudan's diplomatic and discursive failures, Ethiopia's diplomatic and material support and the SPLM's narrative innovations. Beginning with an examination of the ways Sudan continued to lose prestige in Pan-Africanist and socialist networks, the chapter will briefly analyse the Sudanese government's international responses to the SPLM. Then, through an exploration of Ethiopia's patronage towards the SPLM, the chapter will reveal how this relationship facilitated the SPLM's access to international networks in the context of the battle for legitimacy. Thereafter, through a close examination of the SPLM's *Manifesto*, the chapter will argue that the SPLM's new narrative reconfigured the discursive terrain of the "Southern Problem" and enabled the Movement to construct a progressive and credible image abroad to the very audiences the Sudanese government relinquished.

Sudan's Discursive Drift and Diplomatic Decline

By 1985, Nimeiri had been toppled in a bloodless coup that led to a transitional military government, followed by a quick succession of parliamentary regimes under the leadership of Abdel Rahman Swar al-Dahab and Ahmed al-Mirghani, who, respectively, served as president, as well as Al-Jazuli Daf'allah and Saddiq al-Mahdi as prime minister, respectively. The decade ended with a military coup in 1989 that brought Omar al-Bashir to power. As a result, the 1980s were a tumultuous decade in Sudan's domestic and international politics. In the absence of a concerted deployment of diplomatic and discursive resources akin to Mahgoub's and Nimeiri's administrations (in the latter's early years), the Sudanese governments of the 1980s lacked a sophisticated approach to addressing the "Southern Problem" internationally.

Sudan's abandonment of its "deflective diplomacy" strategy impacted the development of its international "Southern Problem" discourse in the 1980s. With declining international approval, the return to war in 1983 further diminished the credence of the Sudanese government's established narrative of the "Southern Problem" and it shifted 'narrative authority' away from the Sudanese government to the Southern rebels.[12] As Ronald Krebs has shown, the failure of political leaders 'to align their rhetoric to the moment' allows 'alternative narratives and policies to proliferate'.[13] Failing to rise to the occasion, the Sudanese government neither revived Joseph U. Garang's narrative of Sudan's class struggle, nor innovated a new narrative to explain the collapse of peace and its inability to solve the "Southern Problem". Instead, it criticised Ethiopia and the SPLM abroad.

Throughout the dramatic changes that took place in the country, the administrations between 1983 and 1989 relied on a relatively rudimentary discourse. The Sudanese government frequently used its English-language *Sudan News Letter* publication that it disseminated through the Sudanese embassies abroad as a channel through which to offer the official narrative of the country's return to war. The government framed the conflict as merely a result of external interference. From as early as June 1983, President Nimeiri publicly named the interfering parties on the BBC's "This Week in Africa", alleging that Ethiopia and Libya served as the main backers of the SPLM.[14] The Sudanese government continued publicising these allegations throughout the decade, only removing Libya from the list of foreign conspirators after the fall of Nimeiri, when Ghaddafi's ally, al-Mahdi, came to power in 1986. The government publicly claimed to have evidence that 'the Sudan rebel movement was based inside Ethiopian territories and it has a radio transmission and training camps there'.[15] The Sudanese government portrayed the war as a result of Ethiopia violating its national sovereignty. For example, at the East and Central African Countries Summit in Khartoum in June 1987, Prime Minister al-Mahdi reportedly claimed that '[w]hat we face in the South is not a local mutiny but a tool of foreign invasion'.[16] In addition to portraying the rebels in the South as pawns, in 1988 the government also characterised the rebels as 'a handful of Sudanese traitors'.[17] This attempt to discredit and minimise the threat that the rebel forces represented was designed to conceal the magnitude of the military threat they posed to the state. At the time the number of SPLM soldiers rivalled that of the Sudan Armed Forces—for example, in 1989, the SPLM had 70,000 soldiers, whereas the Sudan Armed Forces had 65,000.[18]

According to the *Sudan News Letter*, in July 1987, during a six-day tour of Saudi Arabia, Iraq, Kuwait and Qatar, Prime Minister al-Mahdi 'announced Sudan's intention of launching an international campaign at the UN, OAU, and the Arab League to expose that the prevailing rebellion is not a mere internal question but an explicit foreign intervention'.[19] Evidence of the anticipated international campaign remains elusive. However, the announcement in a diplomatic publication suggests that the Sudanese government aimed to convince international audiences that the war was not a result of the government's failure to govern its country peacefully. While this argument represents the continuation of earlier blame discourses (although the earlier were directed at the British colonial administration), it resourcefully inverted the Sudanese government's insistence in the early 1960s that the first war in the South is best characterised as an internal matter rather than that of foreign affairs. Thus, in the 1980s, various Sudanese administrations relied on a discourse that blamed foreign backers for its war in the South and vilified the rebel movement. After Nimeiri's government consequently abdicated its status within Pan-Africanist and socialist networks, the Sudanese government failed to maintain its discursive and diplomatic upper hand over the rebels from the South.

Ethiopia's Diplomatic and Military Support for the New Southern-Led Movement

In light of the changes in Sudan's foreign policy, grasping the geopolitical context of the Horn of Africa is imperative to understanding the relationship that developed between the Ethiopian government and the SPLM. On the western frontier of Ethiopia, competition for dominance emerged between the newly minted SPLM and the remnants of Anya-Nya II it had not absorbed, based in part on political differences. The latter sought to revive the historical aspirations for Southern Sudanese independence, while the SPLM, as we will shortly see, abandoned the traditional Southern rebel outlook. The Ethiopian government had ordered Anya-Nya II to integrate its forces with the SPLM, but it retreated into the surrounding bushlands instead.[20] The SPLM's leader, John Garang de Mabior (unrelated to Joseph U. Garang), rejected its subsequent reconciliation efforts and instead 'adopted the heavy-handed militarism' and 'proceeded to hunt down his Anyanya II rivals, who swiftly fled back to Sudan'.[21] Anya-Nya II subsequently formed a military alliance with the Nimeiri government prior to Nimeiri's toppling in 1985. Nimeiri's successors continued using them as proxy forces in the South to combat the SPLM.[22] With these groups forming part of Khartoum's counter-insurgency strategy against the SPLM, Addis Ababa responded with increased support for the SPLM.

During the SPLM's contested emergence, Ethiopia provided more support to the Movement than it had done for its predecessors. Sudan's rumours were right. Libya also supported the Movement briefly by providing military hardware.[23] However, after the 1985 coup in Khartoum, Libya started supporting the succeeding Saddiq al-Mahdi administration in Sudan, thus halting all support of the SPLM.[24] From 1986, the SPLM relied heavily on Ethiopia and 'served as a local security force' for the Derg government in return.[25]

It fought in support of the Derg against the Oromo Liberation Front (OLF), reasoning that the OLF's alliance with Khartoum justified the SPLM's involvement in the proxy conflict.[26] The SPLM was aware that Sudan supported 'various Ethiopian Rebel groups' (including the Oromo Liberation Front (OLF), the Eritrean People's Liberation Front (EPLF), the Gambella People's Liberation Front (GPLM)).[27] The SPLM's military support strengthened the allegiance between Mengistu and Garang.[28] Equally, Mengistu provided the SPLM with substantial support, ranging from access to training bases (in Bilpam, Bongo, Dimma and Pagak) and refugee camps (mainly Itang) in the Gambella region, as well as freedom of movement in and out of Ethiopia[29] Furthermore, Ethiopia hosted approximately 400,000 Southern Sudanese refugees in the 1980s.[30] It occasionally gave the SPLM access to Ethiopian air planes to make air-drops in Sudan.[31] In addition to the SPLM's headquarters in western Ethiopia, the Ethiopian government provided Garang with a liaison office in Addis Ababa, where international leaders could contact him, and with a house for his family in the city.[32]

Most importantly, the Derg made Ethiopia's socialist networks available to the SPLM. Ethiopia formed part of a hotly contested site for Cold War superpowers, a region the West dubbed "the crescent of crisis", referring to the stretch of Third World countries from Afghanistan through Iran to the Horn of Africa that had experienced revolutions in the 1970s.[33] Considered 'the most important Marxist-inspired transformation in Africa during the Cold War', the Derg subsequently formed an ideologically and pragmatically informed alliance with Moscow, which resulted in the USSR's 'most important intervention in Africa'.[34] In the context of the wider rivalry, the Soviet Union invested in the consolidation of the Ethiopian revolution.[35] During the 1980s, Soviet arms in Ethiopia constituted an investment of around $7 billion.[36] The Derg's involvement in Sudan had the blessing of the USSR. In fact, Woodward suggests that 'the Soviets were as ready as the Ethiopians to see the arming of the SPLM in southern Sudan'.[37] Cuba, having intervened significantly in Ethiopia during the Ogaden War (1977–1978), offered training to SPLM soldiers on site and sent a number of SPLM officers to the Caribbean country for advanced military and political training.[38] In addition, approximately 600 Southern Sudanese refugee youth received scholarships to study in Havana with the aim of returning to Sudan with skills, principally medical, needed to build the SPLM's "New Sudan".[39] Although the SPLM's support from the Soviet Union was mediated through Ethiopia and support from Cuba was modest, these relationships gave the SPLM clout in the liberation and socialist networks in Africa and further afield.

Private support from businesspersons involved with African liberation movements also facilitated the SPLM's access to these networks. The controversial business tycoon Roland Walter "Tiny" Rowland ran a British-based multinational corporation, Lonrho, which had investments in various African countries. He played a central role in forging what would become one of Sudan's largest public-private partnerships (PPP), and Lonrho's biggest undertaking in the 1970s, the Kenana Sugar Scheme.[40] But the relationship between Lonrho and the Sudanese government ended in May 1977 during the construction phase due to problems between shareholders, and Lonrho was consequently dismissed.[41] Thereafter, having supported southern African liberation movements in the past,[42] Rowland became the SPLM's 'earliest financial backer'.[43] Rowland allegedly played a significant role in helping the SPLM gain military weaponry as well as diplomatic access to 'some of the former Front Line States of southern Africa'.[44] These factors led to the SPLM gaining access to the network of interconnected southern African governments and liberation movements, and it could accrue diplomatic capital by association.

By the late 1980s, the list of African countries that offered the SPLM support included Angola, Namibia, Zambia, Mozambique, Zimbabwe and Uganda.[45] They provided material support (weapons and uniforms), and occasionally, representatives from these countries or liberation movements visited the training camps and addressed the SPLM soldiers.[46] The SPLM's military successes, which were partly enabled by external support, made the Movement a substantial force in the international affairs of the region. For example, when the SPLM won control over the Sudanese borders with Zaïre (now the Democratic Republic of the Congo (DRC)), the Central African Republic, Kenya, Uganda and Ethiopia, it became clear to analysts that 'diplomacy notwithstanding, as a matter of practical reality, the governments of these five neighbouring countries will now have to deal with the SPLA authorities when managing these international frontiers'.[47]

Throughout the 1980s, the SPLM negotiated a mutually beneficial dependence with the Ethiopian government, which included gaining access to the Derg's international socialist and Africa liberation networks. By the end of the decade, Sudan's civil war had drawn the OAU's attention once again to the "Southern Problem". While chairing the

OAU Commission in 1989 and 1990, Hosni Mubarak, possibly motivated by Egypt's geopolitical interests,[48] attempted to broker peace between the Sudanese state and the SPLM. Collaborating with key heads of state from Ethiopia, Kenya, Uganda and the DRC, in the search of peace, Mubarak also specifically drew on the diplomacy of Zambia's Kaunda, Zimbabwe's Mugabe and Nigeria's Babangida. He also hosted the SPLM twice in Cairo in 1989 and 1990, and on one occasion, he televised a meeting for the Egyptian public and the wider Arab world.[49] These occasions provided the SPLM with international audiences to communicate its political discourse, despite the failure of these efforts to secure a lasting ceasefire.

The "New Sudan" Discourse

Through a protracted process, a high-ranking officer who had also defected from the SAF, John Garang emerged as the leader of the conjoined political and military wings of the SPLM, with the backing of the Ethiopian government.[50] An intellectual and a member of the Southern political elite, Garang had his education at Rumbek Secondary School interrupted by the first civil war. Garang was expelled from school for participating in the student strikes of 1962 and travelled through Uganda, Kenya and Tanzania as a refugee.[51] He completed high school in Lushoto, Tanzania. Upon graduation, he taught mathematics at a secondary school in Karatina, Kenya, and thereafter obtained a scholarship to study economics at Grinnell College in Iowa, USA, where he graduated in 1969.[52] He then returned to Tanzania to study at the University of Dar es Salaam (UDS) as a Watson Fellow.[53] The experience in Dar radicalised Garang, as UDS 'soon became an international community of liberation fighters'.[54] He became a member of the University Students African Revolutionary Front (USARF), a Pan-African student organisation previously known as the Socialist Club, which had close relations with the Mozambican liberation movement, Frente de Libertação de Moçambique (FRELIMO).[55] Through the USARF, he was exposed to the Pan-Africanist and Marxist intellectual Walter Rodney.[56] While at UDS, Garang decided to leave Tanzania to join the Anya-Nya rebellion in South Sudan in 1970. After the 1972 Addis Ababa Peace Agreement, he attended military training at Fort Benning in Georgia, USA, and then pursued a PhD in Agricultural Economics at Iowa State University, graduating in 1981. Upon his return to Sudan, he joined the research leadership team for the military and lectured at the military academy and the University of Khartoum's faculty of agriculture on a part-time basis. It is likely that the combination of Garang's academic and military accolades inclined Mengistu to support his SPLM.[57] As we will see, his intellectual foundation influenced the SPLM's discourses.

Beginning with a brief outline of the approach the SPLM employed to reach a wide variety of audiences, this section will examine the SPLM's discursive strategies to transform the terrain upon which the narrative battle was fought. In Ethiopia, the SPLM's memoranda to its host government not only presented opportunities for the Movement to list its needs, but also to delineate the kind of revolution the SPLM sought to bring about. Garang articulated the SPLM's identity in subtle ways throughout the reports. For example, in the report submitted to Ethiopia in June 1987, the Movement's forecasts included the establishment of an SPLM provisional administration inside Sudan, described in the reports as the 'United New Sudan'.[58] Moreover, Garang stated that he expected to establish it in May 1988, at which point he had planned to have an 'effective presence' in the southern parts of the Northern provinces of Kordofan and Blue Nile 'so our detractors will not find objective grounds to accuse us of secession as we would have citizens from these [Northern] areas in the Provisional Administration'.[59] Thus, the SPLM's military strategy matched its political discourse.

Beyond Ethiopia, the SPLM leadership targeted strategic audiences with its discourses. In his letters to their chief patron, Ethiopia, Garang emphasised the importance of the SPLM's propaganda production as a means through which to 'intensify contacts with African and Arab countries and to solicit for material and political support from any sympathetic countries and organizations'.[60] By recognising Arab countries as potential allies, the SPLM distinguished itself programmatically from its revolutionary predecessors in Southern Sudan. As we have seen, having conceived of the two regions of Sudan as racially at odds and publicly attacking the Sudanese government for being a member of the Arab League, Southern rebels from the 1960s precluded the Arab world from its potential supporters. With new audiences in mind, the SPLM leadership prioritised controlling the Movement's image abroad through carefully considered publicity campaigns. It requested Ethiopia's assistance to establish a printing facility for the *New Sudan Magazine*, the Movement's intermittent propaganda outlet, which it had planned to publish in English and Arabic in order to access a diverse readership.[61] Historically, Southern rebel groups had published predominantly in English, and occasionally in Southern Sudanese or other European languages. Arabic had come to represent the language of the oppressive North. Even though the SPLM only published the first volume of the *New Sudan Magazine* in English in 1993, from Nairobi after the Mengistu regime fell, it continued attempting to engage Arab-speaking audiences.[62]

In the 1980s, the SPLM's publicity strategy included establishing a radio station, "Radio SPLA: The Voice of the Revolutionary Armed Struggle".[63] Established in October 1984, the multilingual station, broadcasting in English, Arabic and some Sudanese languages, was intended to both gather new recruits within Sudan and to inform listeners abroad. By 1989, Radio SPLA had become more popular inside Sudan than the government-run Radio Omdurman, having quickly become 'essential listening right across Sudan'.[64] Outside Sudan, it was recognised as 'invaluable as a source of information about the developments in Sudan'.[65] The medium was significant to the SPLM. Garang called Radio SPLA 'an unconventional Battalion' that was an instrument for 'combating the enemy's obnoxious lies and propaganda'.[66] Thus, Garang used the radio station to show his 'internationalist' view: he announced his offer on Radio SPLA in September 1990, to send at least 500 SPLM soldiers to 'defend Saudi Arabia and to help restore the sovereignty of Kuwait', during the Gulf War.[67] Garang sought in this way to capitalise on Khartoum's hostile relations with Riyadh at the time.[68] Subsequently, the Sudanese government accused Saudi Arabia of supporting the SPLM in this same period.[69] This SPLM initiative signalled its embrace of the Arab world, indicating a sharp disjuncture from the earlier Southern Sudanese rebel movements. Moreover, Movement representatives in Arab and African countries were told to frame the conflict as 'not polarized on religious and racial lines'.[70] In so doing, the SPLM aimed to assure international audiences that ethno-nationalism, racial thinking and separatism did not drive the insurgency.

With these platforms in place, as the Commander-in-Chief, Garang understood a significant part of his role as providing discursive leadership to the Movement by crafting and safeguarding the SPLM's image. Complaints levelled against John Garang in an open letter in 1991, written by Lam Akol, a former member of the Political-Military High Command (PMHC), 'the highest decision-making body of the SPLM/A', reveal this.[71] He alleged that Garang

> is the Director of Radio SPLA as well as its news editor. Any contribution to the radio must be sanctioned by him personally … High Command members are not informed of Garang's visits abroad before they occur and consequently they do not know who is in charge on his absence. After the visits no proper briefing about them is given to the PMHC. In the same vein, other delegations on missions abroad never report to the PMHC. Thus, members of the PMHC are not in [the] picture of the political and diplomatic activities of the Movement abroad.[72]

In addition to highlighting Garang's dominant leadership style, this grievance also indicated that controlling the SPLM discourse was as important to him as political representation abroad.

This was because Garang concluded that SPLM discourses served an important role in the SPLM's campaign against the Sudanese government. The Movement's debut propaganda document, the *Manifesto*, represents the consummate articulation of the SPLM's aims and its discursive reimagining of the "Southern Problem" in the 1980s. Published in 1983 in English, it targeted both international and local audiences. Lam Akol, a member of the SPLM who fell out with Garang in 1991, suggested that the widely circulated version of the *Manifesto* was 'amended in Tripoli in March 1984 … but, curiously enough, the date of publication to this day still remains to be 31st July 1983'.[73] Although Akol did not offer a reason, he suggested that the backdating of the *Manifesto* was proof of Garang's duplicity. It can be inferred that the backdating was somehow politically expedient. Regardless, independent international, English-language publications, including the *Horn of Africa Journal*, which is dedicated to Ethiopian-Sudanese relations, reproduced the *Manifesto* for its readership to understand the Movement in its own terms.[74] The *Horn of Africa* described a key contribution of the *Manifesto* as its 'endeavours to some extent to rewrite, Sudanese history'.[75] Due to the SPLM's internal coup attempt and the fall of the Derg regime in 1991, the SPLM changed in ways that represented significant departures from the *Manifesto*.[76] Thus, the document is arguably most relevant to understanding the Movement in its formative years in the 1980s. The following analysis provides a brief window into the SPLM's discursive innovations.

Reflecting the historical moment of its production, the *Manifesto* captured frustration with the failures of the post-independence era. By the early 1980s, many African nationalist leaders had lost credibility due to rising allegations of corruption, debt crises exacerbated by structural adjustment and stabilisation policies, general economic stagnation and stunted industrial development.[77] The SPLM attributed the failure of the earlier generation of nationalist leaders to truly decolonise Africa to their compromised class position. *The Manifesto* claimed that

> [w]hen it became clear that genuine wars of liberation were imminent and would result in total de-colonization and establishment of genuine independent states in Africa, colonialism struck a deal with the emerging African bourgeoisfied [sic] bureaucratic elite.[78]

This interpretation of decolonisation reflects Marxist conceptions of class conflict often attributed to Frantz Fanon, to which Walter Rodney and other UDS intellectuals also subscribed.[79] The *Manifesto*'s critique of African elites allowed the SPLM to situate the failures of post-colonial Sudanese governments in a discourse of disappointment in African nationalism, thus making it legible to a wide range of audiences. The SPLM thus attempted to both discredit the Sudanese government and legitimise itself. By implying that 'genuine' independence would be a product of 'genuine wars of liberation', the document sought to justify its armed rebellion. 'Genuine' insurgency was needed to unseat the co-opted 'elite'. The SPLM thereby framed itself as a revolutionary movement of the masses that could complete Sudan's unfinished decolonisation. The SPLM thus re-appropriated and subverted the Sudanese government's narrative of authenticity. It challenged the genuineness of Sudan's independence by placing the word "independence" in inverted commas with reference to Sudan throughout the *Manifesto*.[80] Unlike its predecessors who argued that Southern Sudan experienced independence as Arab Northern colonialism, the SPLM suggested that the political elite in Khartoum subjected the "masses" all across Sudan to their class-based rule, which was reminiscent, if not a continuation, of colonialism.

The *Manifesto* also introduced a novel conceptualisation of the "Southern Problem". The SPLM employed new language to deliberately signal its distinctive aims in comparison to earlier Sudanese rebels from the South:

> The so-called "Problem of Southern Sudan" is really a general problem in the Sudan. It is generally a "problem of Backward Areas" in the whole country that is particularized and exacerbated in the South by successive oppressive minority clique regimes in Khartoum. ... in fact, the problem has its origins in the spread of capitalism and colonialism towards the end of the last century.[81]

By evoking economic exploitation, the SPLM fashioned a leftist political identity for itself. It represents a distinct disjuncture from the Sudan African National Union (SANU)'s discursive tradition of upholding Southern Sudanese exceptionalism on the basis of racial distinction and oppression. The *Manifesto* ironically also bears the marks of the discourses originating from the Sudan Communist Party's Joseph U. Garang—excluding his occasional culturally demeaning references to the South. As we saw in Chap. 9, Nimeiri's government used Joseph U. Garang's socialist discourses to sanitise the country's image abroad and to seek legitimacy in international socialist networks. In the 1980s, in a volte-face, John Garang's SPLM appropriated and modified the Nimeiri government's socialist discourses to challenge the very same Nimeiri administration and subsequent Sudanese governments. The SPLM thus occupied the government's discursive terrain.

The consensus in much of the literature that the SPLM's socialism is owed to a reliance on Mengistu's Socialist Derg is incomplete. For example, referring to the *Manifesto*, Johnson posited that 'much of the language may have been borrowed from the movement's Ethiopian patrons'.[82] Rolandsen similarly suggests that the SPLM 'published a quasi-Marxist manifesto allegedly to please Mengistu'.[83] A closer examination of the Sudanese discursive traditions of the "Southern Problem" reveals that the SPLM could have drawn from multiple influences that it perceived to have currency abroad, from Nimeiri's socialist politics, from John Garang's extensive exposure to socialism in Tanzania and from his enduring interest in the ideology while teaching at the University of Khartoum, where he was known to have lectured on topics such as political economy and socialism.[84] Thus, the SPLM's reconstruction of the "Southern Problem" ought to be understood as part of an iterative process in which it renegotiated the discursive remit in the ongoing narrative battle with the Khartoum political establishment. Despite the transformative power of their relations, the Derg was not the only source of the SPLM's intellectual fodder. In short, the *Manifesto* was a product of historical bricolage, not short-term mimicry.

Not only did the SPLM project a socialist image, it also inventively defined itself as nationalist. The SPLM rooted its own emergence in a history that preceded Sudan's second civil war (which began in 1983) and that was wider than the South, as it aimed to encompass other margins of the Sudanese state. It specifically portrayed itself as a continuation of 'the Liberation Movements in the backward areas of the Sudan', which included 'Anya-nya in the South', various groups 'in the West and [the] Beja Congress in the East'.[85] Marxist rhetoric, specifically the lexicon of Walter Rodney's Dependency Theory, made the SPLM's new nationalist discourse possible. By conceiving of the "Problem" in terms of an inequitable distribution of resources, the SPLM could keep the Southern rebel narrative of dispossession but apply it to a broader, heterogeneous periphery and a deracialised core.[86] The SPLM destabilised the racial and religious binary that had inadvertently constrained former Southern rebels by claiming to inhabit an identity and championing a cause that was more expansive and inclusive than its predecessors. The *Manifesto* clarified that

> [t]he term "The North" is used throughout the Manifesto to refer to those areas in Northern Sudan in which peripheral development became necessary in order to facilitate cheap extraction of surplus by the colonial regime. It therefore includes the old Province of Khartoum and Blue Nile, and exclude [sic] all the other areas in Northern Sudan. The old Provinces of Darfur, Kordofan, Kassala and Northern Province are underdeveloped areas just like the Southern Provinces of Bhar [sic] el Ghazal, Equatoria and Upper Nile that are known as Southern Sudan.[87]

It foregrounded the factitious nature of the region 'known as Southern Sudan' by using the seemingly neutral phrase 'the Southern Provinces'. As we have seen in Chap. 4, the publications of Abboud's regime on the "Southern Problem" in the 1960s often used the same phrasing in order to counter the discourses of the Southern rebels who naturalised the North-South racial binary. Moreover, it posited that Khartoum's 'clique regimes' constituted the enemy because of their economic and political, but not racial or religious, supremacy.[88] The *Manifesto* claimed that the Khartoum political elite used religion to divide the disgruntled people of the South from those of the neglected parts of the North, in order to successfully conquer them.[89] Because they effectively inhibited Sudanese people on the periphery from recognising their commonalities, the Sudanese elite were described as 'anti-liberation' in the *Manifesto*.[90]

To solidify its nationalist claims, the SPLM intentionally distanced itself from Southern Sudanese secessionism. With a Southerner as the leader, the overwhelming majority of SPLM soldiers hailing from the South and the armed struggle taking place in Southern Sudan, the SPLM could easily be mistaken for a liberation movement for the South. It sought to dispel the notion and to distinguish itself from the Southern liberation tradition by constructing an unfavourable narrative of Southern secessionism:

> When Sudan became "independent" in January 1956, colonial jobs were "unfairly" divided between the North and South. The Southern elite felt cheated and betrayed by British colonialism. … The objectives and aims of Anya-nya I therefore centred around jobs and job titles.[91]

By placing the word "unfairly" in quotation marks, the SPLM opened a critical pillar in the conventional construction of the "Southern Problem" up for scrutiny. Was Sudanisation in fact unfair? To whom? What were their interests? This new narration of Southern history introduced doubt to the legitimacy of the leadership of the old guard. The *Manifesto* claimed that the spark of the first civil war was in fact the "unfair" 'distribution of colonial jobs between the Southern and Northern bourgeosified [sic] bureaucratic elites'.[92] Therefore, the SPLM opposed 'the jobbist character of Anya-nya I' and argued that, as a result, those leaders 'compromised the interests of the masses in return for jobs'.[93] Distancing itself from the history of failed Southern rebellions, the *Manifesto* contrasted the SPLM and Anya-Nya.

After distinguishing itself historically, the SPLM used the same argument to discredit Anya-Nya II. The *Manifesto* narrated the history of the 1970s as follows: the 1972 Addis Ababa Peace Agreement required the incorporation of 6000 Anya-Nya soldiers into the Sudan Armed Forces and the provision of 'unproductive' civil service jobs for the remaining 32,000, paid out of a fund for the rehabilitation and resettlement of former rebels.[94] However, when money from the fund was drained after two years, the ex-combatants were left without employment. As a result, in the mid-1970s, the ex-guerrillas began organising and established Anya-Nya II to confront the Sudanese government. In light of this, the SPLM argued that

> [t]he origins and objectives of Anya-nya II were therefore similar to those of Anya-nya I; both were dissatisfied with the jobs offered or denied them by the Northern and Southern bourgeosified [sic] ruling elites.[95]

Most importantly, the SPLM aimed to distinguish itself from its counterpart by characterising it as opportunistic and parochial. The *Manifesto* averred that:

> It must be reiterated that the principal objective of the SPLA is not separation for the South. The South is an integral and inseparable part of the

> Sudan. Africa has been fragmented sufficiently enough by colonialism and neo-colonialism and its further fragmentation can only be in the interests of her enemies.[96]

The SPLM thus revived discursive strategies that the Sudanese government had designed to condemn Southern secessionists. The SPLM opposed both the Southern secessionists and the Sudanese government, by using the latter's arguments to dismiss the former and building on the antipathy of the former to oppose the latter. The *Manifesto* epitomises a discursive rebellion against both, replete with dexterous disjunctures and continuities of previous constructions of the "Southern Problem".

The *Manifesto* further posited that Southern secession would lead to the 'imminent, latent and impending disintegration and fragmentation of the Sudan'.[97] This was the first reference in an international publication on the "Southern Problem" (produced by either the government or rebels) that suggested that Southern secession might set a negative precedent, not just for Africa, but for Sudan itself:

> The separatist attitude that has developed in the South since 1955 has caught the imagination of the backward areas in Northern Sudan ... If left unchecked, these separatist movements in the South, East and the West coupled with the stubborn determination of a repressive minority clique regime in Khartoum to hang on to power in the Sudan at all costs will lead to the total disintegration of the Sudan.[98]

Only the SPLM could combat this balkanisation by providing 'a correct solution': the establishment of 'a United Socialist Sudan'.[99]

Although this concept was new to the rebel discourses, the Movement's Chairperson had long embraced the notion of a 'United New Sudan'. A brief examination of John Garang's early writings suggests that he had held a version of a nationalist position from as early as 1972. In a widely circulated open letter to the Commander-in-Chief of the Anya-Nya forces and the Southern Sudan Liberation Movement (SSLM), Joseph Lagu, on the eve of the 1972 Addis Ababa Peace Agreement, Garang expressed his opposition.[100] The 27-year-old captain's letter was circulated at the time and has been republished since.[101] It was in this document that Garang introduced the idea of the 'New Sudan'. He maintained that '[t]he central problem of the Sudanese war is the dominance of Arab Nationalism'.[102]

These 'forces of Arab nationalism' were particularly ill-equipped and unwilling to manage a 'multi-nationality country' and they deliberately undermined the emergence of a truly integrated nationalism.[103] He continued that Sudan required 'a correct consistent Social Democratic solution' and criticised the historical attempts at what he called '"local autonomy" within the context of a United Arab Sudan'.[104] Instead, the young Garang maintained that 'the Sudanese crises' (not 'the "Southern Problem"') could only be solved through one of two options:

> The birth of two nation-states out of the present (geographical) Sudan or political autonomy for both the South and the North (and/ or any other part that so demands) in a federal United New Sudan.[105]

He thus did not conceive of secession as the only solution to the 'crises'. In the rest of the letter he capitalised 'the United NEW Sudan', to emphasise that a transformation, 'a SYNTHESIS', of all the parts of Sudan was essential to counter the political hegemony of Arab nationalism.[106] In summation, echoing ideas from multiple sources, the *Manifesto* framed the Movement as a mass-based, progressive, socialist and nationalist movement. It reconceptualised what was previously known as the "Southern Problem".[107] The SPLM used a materialist conception of history, which enabled it to discard the racial claims of earlier Southern rebel movements and consequently claim that it represented the entire Sudan and not just the South.

The SPLM's rhetorical and conceptual shift stands in sharp contrast with the discursive hangover of the SPLM's contemporaries in other rebel movements in the 1980s. Joseph Lagu, having become Vice-President of Sudan after the 1972 Addis Ababa Peace Agreement, continued framing the Sudanese struggle in terms of racial discrimination when war erupted again. For example, in a letter he wrote to US Vice-President George Bush in 1985 explaining Sudan's return to war, Lagu suggested that 'the Southern struggle only amounts to what was a struggle for Civil rights in the United States of America some years back'.[108] He was not alone. Other renowned figures from the first civil war emphasised the significance of the Sudanese racial fault line. Vocal proponents of this narrative included Gordon Muortat-Mayen, an exile leader, who did not accept the 1972 Addis Ababa Peace Agreement. In his regular newsletters published in London during Sudan's second civil war, Muortat-Mayen included snippets of the

African media coverage of the war that supported his construction of the conflict in Sudan. In 1983, he quoted a Southern Sudanese reporter stating that

> [t]he Northern soldiers are now committing worst [sic] atrocities in the South, compares [sic] with the one of South Africa. For example, the killing of civilians, the burning of houses, huts, and the cutting of children [sic] hands and throwing them into the burning houses or huts.[109]

The gruesome horrors of the war aside, for Muortat-Mayen, comparing Sudan to South Africa was in keeping with a well-rehearsed rhetorical strategy of drawing an analogy between Sudan and Apartheid South Africa. To him, like the Southern rebels before him, the war occurred within a binary between 'Southern freedom fighters and the Northern Army of occupation'.[110]

Conclusion

A combination of factors created a favourable environment for the SPLM to win allies in African liberation and socialist international networks. These included the decline of Sudan's standing among the same audiences, the Derg regime's military and diplomatic support, and the SPLM's discursive innovations and strategies. The Sudanese government failed to align its narrative in the renewed war, and in the vacuum, the SPLM transcended the traditional rebel narrative and reimagined the discursive parameters of the "Southern Problem". Since the SPLM had integrated the socialist discourse of Nimeiri's government into its new narrative, the Sudanese government could not refute the SPLM's narrative as it would further discredit itself. By redefining 'the war's underlying rationale',[111] the SPLM not only deviated from the established Southern rebel narrative, but also challenged the Sudanese government's dominant narrative. The SPLM '[closed] off routes of acceptable rebuttal'[112] from the Sudanese government by framing the war as a result of 'a betrayal' of Sudan's socialist vision 'properly conceived'.[113] The SPLM *Manifesto* thus represented a discursively strategic move to foreclose rhetorical opposition on the one hand, and to gain access to the audiences that supported the Sudanese government in the late 1960s and the 1970s on the other.

Notes

1. After a meeting at Port Said with Saddiq al-Mahdi and the Muslim Brothers leader Hassan al-Turabi in 1977, Nimeiri pursued a more religiously inclined political line as it became politically expedient for him to do so. Nimieri appointed Turabi to serve as attorney general and offered other prominent Islamists positions in the judiciary as well as in the Sudanese Socialist Union. For the in-depth study of the politicisation of Islam during this period, see: G. Warburg, 'Mahdism and Islamism in Sudan', *International Journal of Middle East Studies*, 27/ 2 (1995), pp. 219–236.
2. J. Leach, *War and Politics in Sudan: Cultural Identities and the Challenges of the Peace Process* (London, 2013), pp. 163–164.
3. E. N. Wakoson, 'The Politics of Southern self-government 1972–83', in M. W. Daly and A. A. Sikainga (ed), *Civil War in the Sudan*, pp. 27–50.
4. Johnson, *The Root Causes*, p. 59.
5. L. Aalen, 'Ethiopian state support to insurgency in Southern Sudan from 1962 to 1983: local, regional and global connections', *Journal of Eastern African Studies*, 8/ 4 (2014), p. 632
6. Johnson, *The Root Causes*, p. 59.
7. D. H. Johnson, 'The Sudan People's Liberation Army and the Problem of Factionalism', in C. Clapham (ed), *African Guerrillas* (Oxford, 1998), p. 57.
8. G. Prunier, *From Peace to War: The Southern Sudan, 1972–1984* (Hull, 1986).
9. D. Johnson and G. Prunier, 'The Foundation and Expansion of the Sudan People's Liberation Army', in M. W. Daly and A. A. Sikainga (eds.) *Civil War in the Sudan* (London, 1993), pp. 120–121.
10. T. Teklu, J. von Braum, E. Zaki, 'Drought and Famine Relationships in Sudan: Policy Implications', Research Report 88, International Food Policy Research Institute, 1991. J. O'Brien, 'Sowing the seeds of famine: the political economy of food deficits in Sudan', *Review of African Political Economy*, 12/ 33, (1985) pp. 23–32.
11. LeRiche and Arnold, *South Sudan*, pp. 61–62, 256. A. Madut Arop, Sudan's Painful Road to Peace: A Full Story of the Founding and Development of the SPLM/SPLA, (2006), p. 26. Johnson. *The Root Causes*, pp. 59–62.
12. R. R. Krebs, 'How Dominant Narratives Rise and Fall: Military Conflict, Politics, and the Cold War Consensus', *International Organization*, 69/4 (2015): 840.
13. R. R. Krebs, 'Tell Me a Story: FDR, Narrative, and the Making of the Second World War', *Security Studies*, 24/1 (2015): 168.

14. 'June–July 1983: Report No. 3 on the Current Political Situation in Southern Sudan', G. Muortat-Mayen, Chairman of the Anyanya Patriotic Front, 4 August 1983, Allison Papers, SAD 803/6/6-7.
15. Embassy of the Republic of Sudan, *Sudan News Letter*, no. 3 (19 August 1987), p. 3.
16. Embassy of the Republic of Sudan, 'African Summit in Sudan', *Sudan News Letter*, no. 1 (1 July 1987), p. 1.
17. Embassy of the Republic of Sudan, *Sudan News Letter*, no. 6 (7 Jan 1988), p. 5.
18. M. LeRiche and M. Arnold, *South Sudan: From Revolution to Independence* (London, 2012) p. 67.
19. Embassy of the Republic of Sudan, *Sudan News Letter*, no. 2 (15 July 1987), p. 1.
20. D. Johnson, 'The Nuer Civil War', in, Maj-Britt Johannsen and Niels Kastfelt (eds.), *Sudanese Society in the Context of Civil War* (Copenhagen, 2001), p. 6. Johnson highlights the militarisation of ethnicity that occurred as a result of the conflict between the SPLA and Anya-Nya II (pp. 4–8).
21. S. E. Hutchinson, 'A Curse from God? Religious and political dimensions of the post-1991 rise of ethnic violence in South Sudan', *Journal of Modern African Studies*, 39/2 (2001), p. 311.
22. Johnson, 'The (SPLA)', p. 61.
23. Johnson, 'The (SPLA)', p. 58.
24. Ibid, p. 60.
25. Woodward, *The Horn of Africa*, p. 179.
26. Johnson, 'The (SPLA)', p. 60.
27. 'Working Paper', 5 Jan, 1991, p. 1, Campaign File 627, Government of Ethiopia Ministry of Defence Archives (henceforth MOD).
28. To illustrate the influence the Ethiopian government had on the SPLM, a senior member of the Movement, Commander Kerubino Bol, appealed to Mengistu when he wanted recourse for Garang's domineering leadership style. Upon hearing the accusation, Mengistu alerted Garang of the act of insubordination, and Garang swiftly arrested and detained Kerubino Bol from 1987 until 1992. Johnson, 'The (SPLA)', p. 60. Johnson, *The Root Causes*, 92. J. Rone, 'Behind the Red Line: Political Repression in Sudan', Human Rights Watch (1996), pp. 318–319.
29. For more details of the specific military campaigns, see: Johnson, 'The (SPLA)', p. 58, and M. A. Kuol, *Administration of Justice in the (SPLA/M) Liberated Areas: Court Cases in War Torn Southern Sudan* (Oxford, 1997); and K. Fukui and J. Markakis, *Ethnicity and Conflict in the Horn of Africa* (London, 1994).
30. Sudan Democratic Gazette, no. 15 (August 1991), p. 5.

31. Letter from Osman to GHQS, 23 Nov. 1987, Campaign File 428, MOD.
32. Sudan Democratic Gazette, no. 14 (July 1991), p. 3.
33. F. Halliday, 'The Arc of Crisis and the New Cold War', *MERIP Reports*, No. 100/101, (1981), pp. 14–25.
34. Westad, *The Global Cold War*, p. 251.
35. See: R. Yordanov, *The Soviet Union and the Horn of Africa during the Cold War: Between ideology and pragmatism* (Lanham, 2016); R. Patman, *The Soviet Union in the Horn of Africa: The diplomacy of intervention and disengagement* (Cambridge, 2009); D. Korn, *Ethiopia, the United States and the Soviet Union* (London, 1986).
36. P. Woodward, *The Horn of Africa: Politics and international relations* (London, 2002), p. 142. For example, David Kinsella shows that in November 1987 alone, 'the two countries signed another arms agreement, this one for $2 billion worth of equipment over four years'. D.T. Kinsella, 'In the Shadow of Giants: Superpower arms transfers and Third World conflict during the Cold War' (Ph.D. thesis, Yale University, 1993), p. 211.
37. Woodward, *Horn of Africa*, 142.
38. Letter from Thunder to Fire, 24 Dec. 1987, Campaign File 428, MOD. Also see: Woodward, *Horn of Africa*, p. 123.
39. J. Rone, *Children in Sudan: Slaves, Street Children and Child Soldiers* (Human Rights Watch/Africa Human Rights Watch, 1995) pp. 69–71.
40. O. A. El Nazir and G. D. Desai, *Kenana Kingdom of Green Gold: Grand Multinational Venture in the Desert of Sudan* (London, 2001), p. 48.
41. Ibid, p. 18, 84–85.
42. Zambia's African nationalist Kenneth Kaunda was a close associate of Rowland. See: K. Good, 'Zambia and the Liberation of South Africa', *Journal of Modern African Studies*, 25/3 (1987), pp. 525–526; M. Larmer, 'Chronicle of a Coup Foretold: Valentine Musakanya and the 1980 coup attempt in Zambia', *Journal of African History*, 51 (2010), p. 398. Rowland also supported Joshua Nkomo of the Zimbabwe African Patriotic Front as well as the National Union for the Total Independence of Angola (UNITA). K. Eriksen, 'Zambia: Class formation and détente', *Review of African Political Economy*, 4/9 (1977), p. 25. For Lonrho's involvement in Mozambique in the 1980s, see: M. A. Pitcher, 'Recreating colonialism or restructuring the state? Privatisation and politics in Mozambique', *Journal of Southern African Studies*, 22/ 1 (1996), pp. 49–74.
43. Johnson, *The Root Causes*, p. 46.
44. Ibid, p. 85.
45. Interview with Wol (pseudonym), conducted by Sebabatso Manoeli, Durham, 7 Nov. 2014. Interview with Dr John Gai Yoh, conducted by Sebabatso Manoeli, Telephonically, 2 July 2013. Durham. Johnson, *Root Causes*, pp. 95, 120.

46. Interview with Wol.
47. Sudan Democratic Gazette, no. 8, January 1991, p. 3.
48. Egypt-Sudanese relations soured a few months after Omar al-Bashir took power in June 1989, when Bashir's regime harboured Egyptian Islamic fundamentalist Omer Abdel Rahman. S. M. Makinda, 'Islamisation and Politics in Sudan', *Australian Journal of Political Science*, 28/1 (1993), p. 131. M. Burr and R. O. Collins, *Revolutionary Sudan: Hasan Al-Turabi and the Islamist State, 1989–2000* (Leiden, 2003).
49. Sudan Democratic Gazette, no. 3 (August 1990), pp. 4–7.
50. Madut-Arop, *Sudan's Painful Road*, pp. 67–74.
51. P. Wël, 'Editorial Introduction', in P. Wël (ed), *The Genius of Dr. John Garang: The essential writings and speeches of the late SPLM/A's leader, Dr. John Garang de Mabior*, Vol. 1 (Kongor, South Sudan, 2013), p. 1.
52. Ibid, p. 2.
53. 'John Garang De Mabior: A Background Note', *Horn of Africa*, 8/1 (1985), p. 72. M. LeRiche, 'John Garang DeMabior', in H. Louis Gates Jr., and E. Akyeampong (eds), *Dictionary of African Biography* (New York, 2012).
54. W. Reno, *Warfare in Independent Africa* (Cambridge, 2011), p. 7.
55. P. Roessler and H. Verhoeven, *Why Comrades Go to War: Liberation Politics and the Outbreak of Africa's Deadliest Conflict* (London, 2016), p. 38.
56. H. Campbell, 'The Impact of Walter Rodney and Progressive Scholars on the Dar es Salaam School', *Social and Economic Studies*, 40/2 (1991), pp. 99–135.
57. Hutchinson, '"A Curse from God?"', p. 311.
58. Garang, 'Memorandum No. 5', p. 1, Campaign File 70, MOD.
59. Ibid.
60. Garang, 'Annex to Memorandum No. 5', p. 2, Campaign File 70, MOD.
61. Garang, 'Memorandum No. 5', p. 6, Campaign File 70, MOD.
62. J. M. Alley, 'Southern Sudanese women and children: the saddest victims of the Sudanese conflict', *The Sudan Newsletter*, 4/3 (1994). Pax Sudani Network, 'Rampant Raids and Cases of Slavery', *Sudan*, 3/3 (1993), p. 37. The movement also established a key English-language publication, the *SPLM/SPLA Update*, which ran from 1992 to 2004 and was disseminated throughout East Africa free of charge. It is unclear what became of the Arabic periodicals. C. Tounsel, '"God will crown us": The Construction of Religious Nationalism in Southern Sudan, 1898–2011', (Ph.D. thesis, University of Michigan, 2015), pp. 348, 359.
63. Madut-Arop, *Sudan's Painful Road to Peace*, p. 103. Radio SPLA was located in the suburb of Naru in Addis Ababa, Ethiopia.

64. Woodward, *Horn of Africa*, p. 123. M. A. M. Guarak, *Integration and Fragmentation of the Sudan: An African Renaissance* (Bloomington, 2011), p. 284
65. *Sudan Democratic Gazette*, No. 14, July 1991, p. 2.
66. Quoted taken from Madut-Arop, *Sudan's Painful Road to Peace*, p. 104.
67. *Sudan Democratic Gazette*, No. 5, October 1990, p. 5.
68. Ibid.
69. J. Abadi, 'Israel and Sudan: The Saga of an Enigmatic Relationship', *Middle Eastern Studies*, 35 (1999) p. 32.
70. Garang, 'Annex to Memorandum No. 5', p. 2, Campaign, 70, MOD.
71. Rolandsen, *Guerrilla Government*, p. 29. The PMHC was abolished in 1993.
72. 'L. Akol, 'Why Garang Must Go Now', July 1991', in P. Wël, *The Genius of Dr. John Garang: Letters and radio messages of the late SPLM/A's Leader, Dr. John Garang de Mabior*, Vol. 2 (Kongor, 2012), pp. 139–140.
73. L. Akol, *SPLM/SPLA: inside an African revolution* (Khartoum, 2001), p. 210.
74. L. Baissa, 'Stated Position of the Rebels', *Horn of Africa*, 8/1 (1985), pp. 39–46. L. Baissa, 'Involvement of Ethiopia and Libya', *Horn of Africa*, 8/ 1 (1985), p. 56.
75. 'Stated Position of the Rebels', *Horn of Africa*, 8/ 1 (1985), p. 39.
76. For instance, the SPLM increasingly embraced a secessionist political agenda in the 1990s, a position that was marginalised in the 1980s.
77. P.T. Mkandawire, and C.C. Soludo, *Our continent, our future: African perspectives on structural adjustment.* (Dakar, 1999). J. Herbst, 'The Structural Adjustment of Politics in Africa', *World Development* 18, 7 (1990), 949–958.
78. SPLM, *Manifesto* (Addis Ababa, 1983), p. 2.
79. F. Fanon, *The Wretched of the Earth* (New York, 1963). J. P. Sharp, 'Geopolitics at the margins? Reconsidering genealogies of critical geopolitics', *Political Geography*, 37 (2013), p. 26. W. Rodney, 'Contemporary Political Trends in the English Speaking Caribbean', *The Black Scholar*, 7/1 (1975), p. 15–21. W. Rodney, 'Black Scholar Interviews: Walter Rodney', *The Black Scholar*, 6/3 (1974), pp. 40, 42. M. Bedasse, 'A Pan-African Imagined Community: Anti-Colonialism, Rastafarians and Post-Colonial Tanzania, 1961–1992' (Ph.D. thesis, University of Miami, 2010), pp. 33, 88.
80. For example, see, SPLM, *Manifesto*, pp. 4, 7.
81. Ibid, p. 1.
82. Johnson, *Root Causes*, p. 63.
83. Rolandsen, *Guerrilla Government*, p. 27.
84. LeRiche and Arnold, *South Sudan*, p. 260, note 25.
85. Ibid, p. 4.

86. E. Thomas, *South Sudan: A Slow Liberation* (London, 2015), pp. 115–116. A. Idris, *Identity, Citizenship, and Violence in Two Sudans: Reimagining a Common Future* (New York, 2013), p. 97.
87. SPLM, *Manifesto*, pp. 4–5.
88. Ibid, p. 1.
89. Ibid, p. 5.
90. Ibid.
91. Ibid, pp. 7–8.
92. Ibid, p. 8.
93. Ibid, pp. 8–9.
94. Ibid, p. 13.
95. Ibid, pp. 13–14.
96. Ibid, pp. 16–17.
97. Ibid, p. 17.
98. Ibid, p. 17.
99. Ibid, p. 25.
100. 'An Excerpt from Captain John Garang's 1972 Letter to Gen. Joseph Lagu of Anyanya One, January 24, 1972', in Wël, *The Genius of Dr. John Garang*, p. 20.
101. L. A. Deng, *The Power of Creative Reasoning: The Ideas and Vision of John Garang* (Bloomington, IN, 2013) p. 114.
102. 'An Excerpt from Captain John Garang's 1972 Letter', p. 20.
103. Ibid, p. 20.
104. Ibid, p. 21.
105. Ibid, pp. 20–21.
106. Ibid, p. 21.
107. Ibid, p. 26.
108. 'Notes for HE Vice President George Bush of the United States of America', Joseph Lagu, 6 March 1985, SAD 803/6/49–51.
109. 'August–October 1983: Report Number 4 on the Current Political Situation in South Sudan', G. Muortat-Mayen, Chairman of the Anyanya Patriotic Front, 31 October 1983, p. 9, Allison Papers, SAD 803/6/8-16.
110. Ibid.
111. R. R. Krebs, 'How Dominant Narratives Rise and Fall: Military Conflict, Politics, and the Cold War Consensus', *International Organization*, 69/4 (2015): 840.
112. Krebs and Jackson, 'Twisting Tongues and Twisting Arms', 44–45.
113. Krebs, 'How Dominant Narratives Rise and Fall', 840.

CHAPTER 11

Conclusion

> I was born and raised in Northern Sudan, and I only believed that Northern Sudan is an Arab country because this is what we were taught in schools. … we could not think at that time, that there is something wrong with this. My liberation happened in – you'll be surprised – when I left the Sudan. … I was working at the UN [in New York City] … The United States was very bad when it comes to race, even in the east, even in the capital. But things were brewing at that time, I was there when Martin Luther made his March and I could see that what he was calling for, and calling it separation, is something we are doing here in the Sudan all the time… That is one [fact]. But another … was the fact that it was not the Blacks who were alone in the fight. I've seen many of the white students … who were fighting against this. And I just started asking myself why don't we do this, why do we accept this, if even people who belong to the other race, the "superior" race saw it and fought against it?[1] (Interview with Malik, Former Minister of Foreign Affairs, Sudan)

Martin Luther King Jr.'s March on Washington in August 1963, during which he stood atop the Lincoln Memorial to give his acclaimed "I Have a Dream" speech, sparked the world's imagination. Similarly inspired by the historic March, in this excerpt, a retired Sudanese diplomat of Arab descent disclosed a personal account of his political awakening. Witnessing the American civil rights movement enabled him to see Sudan's political conflict in the South through borrowed eyes. He began to perceive the Arab character of the Sudanese nation-state as exclusionary. To him, this

S. C. Manoeli, *Sudan's "Southern Problem"*, African Histories and Modernities, https://doi.org/10.1007/978-3-030-28771-9_11

revelation constituted a 'liberation' which strikingly occurred outside the confines of his country. It impressed upon him the possibility of a multiracial alliance, in which he could stand in solidarity with Southerners as an ally. His liberation came not only with a diagnosis of the country's segregation, but also with the awareness that his identity in Sudan was comparable with that of whites in the US. He thus became aware of his social location and power relative to Southerners, and implicitly compared the bourgeoning Southern Sudanese political struggle to the African-American struggle for equality. Unbeknown to him, from December 1962 to the close of 1963, in New York and other cities in Africa and Europe, Southern Sudanese rebels in exile began pleading publicly that the rebellion in the South should be understood in exactly the same terms as Malik's epiphany.[2] The Sudanese government responded by developing an opposing public narrative of the conflict in the South that eschewed race. The evolution of these competing narratives as they interacted abroad has been the focus of this book.

Malik's experience in the US marked him indelibly. But it took him two decades to act on his convictions. He became the chief political advisor to John Garang, leader of the Southern-led rebel movement, the Sudan People's Liberation Movement and Army (SPLM), from the late 1980s. I did not ask him what accounted for the delay, partly because I did not want to ask him to defend his life choices, and partly because I assumed that his diplomatic career precluded such a radical stance. Then only 32, it is unlikely that he could have become the Minister of Foreign Affairs less than a decade later and attained other international positions of prominence had he embraced the Southern cause. Acknowledging Southern Sudanese political grievances was highly unpopular among the traditional power brokers in Khartoum and no other influential Northern Arab Sudanese politician had openly supported Southern Sudanese rebels before Malik. The period between Malik's epiphany and his response also coincided with the two decades in which the Sudanese government offered the most effective international rebuttal to the rebel discourses on the "Southern Problem".[3]

This book has argued that a critical part of understanding the civil wars in Southern Sudan between 1961 and 1991 requires understanding how they were projected and imagined abroad. Building on John Peel's argument that 'narrative empowers', the book has focused on narrative-making as a site of political contestation.[4] It has taken the discourses of Southern Sudanese rebels seriously. It showed that Sudanese governments have engaged with Southern rebels as diplomatic rivals, in part due to their influential discourses. It explored how their competing narratives interacted abroad in divergent bids to attain international legitimacy. These discourses were consequential abroad. They contributed to informing diplomatic action and inspiring solidarity.

The book builds on a number of works on discourses pertaining to Southern political belonging. These include Rolandsen and Leonardi's work on the Sudanese government discourses of violence that justified the use of excessively punitive measures against Southern Sudanese rebels between 1955 and 1960[5]; Leonardi and Vaughan's work on the practices and discourses of citizenship in Southern and Western Sudan in the 1940s and 1950s[6]; and Willis' work on the challenges that politicians from the Southern region faced while attempting to represent and forge the South as a political community.[7] The book moves on from the domestic political domain that these works focus on, and places both government and Southern Sudanese international discourses in a single frame. It has argued for placing the narrative constructions of these two sets of actors in one frame since they did in fact compete on those terms in front of international audiences at the Round Table Conference, at several Organisation of African Unity (OAU) meetings, in the international press, in letter-writing campaigns and in their respective political imaginations.

The book argued that the Sudan African National Union (SANU) played an indispensable role in formulating the dominant international rebel discourse on the "Southern Problem". Constructed in the early 1960s, this discourse relied on a racialised lexicon replete with references to Southern Sudanese people as "Negroes", "Blacks", "Azanians" and "Africans", and alleging that they were racially distinct from the "Arab" or "Arabised" Northerners. SANU employed the colonial discourse of Sudan's racial binary in order to explain the oppression that its putative constituencies experienced. In the Condominium period, the discourse of the racial binary had been used to construct a narrative of incompatibility between the two regions, which the Condominium government conceived of as discrete. SANU also argued that the racial oppression of Southerners by Northerners in the post-independence period proved their political incompatibility. This racial dualism made secession the logical solution to the "Southern Problem". Moreover, these rigid racial categories allowed SANU, in the wake of decolonisation, in the aftermath of Negritude and in the moment of the rise of Pan-Africanist solidarity, to make claims to Black Nationalism. This racialised formulation of the

"Southern Problem" required a certain packaging in order to evoke sympathy from international audiences. Thus, as the world's attention was drawn to Apartheid South Africa after the Sharpeville Massacre of 1960, Southern Sudanese rebels increasingly compared the Southern Sudanese cause with that of Black people in South Africa. They also, less frequently, drew analogies between Sudan and states like the US and Nazi Germany that were infamous for their racism in past and present international discourses.

Curiously, race as an identity paradigm is not defined in any of the narratives. While the Sudanese government of the early 1960s partially subscribed to the then outdated biological conception of race, it also did not provide a working definition of this social marker of difference. Neither acknowledged the slippery nature of the term and both relied on its vagueness to advance their respective agendas. The rebels at times alluded to skin colour as a criterion of racial difference, for example, in *The Problem of Southern Sudan*, Oduho and Deng mentioned that Southerners experience oppression because 'their skin pigment differs, slightly in some cases'.[8]Augmenting the argument that slight 'physical differences' could produce racism,[9] Richard Gray explained that 'the Southerner *feels* himself to be an African', and that 'Southerners *see* the problem today as a fight for racial equality'.[10] Although acknowledged as partly physiological, race here was described in highly subjective and emotive terms. On other occasions, we saw that SANU acknowledged that the "Arabs" were 'no browner than some Bantu people',[11] suggesting that race was more than colour. These efforts represented SANU's blunt attempts at formulating Sudanese racial thought. Despite the limitations of applying popular internationalised conceptions of race to the Southern Sudanese case, SANU employed the language of Negritude and Black Nationalism to make the cause legible to particular audiences abroad.

While this vagueness was useful in some respects, not defining race in their debates left Southern rebels vulnerable. It enabled William Deng to acquiesce that Sudan's 'races have been mixing over the centuries', and to thus backtrack on demanding self-determination on the basis of racial difference.[12] As we saw, the Sudanese state had already unravelled the "Arab" and "African" binary by arguing that the country lacked racial purity, thus enabling it to suggest that the country therefore lacked racial discrimination. On occasion it used the small group of pro-government Southern politicians in Khartoum as spokespersons and specimens to prove that racial discrimination was absent in the country. The lack of a precise definition meant that the Sudanese government could simultaneously evade questions concerning race, while marshalling subtle cues such as showcasing co-opted Southerners in international publications and conferences, as well as associating with groups opposing Apartheid, Southern Rhodesia and Portuguese colonialism, to give the appearance of non-racialism and anti-racism.

As we have seen, the distinctive intellectual milieu of Third World politics during the Cold War made a range of discursive strategies available to both sets of actors. Part of the failure of SANU's appeals to Black internationalist networks stemmed from the Khartoum elite having long established connections in that group. Mahgoub had been entrenched in international Black liberation networks in London from the 1940s. He maintained friendships with the African Nationalist leaders who decolonised strategic countries in Africa—Ghana and Kenya—and with journalists like George Padmore who inscribed Sudan in anti-colonial networks. Black Nationalism and Pan-Africanism had gatekeepers, which included the OAU's African Liberation Committee (ALC) Committee of Nine, as well as the liberation movements which were recognised by the OAU as fighting legitimate struggles against imperialism. Sudanese governments—all the way from Abboud through Mahgoub and Nimeiri's administrations—were not only connected to these networks, they became vital contributors to African liberation movements and consequently usurped the attention of the very audiences the Southern rebels sought to influence. We saw how socialist internationalist networks increasingly became important to the Sudanese government of Nimeiri in the 1970s, and how his decline left a lacuna that produced an opportunity for the SPLM to capitalise on the government's socialist discourses. The SPLM crafted a new rebel narrative. It elided both race and religion as the grounds of oppression on Sudan's peripheries of which the South was one. By choosing a materialist interpretation of the "Southern Problem", rebranded as 'a general problem of Sudan', and under the patronage of the Derg regime in Ethiopia, the SPLM inserted itself into international socialist networks.[13]

I have shown that these political actors participated in a dynamic intellectual duel, in which their views at times diverged, and at other times, they shifted discursive terrains and appropriated their opponents' positions, through politically perceptive, quick-witted manoeuvres. This book represents a step towards understanding the construction, dissemination, consumption and reproduction of rebel discourses and their interaction with state discourses designed for international audiences. It has shown how these discourses were contested in a variety of diplomatic arenas.

The protracted struggle over how various international audiences interpreted the "Southern Problem" continued beyond the seismic shifts that occurred within Southern Sudanese and international politics in 1991. After its internal schism and the emergence of a unipolar international system, the SPLM mainstream (as it came to be known) sought to reform its image by adopting a democratic persona. In his study on the reasons for the SPLM's liberalisation and internal reform in the period between 1991 and 1994, Øystein Rolandsen explained that the impetus was 'the SPLM/A's concern for its external image[,] and expectations and pressure from Western countries and foreign organisations'.[14] One can view these changes in the 1990s as an attempt by the SPLM to salvage a reputation it had acquired in the 1980s and lost as a result of the 1991 split, and the loss of the Derg's support. Uncovering a different narrative, Christopher Tounsel argues that the SPLM increasingly espoused a 'martial theology' discourse in the post-1991 period, particularly in the context of the Islamist al-Bashir regime in Khartoum.[15] These studies continue where this book ends and complement it by revealing the different discourses that vied for dominance among Southern Sudanese rebels in the post-Cold War era.

The interplay of discourse and diplomacy highlighted in this book occurred in a period in which African governments represented significant sources of international legitimacy, alongside Western and Eastern audiences, for Southern Sudanese rebels. The book allows us to see how legitimacy was contested in this particular international system. This battle, however, did not constitute "extraversion" in the sense understood by Jean-Francois Bayart.[16] Bayart conceptualises Africa's insertion into world history as shaped by the material inequalities the continent experienced and its resultant marginality and dependency. More specifically, Bayart frames African elites as a group of actors who, in their 'thirst for the West', participate internationally primarily in pursuit of Western patronage.[17] My findings suggest that Southern Sudan's exile politicians had a "thirst" for a much wider variety of audiences. Their modalities of outward-ness were more akin to 'rebel diplomacy'.[18] The focus here is on rebels as intellectual and diplomatic actors who sought to 'narrativize the nation' on the margins of a Cold War international system.[19] I have interpreted rebel texts regarding the "Southern Problem" not as means to extractive ends, but as expressions of rebel political thought. These ideas reveal Sudan's internationally contested nationalist projects.

These innovative approaches to understanding the rebellions in Southern Sudan offer important new insights. By focusing on these narrative battles, we are able to reframe groups like SANU that have been dismissed as political failures. I have provocatively argued that the fratricidal SANU played a more definitive role in the narrative battle of the 1960s than the SSLM, even though the latter played a militarily significant role as a result of securing Israel's support and successfully negotiating the 1972 Addis Ababa Peace Agreement. The SSLM operated within the discursive terrain that SANU had mapped. Equally, the SPLM's novel discursive contribution has long been reduced to a mimicry of Ethiopia, and its nationalist language is often depicted as 'rhetorical cover' designed to elicit material gain. It has complicated our understanding of the origins and influences of the SPLM discourses described in the *Manifesto*. Overall, it shows that audiences in various parts of Africa and the world consumed and occasionally reproduced Southern Sudanese rebel discourses.

This work also has limitations. The work is an overwhelmingly masculine history. The absence of women's voices limits the understanding of Sudan's narrative battles. SANU did on occasion publish poetry written by a woman,[20] and the SPLM did have women battalions.[21] Engaging with sources that provide a window into women's points of view would have augmented this study. Moreover, the book has not uncovered the complicated political subjectivities and imaginations of the unionist Southern elites in Khartoum. In many ways, the narratives that Santino Deng, Ambrose Wol, William Deng and Joseph U. Garang developed could provide insight into more than their political ends. It could shed light on the survival mechanisms of these Southern elites as they navigated their own peculiar position in Sudan. Building on what Justin Willis describes as the 'unique double marginality' of Southern political elites in the 1960s and 1970s—the state of being privileged relative to the Southern populations they aimed to serve and of being excluded from the Northern political elite—these men experienced a third axis of marginality as they were largely characterised by secessionist Southerners with constituencies as having sold out the South for political gain.[22]

Despite these limitations, the approaches introduced in this work remain important. This exploration of the international dimension of Southern Sudanese rebel narratives as they interacted with the Sudanese government's counter-narratives, and gained traction among various international audiences, raises new questions. For instance, it calls for an examination of the presence of these competing discursive constructions of Southern rebels and the state in academic history-writing on Sudan in the post-independence period. Such a historiographical enquiry could provide insights into the entangled relationships between scholars and political actors on both sides and expand the terrain of contested knowledge production. Examining the intellectual implications of the 'homespun histories' circulated in these narrative battles could prompt debates about Sudan's post-independence historiography.[23] This could take a form similar to Terence Ranger's critical delineation and examination of Zimbabwe's 'patriotic history', 'nationalist history' and 'history of the nation'.[24] Further, it raises comparative questions. How do Sudan's narrative battles compare with the 'War of Words' in Zanzibar that Jonathon Glassman uncovers about a parallel (albeit domestic) contest? He shows that the pre-revolution government also rhetorically maintained a myth of a multiracial Zanzibar 'in which most people were "mixtures of mixtures"', while in actuality maintained a proudly Arab self-identification, devoid of any mixture.[25] This similarity suggests that a comparative study could uncover the ideoscapes of political racial thought in Afro-Arab contests during Africa's Cold War.

This book's reconstruction of Sudan's international narrative battles has established that all 'ways of thinking about the collective self and the collective other', to evoke Glassman's astute words, are indeed 'refashioned from generation to generation, in part from old discursive materials, in part from others newly imagined'.[26] The book has offered an innovative analytical approach by exploring and tracking the evolution of Sudan's competing discourses and diplomacies about race during the country's civil wars in the South. The series of nested arguments that the book has made has drawn on a variety of sources to provide a rich picture of how rebel discourses about the "Southern Problem", produced in and experienced in exile, interacted with government narratives in international venues over a 30-year period.

Notes

1. Interview with Malik (pseudonym), conducted by Sebabatso Manoeli, Khartoum, Sudan, 20 November 2015.
2. Ø. Rolandsen, 'The Making of the Anya-Nya insurgency in the Southern Sudan, 1961–64', *Journal of Eastern African Studies*, 5/2 (2011), p. 216. For more on these articulations of Southern Sudanese grievances, see Chap. 2 of this book.

3. See Chaps. 8 and 9.
4. Peel, 'For who hath Despised', p. 585.
5. Rolandsen and Leonardi, 'Discourses of Violence'.
6. Leonardi and Vaughan, '"We are oppressed and our only way is to write to higher authority"'.
7. Willis, 'The Southern Problem'.
8. Oduho and Deng, *Problem*, p. 59.
9. Gray, 'Introduction', in Oduho and Deng, *Problem*, p. 1.
10. Ibid. Emphasis added.
11. Letter from I. Nyigilo to Foreign Ministers in Uganda, 1963.
12. Letter from SANU to the Prime Minister of the Sudan, Khatim Khalifa, November 1964.
13. SPLM/A, *Manifesto*, p. 1.
14. Rolandsen, *Guerrilla Government*, p. 62.
15. C. Tounsel, 'Khartoum Goliath: SPLM/SPLA Update and Martial Theology during the Second Sudanese Civil War', *Journal of Africana Religions*, 4/2 (2016), pp. 129–153.
16. Bayart, 'Africa in the World', pp. 217–267.
17. Ibid., p. 265.
18. Huang, 'Rebel Diplomacy'.
19. P. Chatterjee, *The Politics of the Governed: Reflections on popular politics in most of the world* (New York, 2004), note 17, p. 8.
20. R. Akuany, 'A Lament by a Southern Sudanese Girl', *Voice of Southern Sudan*, no. 4 (1969), p. 3.
21. For work that focuses on woman in the SPLA, see C. Pinaud, '"We are trained to be married!" Elite formation and ideology in the "girls' battalion" of the Sudan People's Liberation Army', *Journal of Eastern African Studies*, 9/3 (2015), pp. 375–393. A. Weber, 'Barbarian Beasts or Mothers of Invention: Relation of Gendered Fighter and Citizen Images: with a specific case study of Southern Sudan' (PhD thesis, Frele Universität Berlin, 2006).
22. Willis, 'Southern Problem', p. 283.
23. Peterson and Macola, *Recasting the Past.*
24. T. Ranger, 'Nationalist Historiography, Patriotic History and the History of the Nation: the Struggle over the Past in Zimbabwe', *Journal of Southern African Studies*, 30/2 (2004), pp. 215–234.
25. Glassman, *War of Words*, p. 7.
26. Ibid., p. 22.

CHAPTER 12

Epilogue: Narrative-as-Lived—The Meaning of the "New Sudan" to SPLM Soldiers

The epilogue moves beyond the traditional bounds of studies of international relations and diplomacy to explore how rebel discourses shaped the lives of Southern Sudanese rebels in exile. It shows that rebel discourses were not simply narratives-as-told, to evoke John Peel's term,[1] but they in fact, in important ways, defined the realities of ordinary Southern Sudanese rebels in exile. The Sudan People's Liberation Movement (SPLM) soldiers experienced camp life in Ethiopia as a laboratory in which the "New Sudan" discourse was engaged and put into practice. This narrative powerfully shaped the political subjectivities of these soldiers during the 1980s. By extending the book's enquiry to these realms, we can begin to see how rebel discourses of legitimacy reverberated across personal and political fields, shaping far more than the relations between states. In order to engage substantively with soldiers' accounts, it is important to begin by reckoning with the representations of African rebels in scholarship.

Taking Rebel Rhetoric Seriously

As we saw previously, despite the deliberate and unequivocally unionist self-portrayal of the SPLM, some have thought that the Movement, in an attempt to distance itself from the earlier, failed liberation movements from Southern Sudan, 'found that their uncompromising separatist goal isolated them from potential national and regional allies'.[2] In light of these

S. C. Manoeli, *Sudan's "Southern Problem"*, African Histories and Modernities, https://doi.org/10.1007/978-3-030-28771-9_12

benefits and the opportunistic logic they imply, it can be tempting to dismiss the SPLM's commitment to non-sectarian, nationalist reform as simply a strategy of extraversion designed by elite rebels.[3] But, as this epilogue will argue, the SPLM's nationalist rhetoric in the 1980s actually gained traction among foot soldiers such that the externally circulated narrative of the SPLM's commitment to nationalism became an internal myth among SPLM cadres. This internalisation evinces the absence of duplicity in the stated nationalism of the Movement. The epilogue relies on oral testimonies to ascertain the SPLM's exile histories from below, and it seeks to challenge the view that the SPLM rank-and-file soldiers were devoid of ideas, and that the unionist political stance was merely the province of a worldly elite.

More broadly, African guerrillas and insurgents have long been held in suspicion.[4] Explaining this realist perspective, Engelbert and Hummel argue that the low probability of attaining diplomatic recognition for secessionist groups like the SPLM as well as the 'compelling material incentives' of having access to the national coffers leads many 'would-be separatists' to appear to embrace nationalism.[5] William Reno makes a similar case regarding the reasons insurgents desert their regionalist ambitions by asserting that 'international recognition of sovereignty offers material and political advantages to insurgents that exceed the resources that come with de facto control over a specific territory'.[6]

Furthering this realist perspective, in an influential volume on African guerrilla movements, Christopher Clapham labelled the SPLM a 'reform insurgency'[7] and later a 'separatist insurgency'[8] rather than a 'liberation insurgency' (a moniker reserved for the insurgents opposing the white settler states of southern Africa and the Portuguese colonies), in part due to its lack of 'special standing in African international relations' and the assumed ideological vacuity of the Movement.[9] This categorisation matters due to the tendency to accept on face value the legitimacy of the political motivations of African 'liberation' insurgencies in sharp contrast to other kinds of insurgencies. In their continuation of Clapham's work, Bøås and Dunn argue that commitments to 'revolutionary ideological discourse often grounded in variations of Marxist-Leninism or Maoism' also distinguished the 'armed liberation groups' from ones like the SPLM.[10] The view that upholds a narrow conception of 'ideology as understood by Western political science',[11] acknowledging only 'formal political ideas across a left-right continuum', and that also insists on the 'decay of ideology' among African guerrillas[12] ignores the emergence of innovative approaches to nationalism and hinders our ability to understand the ideas that animate African insurgents.[13]

These scholars are right in acknowledging the importance of international recognition to movements like the SPLM. International propaganda constituted a central battlefield for the Movement. However, by only conceiving of these discourses as instrumental rhetoric, we fail to grasp both the ideational political processes at work and the political imaginaries of the guerrillas. This reduction of African insurgency politics to pragmatism seems to stem from disillusionment with African nationalist movements and the fear of being branded as gullible if they take rebel political rhetoric seriously. Departing from this line of reasoning, the epilogue argues that the SPLM's nationalist discourse, dubbed as the "New Sudan" vision,[14] resonated deeply with soldiers as they imbibed it in exile in Gambella, Ethiopia, and that its principles governed SPLM camp life. This chapter contributes to our understanding of the transformations in and the traction of rebel political discourses.

By engaging with the accounts of foot soldiers and mid-level commanders, this chapter examines SPLM soldiers' experiences of recruitment, camp life and political training in exile in Ethiopia in the 1980s. It argues that the SPLM's discursive innovations produced corresponding political subjectivities amongst its soldiers. It allows us to perceive the degree to which the SPLM's new narrative was lived and to discern the place of ideas in the Movement. Drawing from Peel's argument that 'narratives-as-lived are shaped by narratives-as-told', oral histories are used to gain insight into the lived experience of SPLM exiles, to understand how official narratives were transmitted to soldiers and to uncover the extent to which soldiers adopted them.[15]

Compiled from life history interviews conducted in Ethiopia, Uganda and the UK, these soldiers' stories reveal how they lived the Movement's ideas. Soldiers' accounts, however, do not necessarily establish "the truth" about the SPLM in exile, but they do illustrate the memories of a handful of soldiers who were exiled in Ethiopia in the 1980s. These accounts are valuable precisely because they are subjective and reveal how fighters made meaning of the struggle.[16] As data, these memories serve as an entry into the self-imagination of the soldiers as members of an ideationally rich Movement, since oral history represents an effective method through which to investigate the shape of organisational cultures and power relations.[17] They also reveal some of the complex motivations of guerrilla fighters for both joining and remaining in the armed struggle.

On another level, this is a chapter about memory and particularly nostalgia—a state described as one 'of moral pain associated with the forced separation from family and social environment'.[18] It is not, however, the nostalgia that combatants experience in exile as a result of displacement from their regular domicile. In this case, exile in Gambella, Ethiopia, represents a special context in which those who experienced life there not only remember it with fondness but express nostalgia for it in the present context. In this way, the chapter examines the psychosocial dimensions of Southern Sudanese soldiers' lives through their memories of exile. It rejects the tendency to reduce African rebel combatants to violent and morally calloused warlords. Instead, it maintains that the subjectivities and intellectual lives of soldiers can offer crucial insight into the meaning of their wars.

Their personal narratives were entwined in the ongoing fratricide within the SPLM. The renewed crisis in 2013 in South Sudan occurred along patterns reminiscent of the past. As in 2013, Riek Machar led the breakaway faction that caused a major schism within the SPLM in 1991. He was only reconciled to the Movement in 2002, when he signed an agreement with the SPLM that gave him charge over the troops that belonged to the Dok Nuer ethnic group—indicating the extent to which the SPLM had become ethnicised.[19] The 1991 split led to an ethnically based civil war in Southern Sudan in the 1990s between largely Nuer supporters of Riek Machar and Dinka supporters of John Garang.[20] The cyclical nature of the conflict was evident to the soldiers interviewed herein, many of whom had lived through both iterations.

To mitigate the current war affecting the testimonies of the soldiers, a diverse sample of ex-guerrillas that held differing allegiances in the political moment of the interview was obtained. They were willing to speak freely as the 1980s represent a less charged period in SPLM history. Nevertheless, pseudonyms are used in order to protect their identities. Overall, although the present wormed its way into their narratives about the past, the soldiers had sophisticated ways of making sense of the past and distinguishing it from present politics. Before exploring the soldiers' memories, we briefly turn to a discussion of western Ethiopia's local politics to understand the setting the soldiers inhabited.

Gambella: Layered Local Politics

Despite the Ethiopian government's generous welcome, the SPLM's relationship with the local administration in Gambella was fraught with difficulty. The Movement entered into the already tense relationship between the Gambella region and the Derg government. Historically, the region was known as a source of slaves in Ethiopia and the Turco-Egyptian Sudan; and slave raiding continued up until the 1930s.[21] In 1902, Ethiopia had extended its authority to include Gambella by negotiating a formal agreement with the British as the colonial power in bordering Sudan.[22] Thereafter, Gambella remained marginal to the national agenda of every Ethiopian government until the Derg. While Mengistu's socialist agenda prioritised development on the margins of the state, it also led to the purging of local cultural practices and forms of authority to introduce socialist political structures. The policies antagonised local communities. The Derg introduced forced conscription and moved young men from the Gambella region against their will and that of the traditional authorities to the northern battlefronts in the government's conflicts with dissidents.[23] The combination of factors including the stigma of slavery, decades of neglect and an aggressive government policy of erasing local authority structures built up a groundswell of anti-government sentiment.

The Sudanese civil wars introduced new and disruptive variables into the imbricated histories of Gambella. During the first war and the subsequent period of peace, the Sudanese government, in pursuit of rebels, often conducted operations within Ethiopian territory. These raids, according to Ethiopian defence records, damaged the property of 'peaceful Ethiopian inhabitants' and threatened their lives since 'being of the same racial stock, [they] could not have been safely differentiated from the fleeing Southern Sudanese insurgents'.[24]

In this early period, the local population experienced ethno-racial profiling from a foreign state encroaching into their territory without any significant protection from their state. Although the Anuak comprised the largest ethnic group in Gambella in 1980, by the mid-1980s, it had lost its demographic dominance due to the influx of Southern Sudanese refugees into the area during Sudan's second civil war.[25] Although historically the second largest ethnic group, the Nuer's population increased due to Nuer immigration from Southern Sudan. During this period, these refugees also experienced few hurdles to obtaining citizenship,[26] partly because prior to the Derg era, national citizenship was of little value on the borderlands.[27] In a few short years, Gambella became a highly militarised and politicised zone. Moreover, in 1984, the Derg regime resettled between 50,000 and 60,000 highlanders (Amhara and Oromo) into the Gambella region as part of a nationwide programme aimed at developing "unused" agricultural land.[28] The rapid and marked demographic changes led to 'the politicization of ethnicity in Gambella'.[29] In a short time span, the local population experienced both the heavy-handedness of the Derg's authoritarian militarism and new rivalries over resources and political power with the refugees, highlanders and the SPLM.

By the 1980s, Anuak dissidents had established the Gambella People's Liberation Movement (GPLM).[30] Providing this Ethiopian rebel group with financial assistance, the Sudanese government sought to obtain intelligence from the GPLM by exploiting its hostility towards the SPLM.[31] The GPLM received training from other Khartoum allied, anti-Derg forces such as the Tigray People's Liberation Front (TPLF) and was affiliated with other anti-Derg forces such as the Oromo Liberation Front (OLF). In Gambella itself, the GPLM attacked highlanders, government officials, police posts, the SPLM and government development projects. These actions led to violent confrontations with the state.[32] The region's politics became increasingly ethnicised as all Anuak were treated as dissidents as a result of GPLM activities, further fomenting antagonism between them. Meanwhile, this created an opportunity for the Nuer to strengthen their relationship with the Ethiopian state.

As a result of Gambella's layered local politics, the SPLM initially experienced significant insecurity in Ethiopia but did not have the right to expel the antagonistic Sudanese political groups from the area, despite the Derg's considerable support. Even 18 months into establishing its headquarters in western Ethiopia, the SPLM continued to face opposition from Southern factions unwilling to concede to Garang's leadership. For instance, in a letter to Garang, Col. Kerubino Bol (while he was still a member of the SPLM Political-Military High Command [PMHC]) noted that in Gambella, the SPLM's security was 'constantly threatened', and that soldiers could not retaliate due to their obligation to 'respect Ethiopian authority'.[33] To Kerubino Bol, the militia that refused incorporation into the SPLM were nothing more than 'bandits'. In this letter, Kerubino Bol also identified a certain Bol Kur whom he wanted to arrest for 'agitating refugees in Itang', but Kur received protection from an unidentified source until he finally escaped with another 52 dissenters.[34] Kerubino Bol expressed significant frustration over several others who similarly were 'protected and allowed to organize there and allowed to escape'.[35] He informed the Commander-in-Chief that these 'bandits' organised freely and received arms from an unknown source. He alleged that the Ethiopian public security officer of Gambella District 'was acting in support of these reactionary groups', as the same unidentified official's office was linked to the escape of the leader of one of the SPLM's opponents in the region.[36] The SPLM's leadership saw the Ethiopian authorities in the region as ambivalent, at best. By 1991, the issues had not been entirely resolved as a letter to the Ethiopian Ministry of Defence indicates, in which an SPLM official insisted on highlighting the Movement's need for goodwill on the local level, stating that 'it is necessary to have a sympathetic and highly supportive local administration in both Gambella and Asosa Regions'.[37]

Interviews with Gambella locals corroborate these challenges. I interviewed some Gambella residents who grew up in the region during the 1980s.[38] All the interviewees expressed sympathy with the victims of the war in Sudan, acknowledging that refugees escaped danger to find peace in their midst. However, they tended to resent the symbiotic relationship between the Derg and the SPLM.[39] Alina, a civil servant in the regional administration, explained her misgivings as follows:

> [The Derg] did not protect the indigenous people's right. They instead of protecting its [sic] people, they protect the soldiers of the SPLM. ... The people [were] in many, many problems that time.[40]

The problems Alina referred to include those caused by the SPLM. Eisei Kurimoto, who conducted fieldwork in Gambella in the late 1980s, averred that 'the relation between the local Anywaa [sic] and the SPLM/A was not friendly', as some SPLM soldiers committed atrocities against the local people, such as 'theft, robbery, harassment, rape and killing'; thus, 'they became their enemies'.[41] Alina similarly explained that

> When they were beating one person, or other people, nothing, no one ask them, "why you do this?" There is no right.

Echoing Alina's grievances about the lack of civil protections for original inhabitants, another resident, Daniel, who served in the local government in the 1980s, opined that the Derg gave the SPLM 'excess freedom', and therefore 'there [were] some clashes with the local people'.[42]

The people of Gambella felt under-valued and marginalised by the Derg, which seemed to show more concern for the SPLM than for the locals. The limited accountability for the SPLM's crimes against locals also contributed to their sense of neglect. They interpreted the violence they experienced at the hands of SPLM soldiers as ingratitude for the sacrifices the locals made to host them. Thus, while the SPLM soldiers credited the

Ethiopian government for its exceptional support, it appears that Mengistu's generosity was interpreted by locals as having been in part coloured by the regime's marginalisation of the people of Gambella. Thus, the SPLM's Gambella years occurred at a cross-section of intricate domestic politics. We now turn to a discussion on how SPLM soldiers experienced recruitment and life in the region. Their testimonies will conspicuously omit the unpleasant aspects that the citizens of Gambella recalled. This is mainly because the soldiers focused on SPLM camps within Gambella, which constituted an additional site of the local, national and regional dimensions of the SPLM's relations with the Derg.

The Camp as "Laboratory": Living the SPLM Narrative

The training camps represented a peculiar zone in which the SPLM leadership established governing practices that addressed Sudan's pivotal fault lines and thereby reimagined the country's social relations. As the following testimonies will reveal, the experience of the camp, as a dynamic social and political space, profoundly moulded the subjectivities of SPLM soldiers.[43] The following section engages with their accounts of recruitment in Southern Sudan as well as the journey to the important political terrain of the camp. Further, the section explores the soldiers' experiences of political training, their assimilation of SPLM discourses and how they made meaning of their years in Gambella.

Recruitment

Previously 'just a soldier', Gabriel, now an Episcopal priest and father of five, remembers being recruited by SPLM soldiers who were deployed to his hometown. The soldiers first met with the community elders to obtain permission to enlist fighters, after which, the elders directed them to cattle camps where young men and adolescents spent their days. There, soldiers directly addressed the youth, encouraging them to join the SPLM. Afterwards, Gabriel and his friends thought the trip to Ethiopia could be worthwhile in order 'to have a gun, and not actually to fight with the North'.[44] Chuckling, as he often did throughout the interview, Gabriel stated that his peers joined the SPLM for a variety of reasons but all based on a measure of ignorance regarding the stakes of war. He recounted that some even planned to use the arms to 'loot the cattle from Murle', an ethnic group that often raided cattle from his community in Twic Country. Perhaps the SPLM soldiers countenanced the various motivations because the Murle, as enemies within reach, served as a useful parable for national politics to these, otherwise politically unaware, rural youth.

It appears that the recruiter's promotional speech was also open to interpretation, as it simplified the purpose of the war to only a few pertinent details. Gabriel recalls the SPLM soldier advertising the Movement as follows:

> And he said, "Now, Dr John Garang he got people who are going to support him to give him a gun, and if you go, you will get. They are ready! You will come back with it, and you will carry it." [Chuckles] We don't know what we will do with a gun.[45]

Gabriel poignantly recalled knowing little about weapons, war or politics at age 16. One of the rare moments in which he first faced what he dubbed 'very big politics' occurred when the national language policy changed and his primary school consequently switched the language of instruction from English to Arabic.[46] Besides that, he had distinctly limited reference points for the liberation politics of the South.

When he enlisted, Gabriel said he thought the war would last only three months and told his parents to expect him back shortly. His uncles, who also joined the Movement, encouraged him to participate in the struggle so that he could translate Arabic into Dinka for them in case they needed it. He agreed because 'I am young and they are mature', therefore 'I followed them'.[47] Gabriel thus made the crucial decision to join the exile rebel movement in the context of his community of elders, uncles, parents and peers. Youthful zeal featured in other soldiers' accounts of recruitment. Wol, who had picked up his studies again at a British university in 2014 after the war's outbreak in 1983 had halted his education, joined the SPLM because of peer pressure. Reflecting on his recruitment, he felt in retrospect that

> as a young person at that age – at that time I was about nineteen years – sometimes you rarely calculate the risk that you undertake ... It was confusing to be honest. We didn't understand some of the things, because initially, when we left our schools we did not have a clear idea of what we were going to go through. And the assumption, the assumption was irrational, the

> assumption was that, we are going to go there, spend one or two months then the whole issue will definitely be resolved, then you come back and continue with your studies.[48]

These testimonies illustrate how the recruitment process benefited from the inexperience of the youth. Jonathan, who was only 16 years old when he left Southern Sudan in 1987 to join the SPLM, says he had 'no other options' as he became part of the mass exodus of "lost boys".[49] Jonathan's recruitment occurred in an SPLM-administered town in Southern Sudan, in which a Movement spokesperson conferred with the local paramount chief, youth and women's representatives to discuss the community's responses to the war. They then held rallies in villages to inform residents of the issues, and to educated local audiences, the soldiers referenced the SPLM *Manifesto*.

A recently deposed former South Sudanese diplomat, Bol, joined the Movement at age 13, three years after his older sister and brother. While they were gone, he witnessed a Sudan Armed Forces (SAF) soldier detain and kill his uncle, and an SPLM soldier wrongfully arrest, torture and nearly murder his father. After seeing his father's scarred legs, knees and elbows, he decided to join the SPLM to obtain weapons so he could protect his family and to avenge his father against the SPLM commander who ordered the botched execution. Caught in the crossfire, Bol was initially ambivalent about both warring parties. Yet upon arrival to the SPLM's camps in Ethiopia where he underwent political orientation and training, he was converted to 'the objective and mission of the SPLA'.[50]

Gabriel's political naïvety also ended 'when [he] reached to [sic] Itang, things had changed'.[51] He remembered that as SPLM politicians began introducing him to liberation politics, he encountered Murle as fellow fighters. Another former soldier, Wol, similarly recalled that various soldiers 'had different reasons why they joined, but the Movement had to make sure that everybody abandoned your small issue for a bigger, bigger issue'.[52] Jonathan also experienced the camp as intellectually enlightening, a place where his prejudices and misconceptions were challenged and he was transformed. Perhaps it is no coincidence that his experience in exile concurred with his religious awakening. Since he was too young to officially join the SPLM, he lived in a refugee camp in Itang and became a catechist in a church there, and he eventually helped to set up a Catholic Church in which he preached regularly. As he grew older, he was able to join the SPLM, and when we met in 2015, he was serving as a diplomat of the South Sudanese state abroad.

Because of his tender youth, Gabriel initially did not know why he was fighting and deferred to the wisdom of the Movement's leadership for instruction. By contrast, soldiers who joined at an older age having been workers or students, such as Simon, had lost enough loved ones to the war, to understand and articulate their grievances against the Nimeiri regime.[53] Having joined the SPLM as part of a group of 80 students, then 18 years old, Simon remembers being ready to embrace the SPLM's 'revolutionary spirit' at the moment of recruitment, explaining that 'we were the middle class by then, we were seeing things which were going wrong'.[54] Likewise George, who had been working as a manual labourer at a French company in Southern Sudan for four years, described the early 1980s as a time in which 'the situation was ripe in Sudan for the revolution, because the oppression was very serious'.[55]

Regardless of their various life stages at the point of recruitment, all my interviewees described the camp as a place of enlightenment. In large part, this is because the camp represented the site of their first encounter with the "New Sudan" vision. The interviewees all articulated a similar dialectical schema of their political journey into the SPLM. It comprised of false or limited consciousness at the point of recruitment, followed by ideological transformation in the camp. They all remained in the SPLM, in part, because the political vision presented in the camp resonated with them.

Political Training in the Camp

Soldiers' stories typically include the narrative trope of personal enlightenment. Jocelyn Alexander and JoAnn McGregor's work also shows how Zimbabwe People's Revolutionary Army (ZIPRA) guerrilla narratives describe 'the liberation war as a transformative experience'.[56] By tracing their recruitment processes, border and river crossings, Alexander and McGregor illustrate that former guerrillas often attribute their transformations to their experiences at transitional moments.[57] Not dissimilarly, the SPLM soldiers interviewed described their personal transformations as intellectual illumination that came through exposure to the Movement's ideas. As this section will show, the significance of the SPLM's political training on the lives of the soldiers was the key influence.

By joining the SPLM, these young men joined an explicitly political organisation. Their political socialisation took place through a formal political training course that could span up to six months, running concurrently with military training. Professors from Addis Ababa University as well as Southern Sudanese intellectuals conducted the training of the troops in English and, a Southern Sudanese creole, Juba Arabic. In an ideal context, new recruits would undergo a two-month-long Basic Training programme. After this, the leadership would choose candidates to attend a 12-week officers training programme. After the three months, non-commissioned officers (NCO) and support weapons gunners received special NCO training.[58] Thereafter, they would return to the general training for a four-week unit training session.[59]

The Commander-in-Chief, John Garang, occasionally gave lectures to trainees on the history of injustices enacted by the central government on the South and other peripheral regions of Sudan, explaining the reasons for the war. He continuously drew their attention to the SPLM *Manifesto* as the Movement's creed and to its official penal laws that were meant to govern the army, the Sudan People's Revolutionary Laws. On Sundays, the troops received more general political education, typically through a lecture an SPLM political commissar would give. Beginning by reading the messages that the Chairman had addressed to all units, the commissar read updates about upcoming missions as well the ongoing battles on different fronts, in order to give the soldiers a sense of what their colleagues were doing.[60]

The "New Sudan" vision challenged the vast majority of Southerners who joined the Movement regardless of their background. Now a retired commander, Simon observed that the vision required soldiers of middle-class origin to perform a special role. Ensconced between a minority of soldiers who had accessed tertiary education and the large rural and uneducated base, Simon believed that those with secondary education had the task of what he described as 'pulling the peasants' and explaining the SPLM's unionism in terms they would understand.[61] He did this specifically by holding political discussions every Thursday evening for the soldiers under his command. Simon noted that 'the people from the villages came with different motives ... When we were staying with them, we were telling them the reality.'[62] As a result of his effort to enlighten his comrades, he believed that 'the local people, the peasants, they managed also to understand'.[63] Simon achieved this, in part by using the arts. He encouraged his soldiers to sing 'revolutionary songs' infused with SPLM narratives,[64] and thusly used music 'to recreate the morale of the soldiers' after losing comrades in battle as a way of 'forgetting about the past'.[65] Some of them played a guitar traditionally used in Arabic music, the *rababah*, while others danced.

The Theatre of War: Artistic Modes of Political Education

Senior leaders within the Movement also used the arts as pedagogical tools. In particular, they encouraged a specific narration of Sudanese history as part of the politicisation of the troops. A curious document titled "A Drama for the SPLA Cadets Graduation"[66] offers insight into the artistic aspects of the Movement's political education. Four playwrights, most notably Riek Machar and Pagan Amun, composed the theatrical show of Sudanese history to be performed at the graduation of military trainees. The script, dated 2 September 1984, was among the few English-language documents in the Ethiopian government's Ministry of Defence National Archives. Written for the benefit of the representatives of the host country who attended the ceremony and enacted for the benefit of the wider SPLM troops who witnessed the graduation, the play symbolised the SPLM's articulation of its ideals. The play represents the Movement's institutional self-imagination as well as the revolutionary future to which it aspired.

In the opening scene, an elderly man, donning indigenous attire, heaved his tired limbs onto the stage with assistance. The first of his sons identified as a "Northern Sudanese politician", conspicuously not called Arab in the script, stood robed in a *jellaba*, a traditional Arab loose-fitting garment. The second, dressed in European clothing, is a Southern Sudanese politician, and a third son wearing military uniform, followed. The father rounded his sons up, with the aim of imparting wisdom to all three and to narrate 'the Sudanese people's struggle from Slavery to Colonialism' to them, a history that spanned 1820–1955.[67] Historically, Southern Sudanese rebellions did not identify with the Northern account of the oppression they suffered under the Ottoman Turco-Egyptian occupation that began in the North in 1820 as that coincided with the period in which certain groups from the Northern region enslaved ones from the Southern region and the North, in fact, increased slaving raids after the local Mahdist rebellion dislodged the Ottoman occupiers. Thus, for the SPLM to claim a shared history with the North, beginning in 1820 represented a nationalist act. In this dramatised history, the SPLM playwrights placed both the oppression Northerners experienced and the enslavement of Southerners in a single frame. The father then began asking them how they fared under British colonialism, to which the sons responded by stating that they all suffered. Thereafter, in his moving last words, the father announced that 'Independence' was coming; thus, after having lived through a century of slavery, illicit ivory trade and colonial exploitation, he urged them to remember that the colonialists sought to divide the people and imposed hard times on them, but that he wishes that they would attain 'Unity, Equality and Progress' in the new political era.[68] With this advice, he breathed his last.

The second stage recreated a moment on the eve of independence in which the 'Northern and Southern bourgeoisie' quarrelled over Sudanisation.[69] The older (Northern) brother returned from London, with Sudan's independence in tow, secured in his briefcase. The younger (Southern) brother rejoiced in the freedom they attained and asked how the older sibling divided the jobs. The older stated that he had 'given' the younger three jobs, while he has 'taken' 797.[70] The furious youth then gripped his brother, accusing him of duplicity. The Northern brother quickly freed himself from his brother's hold and asked, with what appeared to be contrived innocence, how he could give the Southerner more jobs when he 'cannot read and write'.[71] To those denigrating words, the Southerner left the stage. Complaining bitterly about this injustice to the third son (the soldier), he vowed to fight the North. According to the script, the soldier then 'rebels, shoots and runs into the bush to wage a guerrilla war', followed by the son now identified as a Southern politician.[72] The scene seems to be designed to elicit from the audience a tinge of sympathy for the middle brother, but his actions are also characterised as somewhat capricious and grounded in a loss of personal advancement rather than in any revolutionary ideals. On the other hand, in a politically charged phrase, the Northerner then exclaimed: 'Allah, Allah, these southerners are meaning it!' The religious act of praying in the Islamic tradition was deliberately scripted to unveil an additional wedge between the brothers. He uttered this prayer upon discovering 'the escalation of the civil war', which was portrayed as an unexpected consequence of his selfish jobs policy.[73] The surprised expression also communicated that the older brother underestimated the South's capacity to mount sustained rebellion.

Centring on the end of the war, the third stage depicted the 1972 Addis Ababa Peace Agreement negotiation. The Northern politician's realisation of the severity of the conflict led him to call upon a Khartoum-based Southerner to gather the Southerners in exile to negotiate. The Southerner in question is given the pseudonym "Abraham", but he represents Abel Alier, who, like Abraham in the play, was made President of the High Executive Council in Southern Sudan at the end of the peace negotiations. The brothers eventually sat to discuss their terms for peace, and the Southern Politician articulated the following:

> We want Regional Autonomy. We want to be ministers, directors, ambassadors, and officers in the armed forces. This is what we've been fighting for the last 17 years (1955–1972).[74]

As in the SPLM *Manifesto*, this monologue that flattened a complex past represented a biting critique of the political leadership of the first generation of Southern rebels whom the SPLM characterised as careerist and devoid of commitment to the Southern people and to any ideology. Nevertheless, the Northern politician responded by granting the men in the room senior positions, essentially buying peace through jobs. In a symbol of concord, the brothers around the table in choral speech declared: 'Unity, No South without North, No North without South'.[75] The audience member likely watched this scene with an ominous sense that these could not be the foundations upon which a lasting peace could be built.

The viewer was to understand that unity was a desirable outcome, but prior to the SPLM, it had only been poorly executed. The final scene, set on the fourth stage representing the post-Addis Ababa period, captures this. A dialogue took place between an old woman and a 'revolutionary soldier' in which she lamented the absence of 'equality and progress', as well as the persistence of war-time deprivations, including the lack of access to schools, healthcare services and food, despite the peace. The soldier responded by expressing his agreement and asserting that the politicians have sold the people out 'for the jobs offered to them'.[76] She then asked him what the people are to do now and the soldier oddly offered a jargon-laden statement, no less to a woman the viewer is supposed to assume is illiterate:

> The solution lies in popular uprising by the Sudanese masses. This armed revolution guided by the Principles of Marxism-Leninism and Proletarian Internationalism will lead to Socialist Transformation of the Sudanese Society.[77]

The ample usage of leftist lexicon in this quote suggests that the SPLM playwrights wanted to signal its ideological alignment with Addis. To this mouthful, the hopeful elderly woman curiously probed about how such a transformation could come about, to which the revolutionary soldier responded with a crescending proclamation: 'By the glorious victory of the SPLA/SPLM. We are the SPLA.'[78] In this concluding scene, an actual battalion joined the revolutionary soldier to shout "SPLA!" three times, after which he fired his weapon for dramatic effect.

Showing fidelity to the *Manifesto*, the moral of the play was: where politicians—Northern and Southern—had failed, revolutionary soldiers under the SPLM's banner would succeed. They would not give in to careerist temptations; instead, the SPLM had the ideology to effect transformative change. The SPLM thus portrayed itself as the harbinger of unity for the whole Sudan. By framing it as an ancestrally mandated mission depicted in the father's commissioning, the SPLM's vision of a united Sudan was portrayed as a matter of destiny. Thus, the play aimed at shaping the ways in which newly minted cadets understood the war to which they were giving their lives, and it also showed the Ethiopian government that the SPLM was committed to national unity and socialism.

Impact of Political Training

The soldiers absorbed the Movement's ideals through artistic and other forms of political training. Despite the preponderance of leftist rhetoric in the play, socialist education featured marginally in the memories the SPLM soldiers discussed with me about their training camps. For example, Simon told me that the "New Sudan" idea was the first thing he learned, and that only secondarily was he taught 'the socialist ideals' through which 'we got the orientation of calling ourselves comrades'.[79] As if reaching for phrases in the recesses of his memory, he described the content of the training as follows: 'We had to undertake some Marxist Lenin, some sort of training [in] dialectical social materialism, and all those books of socialism.'[80]

Concerning the "New Sudan", Jonathan, now a diplomat for the seceded South, was taught to reject separatism. Instead, the leadership challenged him to see the problems of Sudan as stemming from

> only a small clique of learned politicians [that] went and gathered in Khartoum and around Khartoum, and have become the elite that have been ruling. We know that even people in Darfur that they were also suffering like us, people from the Nuba Mountains, people from Funj. And we said … the government *in* the North was not a government *for* the Northerners. So that is where we got this idea of the New Sudan – a Sudan that was circular, a Sudan that is taken from the villages … that was the ideology of the New Sudan.[81]

The "circular Sudan" was a layman's term for Garang's theoretical spatial metaphor described as the "centre-periphery" relations between Khartoum and the rest of Sudan's hinterland in the SPLM's official propaganda. It is not dissimilar from the metropole/core-periphery relations theory developed by dependency theorists at the University of Dar es Salaam where Garang schooled in the late 1960s.[82] This conceptual innovation allowed Southerners to see their disenfranchisement in the context of the inequalities others in Sudan experienced.

Identifying with the "New Sudan" idea became a point of pride for the soldiers. Jonathan emphasised the subversive power of the "New Sudan" vision, '[f]or those who could not dream that anything good could come from the South', he recalled that he wanted it to be known that 'we did not go to the bush for the South, we went to the bush for the Sudan'.[83] Bol similarly remembers embracing the expansive and empowering nature of the "New Sudan" idea. For him, the mission was about 'liberating our brothers, even the ones in the North ... for we are one'.[84] Thus, he assumed a position of power by seeing himself as a liberator of the South as well as a group that was historically seen as oppressive to his people, the Northerners.

Thinking back to when he initially joined the Movement, Simon recounted how Garang explained the vision to him and his peers:

> The concept of the new Sudan was not ... our idea. When we came as students, we were separatists. We were coming for the liberation of the South. So the first thing that we touched – when meeting Dr Garang, he told us there is no need to fight for a smaller place, let us fight for a bigger place. That [sic] why should we run away from people who have really mistreated us, why don't we also work to come to power, to have one Sudan and then we also use the constitution against them. Since they are majority, so we use the constitution to also show them that we are also people, that we can rule them, that the country belongs to all of us. So we embraced that one.[85]

It is remarkable that the political education of the SPLM as an insurgency seems to have produced a measure of faith in political processes and institutions such as the constitution. As indicated above, Simon ensured that everything he learned trickled down to the foot soldiers under his charge. This testimony also indicates that Garang was training the soldiers to become citizens by enfranchising them. Similarly, in his testimony, former foot soldier Jonathan emphasised the primacy of political liberation above military victory:

> We came to know exactly that the problem was not to go to Khartoum one day, to capture Khartoum. But it was [to] restructure the ideology that people who were under Khartoum were going through.[86]

Although inexpertly phrased, by referring to the need for ideological change, Jonathan demonstrated the salience of political thought among SPLM soldiers.

Mandated Multiculturalism

In addition to being political, exile is a relational domain. For example, Christian Williams shows that African National Congress (ANC) soldiers exiled in Kongwa, Tanzania, generated 'affective ties and shared allegiances among Africans of different nationalities'.[87] Though his work specifically focuses on Pan-African relationships, Williams reveals how military camps became spaces for intercultural connection. Training camps can be seen as social spaces in which the ideals and ethos of liberation can be practised in the quotidian aspects of everyday life. The rules that governed SPLM camp life similarly complemented the political training the soldiers received. Soldiers had to grapple with Sudan's racial fault line in their relationships with one another by virtue of the SPLM's unionist position. Jonathan explained the transformation of his racial outlook as follows:

> We came to know when we thought that maybe we were fighting light-skinned persons who call themselves Arabs ... we came to realise when we were young that it is not the Arab because of the skin who is fighting a dark blue man like me.[88]

In a turn of phrase laden with culturally specific ways of conceiving of racial difference, Jonathan describes discovering that difference in skin colour could not justify the war. The Movement thus helped him to complicate and deconstruct a purely racial understanding of the conflict.

While political training may have accounted for some of this enlightenment, the "New Sudan" vision as a 'narrative-as-lived' accounts for much of the inculcation process. David Carr reminds us that narrative can transform even fictions into reality specifically because it shapes human action.[89]

The SPLM's soldiers were made to act upon the Movement's political narrative of inclusion by living in multi-ethnic groups. Bol explained:

> Nobody stays by groups and tribes. When you come, they mix you up during training. Even if your brother will find himself here, [he] will be far. So at that time there was unity among ourselves. Somebody from a different tribe, you feel like he is your real brother.[90]

Nevertheless, living the New Sudan vision was not always easy. Wol's colourful narration of his best friend's striking encounter with Arabs in the SPLM ranks captures this difficulty:

> [H]e was more or less, at the initial stage a separatist, a South Sudanese separatist. So when we reached Bilfam [sic], we found there were already soldiers from the North, SPLA soldiers, Northerners who are already – heh? [gasp] SPLA soldiers. And what happened to this man? He cried with his tears. And he told me, 'Look, if I had known that Northerners have come before' him, he wouldn't have joined the Movement.[91]

Wol explained that over time, 'this friend of mine, he also attended some of the political schools and he became a die-hard unionist'.[92] Not unlike Wol's friend, Jonathan explained that he personally overcame his suspicion of his fellow Arab comrades by realising that

> in the end, they could shout the same "SPLA!", they could sing the same song, they could carry the same gun that I am carrying, and they could also share the same command. That means they are SPLA regardless of their colour, until the end of their lifetime.[93]

Simon shared a similar sentiment that '[i]t was difficult to comprehend in the beginning. But at the end they were doing the work that we were doing. And we were able to really work together.'[94]

In addition to formal training, policies that governed everyday life such as those pertaining to a lingua franca also built fraternal bonds between the soldiers. Wol recalls the leadership encouraging the soldiers to learn other Sudanese languages besides their mother tongues, such that 'even the young ones – most of them became multi- or bi-lingual'.[95] The language policy was aimed at concealing the ethnic differences between the soldiers. It was enforced through social pressure, as Wol remembered: 'It was like a crime to ask someone: "where do you come from?"'[96]

Correspondingly, Wol recalled that the only 'important' questions they could ask each other were: "Who are you?", "What are you doing?", "When did you join the Movement?"[97] It was feared that more invasive questions could be divisive. Wol explained that as a result of these policies, '[t]he feeling of togetherness was overwhelming'.[98]

Jonathan attributes the transformation to the kind of social space camps in exile provided:

> For us, when we were in the SPLA, we did not have these issues of "you are from this group", "you from that group" – including our Arabs, including our Muslims, including our ethnicities. We did not have this culture of pointing of the finger to the people. No, no, no, whenever we are getting people, we are getting new members of our family, new members of our generation, we are very happy. It is not like this one, "if you are not from my tribe, I cannot ..." No, no, no.[99]

The presence of Arabs in the Movement signalled an actual programmatic and paradigmatic shift in the liberation history of the South and of Sudan more broadly. For example, the first major Southern Sudanese rebel movement, Anya-Nya I, typically stationed new recruits to run self-directed operations in their home territories, reinforcing their ethnic affiliation.[100] In contrast, the SPLM transferred troops to new fronts and removed soldiers from their localities to allow them to transcend their local grievances.[101] Both within and outside the camp, in the 1980s, the SPLM's rhetoric, on the main, reflected the lived reality of its soldiers.

The Aftermath of the Gambella Years

The SPLM's robust culture of diversity did not survive. Scholars of organisational cultures of liberation movements tend to emphasise exile's enduring impact, even as the legacies of exile are highly diverse based as on the specific exilic locations. For example, Michael Panzer's work proposes that the Mozambique Liberation Front's (Frente de Libertação de Moçambique (FRELIMO)) authoritarian approach to governance, noticeable once it came into power, developed within its encampments in Tanzania and northern Mozambique.[102] Similarly, Hugh Macmillan argues that the ANC's internal culture of democracy developed, at least partially, among the groups exiled in Zambia.[103] Both Macmillan's and Panzer's works contend that exile can leave an indelible mark on a liberation movement's modes of internal governance for better or worse. Where they trace continuities in organisational habits, this exploration of the SPLM's management of diversity highlights the disjuncture between the 1980s and the present. Despite the impression exile had on the soldiers individually, the drastic changes of 1991, the coup within the Movement and the change of government in Ethiopia that led to the SPLM's expulsion from Ethiopia altered the SPLM's organisational culture. As a result, the SPLM's 'golden years' ended.[104] In the 14 years of war that followed, the Movement's political training was haphazard in the absence of a single exile location in which it could train all of its troops.

The loss of an exile space for most of the army was in many ways a loss of a "laboratory", in which the movement's leadership could experiment with multiculturalism and conduct a robust political programme for all the soldiers. Although the interviewees did not use the term "laboratory" to describe their experiences in Gambella, the term is reminiscent of an SPLM detractor's, Peter Adwok Nyaba, reference to the Movement's adoption of socialism in Ethiopia as an 'experiment'.[105] With withering support from Ethiopia and its leftist networks, which disintegrated with the fall of the Berlin Wall, the SPLM had to reconfigure itself and its external relations strategies in a post-Cold War world. It failed to establish another "laboratory". The SPLM's "New Sudan" vision was a casualty of this traumatic transition. In the new era, troops were based mainly in various parts of Southern Sudan as well as on the borders of Kenya and Uganda, facing at least two sets of opponents: the Sudan Armed Forces and the SPLM breakaway faction.[106] There was less time for political training and ethnic fissures had been accentuated, so the social cohesion that had developed in exile began to fray. This signalled the death of the "New Sudan" vision.

Bol explained that he was baffled when the split occurred in 1991. A soldier of Dinka descent, Bol had received instructions to kill a fellow bodyguard who happened to be of Nuer origin. But he refused to follow the order because he thought it was absurd to kill a person simply on the basis of his ethnicity. At the time, he understood the coup as being the result of Riek Machar's ambitions for power and not somehow representative of all Nuer interest. Not all SPLM soldiers responded as his did, and several Nuer SPLM officers were killed after Riek Machar's breakaway faction attacked two Dinka towns in Southern Sudan.[107] Ironically, when I met Bol, he had recently lost his job in the SPLM based on allegations that he was aligned to the new Riek Machar faction in the current war. He denies these allegations. This incident in 1991 seems to signal the beginning of the SPLM's loss of innocence.

Regardless of the palpable nostalgia in the soldiers' recollections, it is indisputable that the "golden years" were etched onto their memories as a period in which they pursued what they considered a noble struggle. These soldiers believed in the Movement and, on some level, were moved by the political possibilities of the SPLM's "New Sudan" discourse. All the soldiers made extraordinary sacrifices for the SPLM and developed an emotional connection to the organisation. Correspondingly, I asked 55-year-old George to describe what the Movement meant to him and his response illustrates the affective commitment that membership to the SPLM represented to him. Having spent 30 years working in the SPLM's signals unit, intercepting the enemy's radio messages, he was ousted by the Movement leadership in the wake of the current third civil war. When we met, he had recently been released from SPLM detention for allegedly supporting the suspected coup attempt of 2013. He reflected on the meaning of the SPLM as follows:

> Well, it became a part of my life. I believed in it. Because [as a] human being, you are born once, you live once and you die once. And you have a mission to accomplish. So having joined the SPLA/SPLM in the early 80s, I felt that I must accomplish this mission. Although it did not end up nice to me or every family member, and everyone in the South because it was not an easy task. It was taxing. It was taking lives of people. That's where I lost my brother, my elder brother, the one I followed, from my mom. He was killed. He was among the first martyrs who were killed in 1984. He was killed in Pibor on June 26, 1984. So, it was not a simple exercise. But having undertaken that responsibility as a mission, I felt that the SPLM/SPLA is the only thing that I can be in to achieve my dream of liberating myself and liberating my people. Because I have no other option. If I don't remain in it, if I don't achieve the objectives of the SPLM, I will not be living as a human being. You remember, in Sudan there was this class: second-class citizen. We don't count at some point before the war. So it is useless to live. It is useless to call yourself a human being if someone looks at you as third class, you know, you don't belong to his class or high class. It is terrible. SPLM/SPLA was like blood in my veins. That's the way I felt. It was part of me and I am part of it. So that I achieved that dream that [has] convinced me. Because I was completely convinced that the only way out for me to be an independent person is for me to hold on to the objectives and mission of the SPLA.[108]

Despite being subjected to what he considered humiliation in the current political dispensation, George gave this evocative and somewhat existential soliloquy to describe the purpose the SPLM gave to his life.

George's reflections and the epilogue have shown more broadly that SPLM soldiers experienced the camp in exile as a space that enabled them to perform new political identities, and to construct new histories in service of an imagined future, as well as to inhabit more expansive political subjectivities. The training camps in Gambella remain etched onto their memories as the laboratory in which the "New Sudan" was practised in everyday life. As such, the Movement's nationalist rhetoric was embraced by the guerrillas who joined. The SPLM's rhetorical commitments were borne out in its organisational culture. As a result of deliberate politicisation, the external narrative became an internal myth that animated soldiers' understanding of the war and their self-imagination in the 1980s.

Conclusion

The combination of the texts written by elites and the life histories of ordinary rebels allows us not only to contrast but also to see surprising continuities and similarities between positions normally conceived of as irreconcilably adversative. For example, Santino Deng's words in the 1960s, 'There is no such "promised land". This is our country',[109] unexpectedly resonate with those of SPLM soldier Simon, who recounted that 'Dr [John] Garang, he told us ... why should we run away from people who have really mistreated us, why don't we also work to come to power, to have one Sudan ... the country belongs to all of us'.[110] These unexpected similarities show that a chasm did not exist between the perspectives of the unionist Southern political elites aligned to the Sudanese government and those of the Southern rebels. But they did not occur along a simple continuum either. The relationship between their ideas was far more dynamic and shaped by both strategic pragmatism and idealist conviction.

Driven by the same combination and informed by the history of the South's discursive rebellion, the SPLM managed to transform its narrative-as-told into a narrative-as-lived for its soldiers. The SPLM discourses attained taken-for-granted status among the Movement's soldiers during the 1980s. Thus, these insights expand our understanding of rebels as intellectual actors whose political imaginations and commitments are consequential in ways that are too often missed.

Notes

1. Peel, 'For who hath Despised', p. 606.
2. Johnson, SPLM, 54.
3. Jean-François Bayart, "Africa in the World: A History of Extraversion," *African Affairs* 99, no. 395 (2000): 217–267.
4. For a critique of this unwarranted demonisation of warlords, as a sub-category of rebels, see Laura Freeman, "The African Warlord Revisited," *Small Wars & Insurgencies*, 26, no. 5 (2015): 790–810.
5. Pierre Englebert and Rebecca Hummel, "Let's stick together: Understanding Africa's Secessionist Deficit," *African Affairs* 104, no. 416 (2005): 400, 412.
6. William Reno, 'How sovereignty matters: international markets and the political economy of local politics in weak states', in *Intervention and Transnationalism in Africa: Global-local Networks of Power*, ed. Thomas Callaghy, Ronald Kassimir and Robert Latham (Cambridge, 2001), 203.
7. Christopher Clapham, "Introduction: Analysing African Insurgencies," in *African Guerrillas*, ed. Christopher Clapham (Oxford, 1998), 5–9.
8. Christopher Clapham, "*African Guerrillas* Revisited," in *African Guerrillas: Raging Against the Machine,* eds. Morten Bøås and Kevin C. Dunn (Colorado, 2007), 223.
9. Clapham initially characterised the SPLM as possessing 'some elements of the reform agenda' seen in 'reform insurgencies', which seek 'the creation of a new kind of state'. Clapham, 'Introduction,' 6–7.
10. Morten Bøås and Kevin Dunn, "African Guerrilla Politics: Raging Against the Machine?", *African Guerrillas: Raging Against the Machine*, eds. Morten Bøås and Kevin Dunn (Colorado, 2007), 16.
11. Ibid, 17.
12. Ibid, 17.
13. Clapham, *African Guerrillas Revisited*, 224.
14. Francis, M. Deng, ed. *New Sudan in the Making? Essays on a nation in painful search of itself* (Princeton, 2010).
15. John D. Peel, "For Who Hath despised the Day of Small Things? Missionary Narratives, Historical Anthropology," *Comparative Studies in Society and History* 37, 3 (1995): 606.
16. For example, Luise White, "Telling more: Lies, Secrets, and History," *History and Theory* 39, 4 (2000): 11–22.
17. Jocelyn Alexander. "Telling African Cold War Stories: The Personal in the Geopolitical." Keynote lecture presented at the Africa, Eastern Europe and the Dream of International Socialism: New Perspectives on the Global Cold War Seminar Series, St Antony's College, Oxford, 28 October 2016).

18. Filiberto F. de Diego and Carmen V. Ots, "Nostalgia: A conceptual history," *History of Psychiatry* 25, 4, (2014): 404.
19. Douglas H. Johnson, *The Root Causes* of Sudan's Civil Wars: Peace or Truce (Suffolk, 2012), 90–100, 109–110.
20. Sharon E. Hutchinson, "Sudan's Prolonged Second Civil War and the Militarization of Nuer and Dinka Identities," *African Studies Review* 42, 2 (1999): 125–145.
21. J. Young, 'Along Ethiopia's Western Frontier: Gambella and Benishangul in transition', *Journal of Modern African Studies*, 37, 2 (1999), p. 323.
22. B. Zewde, *History of Modern Ethiopia, 1855–1974* (London, 1991), p. 83.
23. Kurimoto, 'Politicisation of Ethnicity', p. 799.
24. 'Joint Communiqué', 26–18 July 1965 Ethiopian Calendar (2 August 1973, Gregorian Calendar), p. 4, Administration 222, MOD.
25. Human Rights Watch (HRW), 'Targeting the Anuak: Human Rights Violations and Crimes against Humanity in Ethiopia's Gambella Region', 17/3 (2005), p. 7.
26. For a fascinating look into the complex discursive responses of Anuak citizens to the changing demographics in Gambella, see D. Feyissa, 'More State than the State? The Anywaa's Call for the Rigidification of the Ethio-Sudanese Border', in D. Feyissa and M. V. Hoehne, *Borders and Borderlands as Resources in the Horn of Africa* (Suffolk, 2010), pp. 27–44.
27. Kurimoto, 'Politicisation', p. 809.
28. HRW, 'Targeting the Anuak', p. 7.
29. E. Kurimoto, 'Politicization of Ethnicity in Gambella', in *Ethiopia in Broader Perspective: Papers of the XIIIth international Conference of Ethiopian Studies, Kyoto, 12–17 December 1997* (Kyoto, 1997).
30. Young, 'Along Ethiopia's', p. 326.
31. Bayissa, *War and Peace*, p. 119. Johnson, 'The Nuer Civil War', p. 8.
32. For example, in May 1987, local police shot 80 Anwak dead and arrested 29 after the GPLM attacked settlers and the police posts. Kurimoto, 'Politicisation of Ethnicity', p. 803.
33. Letter from Kerubino Bol to SPLA Commander-in-Chief, 29 December 1984, p. 1. Campaign File 389, MOD.
34. Ibid.
35. Ibid.
36. Ibid.
37. 'Working Paper', 5 January 1991, p. 5, Campaign File 627, MOD.
38. I conducted the interviews in Gambella mostly in English. On one occasion, I conducted an interview not cited here with the help of translators who translated Anuak to Amharic, and Amharic to English.

39. Interestingly, the destruction of wildlife and agricultural prospects also featured significantly in the interviews as a pernicious outcome of their hospitality to the SPLM and Sudanese refugees.
40. Interview with Alina, conducted by Sebabatso Manoeli, Gambella, Ethiopia, 15 April 2015.
41. Kurimoto, 'Politicisation of Ethnicity', p. 800.
42. Interview with Daniel, conducted by Sebabatso Manoeli, Gambella, Ethiopia, 15 April 2015.
43. See Christian Williams, "Introduction: Thinking Southern Africa from 'the Camp'", *Social Dynamics* 39, 1 (2013): 1–4.
44. Interview with Gabriel, conducted by Sebabatso Manoeli, Addis Ababa, Ethiopia, 2 March 2015.
45. Ibid.
46. See Lilian P. Sanderson and Neville Sanderson, *Education, religion and politics in Southern Sudan, 1899–1964* (London, 1981).
47. Ibid.
48. Interview with Wol, conducted by Sebabatso Manoeli, Durham, UK, 7 November 2014.
49. Interview with Jonathan, conducted by Sebabatso Manoeli, Kampala, Uganda, 30 September 2015.
50. Interview with Bol, conducted by Sebabatso Manoeli, Kampala, Uganda, 25 September 2015.
51. Interview with Gabriel.
52. Interview with Wol.
53. Interview with Simon, conducted by Sebabatso Manoeli, Kampala, Uganda, 26 September 2015.
54. Ibid.
55. Interview with George, conducted by Sebabatso Manoeli, Kampala, Uganda, 29 September 2015.
56. Jocelyn Alexander and Joann McGregor, "War Stories: Guerrilla Narratives of Zimbabwe's Liberation War," *History Workshop Journal*, 57 (2004): 80.
57. Ibid, p. 8.
58. Garang, 'Memorandum No. 5', p. 5, Campaign File 70, MOD, Ethiopia.
59. Ibid.
60. Interview with Simon.
61. Ibid.
62. Ibid.
63. Ibid.
64. Ibid.
65. Ibid.

66. R. Machar, P. Amun, Alfred L. Gore, and Alfred Akwoch, 'A Drama for the SPLA Cadets Graduation', 2 September, 1984, pp. 1–4, Campaign File 389, MOD.
67. Machar, et al., 'Drama', 1.
68. Ibid, p. 2.
69. Ibid.
70. Ibid, p. 3.
71. Ibid.
72. Ibid.
73. Ibid.
74. Ibid, 4.
75. Ibid.
76. Ibid.
77. Ibid.
78. Ibid.
79. Interview with Simon.
80. Ibid.
81. Interview with Jonathan, conducted by Sebabatso Manoeli, Kampala, Uganda, 30 September 2015.
82. "John Garang De Mabior: A Background Note," *Horn of Africa*, 8, no. 1 (1985): 72. Matthew LeRiche, "John Garang De Mabior," in *Dictionary of African Biography,* eds. Henry L. Jr., and Emmanuelle K. Akyeampong (Oxford, 2012).
83. Ibid.
84. Interview with Bol.
85. Interview with Simon.
86. Interview with Jonathon.
87. Christian A. Williams, "Practicing pan-Africanism: an anthropological perspective on exile-host relations at Kongwa, Tanzania," *Anthropology Southern Africa*, 37, 3–4 (2014): 224.
88. Interview with Jonathon.
89. David Carr, *Time, Narrative, and History* (Bloomington, IN, 1986), 59–61.
90. Interview with Bol.
91. Interview with Wol.
92. Ibid.
93. Interview with Jonathon.
94. Interview with Simon.
95. Ibid.
96. Ibid.
97. Ibid.
98. Ibid.

99. Interview with Jonathon.
100. Johnson, "The (SPLA)", p. 58.
101. Johnson, "The (SPLA)", pp. 59, 61.
102. Michael. G. Panzer, "Building a revolutionary constituency: Mozambican refugees and the development of the FRELIMO proto-state, 1964–1968," *Social Dynamics: A Journal of African studies* 39, 1 (2013): 5–23.
103. Hugh Macmillan, "The African National Congress of South Africa in Zambia: The Culture of Exile and the Changing Relationship with Home, 1964–1990," *Journal of Southern African Studies* 35, 2 (2009): 303–329.
104. John Garang referred to the years in Gambella as the SPLM/A's 'golden years'. See "John Garang Speech, Chairman's 22nd anniversary address at a mass rally in Rumbek 16th 2005," cited in *South Sudan: From Revolution to Independence*, by Martin LeRiche and Matthew Arnold (London, 2012), 57, 255–256.
105. Peter. A. Nyaba, *Politics of Liberation in South Sudan: An insider's view* (Kampala, 2000), 42.
106. To a limited degree, the SPLM, under Ugandan patronage, was involved in combatting the Lord's Resistance Army (LRA); see C. R. Day, "*Fates of Rebels: The Politics of Insurgency Survival and Demise*," (PhD, Northwestern University, 2012), 63. James Frkovich, "Limited War and the Ugandan Experience: Implications for African Security," *African Security*, 3, no. 3 (2010), 162. The SPLM also fought against the West Nile Bank Front (WNBF) on behalf of the Ugandan state. John Prendergast, *Crisis Response Humanitarian Band-Aids in Sudan and Somalia* (London, 1997).
107. Johnson, 'The Nuer Civil Wars', 11, 26.
108. Interview with George.
109. Deng and Wol, *Let's Speak the Truth*, p. 17.
110. Interview with Simon.

Bibliography

Interviews Cited

Alina, Gambella, Ethiopia, 15 April 2015.
Bol, Kampala, Uganda, 25 September 2015.
Daniel, Gambella, Ethiopia, 15 April 2015.
Gabriel, Addis Ababa, Ethiopia, 2 March 2015.
George, Kampala, Uganda, 29 September 2015.
John Gai Yoh, Telephonically, 2 July 2013.
Jonathan, Kampala, Uganda, 30 September 2015.
Malik, Khartoum, Sudan, 20 November 2015.
Simon, Kampala, Uganda, 26 September 2015.
Wol, Durham, UK, 7 November 2014.

Archives Consulted (Specific Documents Cited in Endnotes)

African National Congress Liberation Archives, University of Fort Hare, South Africa
Anti-Apartheid Movement Archives, Bodleian Library UK
Archivio Comboniani Roma Comboniani Mission, Archive and Library; Rome (ACR) Italy
Bodleian Library Special Collections
Douglas H. Johnson Personal Papers

S. C. Manoeli, *Sudan's "Southern Problem"*, African Histories and Modernities, https://doi.org/10.1007/978-3-030-28771-9

Ministry of Defence Archives Ethiopia
Newspaper Archive, British Library UK
Sudan Archive, Durham University Libraries; Durham (SAD) England
Sudan National Library Archive
The French Centre for Ethiopian Studies' (CFEE) Newspaper Archive Ethiopia
The Institute of African and Asian Studies at the University of Khartoum Sudan
The National Archives and Library of Ethiopia

Published Books and Articles

Aalen, L. 2014. Ethiopian State Support to Insurgency in Southern Sudan from 1962 to 1983: Local, Regional and Global Connections. *Journal of Eastern African Studies* 8 (4): 626–641.

Abadi, J. 1999. Israel and Sudan: The Saga of an Enigmatic Relationship. *Middle Eastern Studies* 35 (1): 19–41.

Abdelhay, A.K. 2010. The Politics of Writing Tribal Identities in the Sudan: The Case of the Colonial Nuba Policy. *Journal of Multilingual and Multicultural Development* 31 (2): 201–213.

Abdelhay, A., B. Makoni, and S. Makoni. 2010. The Politics of Linguistic Indigenousness in the Sudan. In *Sudan's Wars and Peace Agreements*, ed. J. Spaudling, S. Beswick, C. Fluehr-Lobban, and R.A. Lobban Jr. Newcastle upon Tyne: Cambridge Scholars Publishing.

Abdelwahab, H. 2012. *Influence: Supremacy of Religion on Sudan's Foreign Policy Decision-Making*. Bloomington: AuthorHouse.

Adar, K. 1998. A State Under Siege: The Internationalisation of the Sudanese Civil War. *African Security Review* 7 (1): 44–53.

Africa South of the Sahara: Internal Conflict and External Involvement. 1971. *Strategic Survey* 72 (1): 63–66.

Akol, L. 2001. *SPLM/SPLA: Inside an African Revolution*. Khartoum: Khartoum University Press.

Akol, J. 2005. *I Will Go the Distance: The Story of a "Lost" Sudanese Boy of the Sixties*. Nairobi: Paulines Publications Africa.

Al-Awadi, H. 2004. *In Pursuit of Legitimacy: The Muslim Brothers and Mubarak, 1982–2000*. London: I.B. Tauris.

Albino, O. 1970. *The Sudan: A Southern Viewpoint*. London: Published for the Institute of Race Relations [by] Oxford University Press.

Alexander, J., and J. McGregor. 2004. War Stories: Guerrilla Narratives of Zimbabwe's Liberation War. *History Workshop Journal* 57: 80.

Ali, N.M. 2015. *Gender, Race, and Sudan's Exile Politics: Do We All Belong to This Country?* Lanham: Lexington Books.

Alier, A. 1990. *Southern Sudan: Too Many Agreements Dishonoured*. Exeter: Ithaca Press.

Alley, J.M. 1994. Southern Sudanese Women and Children: The Saddest Victims of the Sudanese Conflict. *The Sudan Newsletter* 4 (3).

Anderson, B. 1991. *Imagined Communities: Reflections on the Origin and Spread of Nationalism*. London/New York: Verso Books.

Anderson, C. 2003. *Eyes off the Prize: The United Nations and the African American Struggle for Human Rights, 1944–1955*. Cambridge: Cambridge University Press.

Andrews, G.R. 1991. *Blacks and Whites in Sao Paulo, Brazil, 1888–1988*. Madison: University of Wisconsin Press.

Anyanya National Organization. 1969. *Resistance: The Story of Southern Sudan*. London: Information Service.

Appiah, K.A. 1990. Racisms. In *Anatomy of Racism*, ed. David Theo Goldberg, 4–5. Minneapolis: University of Minnesota Press.

Ashley, R.K., and R.B.J. Walker. 1990. Introduction: Speaking the Language of Exile: Dissident Thought in International Studies. *International Studies Quarterly* 34 (3): 259–268.

Barber, K., ed. 2006. *Africa's Hidden Histories: Everyday Literacy and Making the Self*. Bloomington: Indiana University Press.

Barkan, E. 1992. *The Retreat of Scientific Racism: Changing Concepts of Race in Britain and the United States Between the World Wars*. Cambridge: Cambridge University Press.

Bayissa, R. 2010. *War and Peace in the Sudan and Its Impact on Ethiopia: The Case of Gambella, 1955–2008*. Addis Ababa: Addis Ababa University Press.

Berger, M. 2008. The Real Cold War Was Hot: The Global Struggle for the Third World. *Intelligence and National Security* 23 (1): 112–126.

Berridge, W.J. 2015. *Civil Uprisings in Modern Sudan: The 'Khartoum Springs' of 1964 and 1985*. London: Bloomsbury Publishing.

Beshir, M.O. 1968. *The Southern Sudan: Background to Conflict*. London: C. Hurst & Company.

———. 1975. *The Southern Sudan: From Conflict to Peace*. London: C. Hurst & Company.

Binaisa, G. 1977. Organization of African Unity and Decolonization: Present and Future Trends. *The Annals of the American Academy of Political and Social Sciences* 432 (1): 52–69.

Bøås, M., and K. Dunn, eds. 2007. *African Guerrillas: Raging Against the Machine*. London: Lynne Rienner Publishers.

Boddy, J. 1992. Managing Tradition: "Superstition" and the making of national identity among Sudanese women refugees. Paper presented at the ASA IV Decennial Conference, The Uses of Knowledge: Global and local relations, St Catherine's College, University of Oxford, July 26–30.

Bones, A. 2006. Canada as an International Actor in Sudan. *African Security Review* 15 (1): 109–114.

Bonilla-Silva, E. 2003. *Racism without Racists: Color-Blind Racism and the Persistence of Racial Inequality in America*. Lanham: Rowman & Littlefield.

Borstelmann, T. 2001. *The Cold War and the Color Line: American Race Relations in the Global Arena*. Cambridge, MA: Harvard University Press.

Boswell, C. 2009. Knowledge, Legitimation and the Politics of Risk: The Function of Research in Public Debates on Migration. *Political Studies* 57 (1): 165–186.

Boutros-Ghali, B. 1996. *The United Nations and Apartheid*. New York: Department of Public Information, United Nations.

Bradbury, M. 1998. Sudan: International Responses to War in the Nuba Mountains. *Review of African Political Economy* 25 (77): 463–474.

Breidlid, A., A.A. Said, A.K. Breidlid, A. Farren, and Y.H. Wawa. 2014. *A Concise History of South Sudan: New and Revised Edition*. Kampala: Fountain Publishers.

Brownell, J. 2014. Diplomatic Lepers: The Katangan and Rhodesian Foreign Missions in the United States and the Politics of Nonrecognition. *International Journal of African Historical Studies* 47 (2): 209–237.

Burr, M. 2003. *Revolutionary Sudan: Hasan al-Turabi and the Islamist State, 1989–2000*. Leiden: Brill.

Carol, S. 2012. *From Jerusalem to the Lion of Judah and Beyond: Israel's Foreign Policy in East Africa*. Bloomington: iUniverse.

Carr, D. 1986. *Time, Narrative, and History*. Bloomington: Indiana University Press.

Clapham, C., ed. 1998. *African Guerrillas*. Oxford: James Currey.

———. 2007. African Guerrillas Revisited. In *African Guerrillas: Raging Against the Machine*, ed. M. Bøås and K.C. Dunn. London: Lynne Rienner Publishers.

Clark-Kazak, C. 2011. *Recounting Migration: Political Narratives of Congolese Young People in Uganda*. Montréal: McGill-Queen's University Press.

Collins, R.O. 1962. *The Southern Sudan, 1883–1898*. New Haven: Yale University Press.

———. 2008. *A History of Modern Sudan*. Cambridge: Cambridge University Press.

Collins, R.O., and F. Deng. 2005. *Civil Wars and Revolution in the Sudan: Essays on the Sudan, Southern Sudan and Darfur, 1962–2004*. Hollywood: Tsehai.

Cooper, F. 1997. The Dialectics of Decolonization: Nationalism and Labor Movements in Postwar French Africa. In *Tensions of Empire: Colonial Cultures in Bourgeois Worlds*, ed. F. Cooper and A. Stoler. Berkley: University of California Press.

———. 2005. *Colonialism in Question: Theory, Knowledge, History*. Berkeley: University of California Press.

Daly, M.W. 1991. *Imperial Sudan: The Anglo-Egyptian Condominium, 1934–1956*. Cambridge: Cambridge University Press.

de Carvalho, B., and I.B. Neumann, eds. 2015. *Small State Status Seeking: Norway's Quest for International Standing*. London: Routledge.

de Waal, A. 2004. The Politics of Destabilisation in the Horn, 1989–2001. In *Islamism and Its Enemies in the Horn of Africa*, ed. A. de Waal, 182–230. London: Hurst Publishers.

Deng, F., ed. 2010. *New Sudan in the Making? Essays on a Nation in Painful Search of Itself.* Trenton: Red Sea Press.

Deng, L.A. 2013. *The Power of Creative Reasoning: The Ideas and Vision of John Garang*, 114. Bloomington: iUniverse.

Deng, L.B. 2014. Political Violence and the Emergence of the Dispute Over Abyei, Sudan, 1950–1983. *Journal of Eastern African Studies* 8 (4): 573–589.

Der Derian, J. 1987. *On Diplomacy: A Genealogy of Western Estrangement.* Oxford: Basil Blackwell Publisher.

Doty, R. 1996. *Imperial Encounters: The Politics of Representation in North-South Relations.* Minneapolis: University of Minnesota Press.

Englebert, P., and R. Hummel. 2005. Let's Stick Together: Understanding Africa's Secessionist Deficit. *African Affairs* 104 (416): 400, 412.

Fabian Colonial Bureau. 1945. *The Sudan: The Road Ahead.* London: Fabian Publications.

Feyissa, D. 2010. More State Than the State? The Anywaa's Call for the Rigidification of the Ethio-Sudanese Border. In *Borders and Borderlands as Resources in the Horn of Africa*, ed. D. Feyissa and M.V. Hoehne, 27–44. Suffolk: James Currey.

Fredrickson, G.M. 2002. *Racism: A Short History*, 153–154. Princeton: Princeton University Press.

Friesel, O. 2015. Changing the American Race Narrative, 1962–1965: Transparency as a Guiding Rule in American Cold War Diplomacy. *Journal of Social History* 49 (1): 168–193.

Fukui, K., and J. Markakis. 1994. *Ethnicity and Conflict in the Horn of Africa.* London: James Currey.

Gallab, A.A. 2008. *The First Islamic Republic: Development and Disintegration of Islamism in the Sudan.* Burlington: Ashgate Publishing.

Garang, J.U. 1971. *The Dilemma of the Southern Intellectual: Is It Justified?* Khartoum: Ministry of Southern Affairs, Democratic Republic of the Sudan.

———. 1983. On Economics and Regional Autonomy. *Review of African Political Economy (RoAPE)* 10 (26): 81–87.

Garang, J., and M. Khalid. 1987. *John Garang Speaks.* London: KPI.

Gavin, M. 1998. Fighting for Legitimacy: Power-Seekers, NGOs, and Image-Creation in Rwanda, 1990–1994. M.Phil. thesis, University of Oxford.

Geiger, S.N.G. 1986. Women's Life Histories: Method and Content. *Signs* 11 (2): 334–351.

Geis, A., and C. Hobson. 2014. The Existence and Use of 'Evil' in International Politics. *International Politics* 51 (4): 417–423.

Gleijeses, P. 2002. *Conflicting Missions: Havana, Washington and Africa, 1969–1976.* Chapel Hill: University of North Carolina Press.

———. 2007. Cuba and the Independence of Namibia. *Cold War History* 7 (2): 285–303.

———. 2013. *Visions of Freedom: Havana, Washington, Pretoria and the Struggle for Southern Africa, 1976–1991*. Chapel Hill: University of North Carolina Press.

Government of Sudan. 1964. *Basic Facts about the Southern Provinces of the Sudan*. Khartoum: Central Office of Information. ACR, A/85/2.

Guarak, M.A.M. 2011. *Integration and Fragmentation of the Sudan: An African Renaissance*. Bloomington: AuthorHouse.

Halisi, C.R.D. 1999. *Black Political Thought in the Making of South African Democracy*. Bloomington: Indiana University Press.

Hall, S. 1980. Encoding/Decoding. In *Culture, Media, Language*, ed. S. Hall, D. Hobson, A. Lawe, and P. Willis, 128–138. London: University of Essex Press.

Halliday, F. 1981. The Arc of Crisis and the New Cold War. *MERIP Reports* 100 (101): 14–25.

Harvey, F. 2015. Fighting for Credibility: US Reputation Building in Asymmetric Conflicts from the Gulf War to Syria, 1991–2013. *Canadian Journal of Political Science* 48 (3): 503–530.

Henderson, K.D.D. 1966. *Sudan Republic*. London: Ernest Benn Ltd.

Heraclides, A. 1987. Janus or Sisyphus? The Southern Problem of the Sudan. *Journal of Modern African Studies* 25 (2): 213–231.

Herbst, S. 2003. Political Authority in a Mediated Age. *Theory and Society* 32 (4): 481–503.

Hesse, B. 2014. Escaping Liberty: Western Hegemony, Black Fugitivity. *Political Theory* 42 (3): 288–313.

Hessler, J. 2006. Death of an African Student in Moscow: Race, Politics, and the Cold War. *Cahiers du Monde Russe* 47 (1): 33–63.

Hirschman, C. 1987. The Meaning and Measurement of Ethnicity in Malaysia: An Analysis of Census Classifications. *Journal of Asian Studies* 46 (3): 552–582.

Holt, P.M. 1970. *The Mahdist State in the Sudan: 1881–1898: A Study of Its Origins, Development and Overthrow*. Oxford: Clarendon Press.

Hooker, J. 1970. *Black Revolutionary: George Padmore's Path from Communism to Pan-Africanism*. New York: Praeger Publishers.

Howell, J. 1973. Politics in the Southern Sudan. *African Affairs* 72 (287): 163–178.

———. 1978. Horn of Africa: Lessons from the Sudan Conflict. *International Affairs* 54 (3): 421–436.

Huang, R. 2016. Rebel Diplomacy in Civil War. *International Security* 40 (4): 89–126.

Human Rights Watch. 2005. Targeting the Anuak: Human Rights Violations and Crimes Against Humanity in Ethiopia's Gambella Region. *Human Rights Watch* 17 (3): 7.

Hutchinson, S. 1999. Sudan's Prolonged Second Civil War and the Militarization of Nuer and Dinka Identities. *African Studies Review* 42 (2): 125–145.

———. 2001. A Curse from God? Religious and Political Dimensions of the Post-1991 Rise of Ethnic Violence in South Sudan. *Journal of Modern African Studies* 39 (2): 307–331.

Idris, A. 2001. *Sudan's Civil War – Slavery, Race and Formational Identities.* Lewiston: Edwin Mellen Press.

———. 2005. *Conflict and Politics of Identity in Sudan.* New York: Palgrave Macmillan.

Ingham, K. 1994. *Obote: A Political Biography.* London: Routledge.

Jackson, R. 1990. *Quasi-States: Sovereignty, International Relations and the Third World.* Cambridge: Cambridge University Press.

Jackson, C. 2012. Speech, Gender and Power: Beyond Testimony. *Development and Change* 43 (5): 999–1023.

James, L., and E. Leake, eds. 2015. *Decolonization and the Cold War: Negotiating Independence.* London: Bloomsbury.

Jedrej, M.C. 2016. The Southern Funj of the Sudan under Anglo-Egyptian Rule, 1900–1933. *Critical African Studies* 8 (1): 8–22.

Jervis, R. 1970. *The Logic of Images in International Relations.* Princeton: Princeton University Press.

John Garang De Mabior: A Background Note. 1985. *Horn of Africa* 8 (1): 72.

Johnson, C.A. 1962. Conferences of Independent African States. *International Organizations* 16 (2): 426–429.

Johnson, D.H. 1993. Prophecy and Mahdism in the Upper Nile: An Examination of Local Experiences of the Mahdiyya in the Southern Sudan. *British Journal of Middle Eastern Studies* 20 (1): 42–56.

———. 2001. The Nuer Civil War. In *Sudanese Society in the Context of Civil War: Papers from a Seminar at the University of Copenhagen, 9–10 February 2001*, ed. M. Johannsen and N. Kastfelt, 3–27. Copenhagen: University of Copenhagen North/South Priority Research Area.

Johnson, C. 2007. *Revolutionaries to Race Leaders: Black Power and the Making of American Politics.* Minneapolis: University of Minnesota Press.

Johnson, D.H. 2011a. *The Root Causes of Sudan's Civil Wars: Peace or Truce.* Kampala: James Currey.

Johnson, H. 2011b. *Waging Peace in Sudan.* Brighton: Sussex Academic Press.

Johnson, D.H. 2016. *Empire and the Nuer: Sources on the Pacification of the Southern Sudan, 1898–1930.* Oxford: Oxford University Press.

Johnson, D.H., and G. Prunier. 1993. The Foundation and Expansion of the Sudan People's Liberation Army. In *Civil War in the Sudan*, ed. M.W. Daly and A.A. Sikainga. London: British Academic Press.

Jok, J.M. 2007. *Sudan: Race, Religion, and Violence.* Oxford: Oneworld.

Kamanu, O.S. 1974. Secession and the Right of Self-Determination: An O.A.U. Dilemma. *The Journal of Modern African Studies* 12 (3): 355–376.

Kasanda, A. 2016. Exploring Pan-Africanism's Theories: From Race-Based Solidarity to Political Unity and beyond. *Journal of African Cultural Studies* 28 (2): 179–195.

Kerr, M.H. 1971. *The Arab Cold War, 1958–1967: A Study of Ideology in Politics*. London: Oxford University Press.

Kevlihan, R. 2007. Beyond Creole Nationalism? Language Policies, Education and the Challenge of State Building in Post-Conflict Southern Sudan. *Ethnopolitics* 6 (4): 513–543.

Khalid, M. 2003. *War and Peace in Sudan: A Tale of Two Countries*. London: Routledge.

Kibreab, G. 2009. Eritrean–Sudanese Relations in Historical Perspective. In *Eritrea's External Relations: Understanding Its Regional Role and Foreign Policy*, ed. Richard Reid, 71–97. London: Cambridge University Press.

Kindersley, N. 2015. Southern Sudanese Narratives of Displacement, and the Ambiguity of "Voice". *History in Africa* 42 (1): 203–237.

Klotz, A. 1995. *Norms in International Relations: The Struggle against Apartheid*. Ithaca: Cornell University Press.

Korn, D. 1986. *Ethiopia, the United States and the Soviet Union*. London: Southern Illinois University Press.

Kramer, R. 2015. The Death of Bassiouni: A Case of Complex Identity in the Sudan. *Canadian Journal of African Studies* 49 (1): 95–107.

Kramer, R.S., R. Lobban, and C. Fluehr-Lobban. 1992. *Historical Dictionary of the Sudan*. London: Scarecrow Press.

Krebs, R.R., and P.T. Jackson. 2007. Twisting Tongues and Twisting Arms: The Power of Political Rhetoric. *European Journal of International Relations* 13 (1): 35–66.

Kuol, M.A. 1997. *Administration of Justice in the (SPLA/M) Liberated Areas: Court Cases in War Torn Southern Sudan*. Oxford: Refugee Studies Programme, University of Oxford.

Kurimoto, E. 1992. Natives and Outsiders: The Historical Experience of the Anywaa of Western Ethiopia. *Journal of Asian and African Studies* 43: 1–43.

———. 1997. Politicization of Ethnicity in Gambella. In Ethiopia in Broader Perspective: Papers of the XIIIth international Conference of Ethiopian Studies, Kyoto, 12–17 December 1997. Kyoto: Shokado Book Sellers.

———. 2002. Fear and Anger: Female Versus Male Narratives among the Anywaa. In *Remapping Ethiopia: Socialism and After*, ed. W. James, D. Donham, E. Kurimoto, and A. Triulzi, 219–238. Oxford: James Currey.

Kustenbauder, M. 2012. The Politicization of Religious Identity in Sudan, with Special Reference to Oral Histories of the Sudanese Diaspora in America. In *Religion on the Move! New Dynamics of Religious Expansion in a Globalizing World*, ed. A. Adogame and S. Shankar. Leiden: Brill Publishers.

Kuyok, K., and A. South. 2015. *Sudan: The Notable Firsts*. Bloomington: AuthorHouse.

Laruni, E. 2015. Regional and Ethnic Identities the Acholi of Northern Uganda, 1950–1968. *Journal of Eastern African Studies* 9 (2): 212–230.

Lasley, T. 2015. Secession, Legitimacy and the Use of Child Soldiers. *Conflict Management and Peace Science* 32 (3): 289–308.

Leach, J. 2013. *War and Politics in Sudan: Cultural Identities and the Challenges of the Peace Process*. London: I.B. Tauris.

Lee, C., ed. 2010. *Making a World after Empire: The Bandung Moment and Its Political Afterlives*. Athens: Ohio University Press.

Leonardi, C. 2015. *Dealing with Government in South Sudan: Histories of Chiefship, Community and State*. Oxford: James Currey.

Leonardi, C., and C. Vaughan. 2016. "We Are Oppressed and Our Only Way Is to Write to Higher Authority" the Politics of Claim and Complaint in the Peripheries of Condominium Sudan. In *Citizenship, Belonging, and Political Community in Africa: Dialogues between Past and Present*, ed. E. Hunter. Athens: Ohio University Press.

LeRiche, M. 2012. John Garang DeMabior. In *Dictionary of African Biography*, ed. H.L. Gates Jr. and E. Akyeampong. New York: Oxford University Press.

LeRiche, M., and M. Arnold. 2012. *South Sudan: From Revolution to Independence*. London: Hurst.

Lesch, A.M. 1998. *The Sudan: Contested National Identities*. Bloomington: Indiana University Press.

Lissoni, A. 2009. Transformations in the ANC External Mission and Umkhontho we Sizwe, c. 1960–1969. *Journal of Southern African Studies* 35 (2): 287–301.

Macmillan, H. 2009. The African National Congress of South Africa in Zambia: The Culture of Exile and the Changing Relationship with Home, 1964–1990. *Journal of Southern African Studies* 35: 2.

———. 2013. *The Lusaka Years: The ANC in Exile in Zambia, 1963–1994*. Auckland Park: Jacana.

Madut-Arop, A. 2006. *Sudan's Painful Road to Peace: A Full Story of The Founding and Development of SPLM/SPLA*. Charleston: BookSurge.

Magaziner, D. 2010. *The Law and the Prophets: Black Consciousness in South Africa, 1968–1977*. Athens: Ohio University Press.

Mahgoub, M.A. 1974. *Democracy on Trial: Reflections on Arab and African Politics*. London: Andre Deutsch Ltd Publishers.

Malkki, L.H. 1995. Refugees and Exile: From 'Refugee Studies' to the National Order of Things. *Annual Review of Anthropology* 24: 495–523.

Malwal, B. 2015. *Sudan and South Sudan: From One to Two*. Basingstoke: Springer.

Medani, K.M. 2012. The Horn of Africa in the Shadow of the Cold War: Understanding the Partition of Sudan from a Regional Perspective. *Journal of North African Studies* 17 (2): 275–294.

Merkx, J. 2002. Refugee Identities and Relief in an African Borderland: A Study of Northern Uganda and Southern Sudan. *Refugee Survey Quarterly* 21 (1–2): 113–146.

Mollan, S. 2008. Business, State and Economy: Cotton and the Anglo-Egyptian Sudan, 1919–1939. *African Economic History* 36: 95–123.

Morrow, S., B. Maaba, and L. Pulumani. 2004. *Education in Exile: SOMAFCO, the ANC School in Tanzania, 1978–1992*. Cape Town: HSRC Press.

Mukhtar, A. 2004. The Crisis of Identity in Northern Sudan: The Dilemma of a Black People with a White Culture. In *Race and Identity in the Nile Valley: Ancient and Modern Perspectives*, ed. C. Fluehr-Lobban and K. Rhodes, 207–240. Trenton: Red Sea Press.

Natsios, A. 2012. *Sudan, South Sudan, and Darfur: What Everyone Needs to Know*. Oxford: Oxford University Press.

Nhial, A.A.J., Nur Tawir Kafi, and Eltigani Seisi. 1993. Human Rights Abuses in Sudan. *Review of African Political Economy* 20 (58): 110–118.

Nimblock, T. 1987. *Class and Power in Sudan: The Dynamics of Sudanese Politics, 1898–1985*. Basingstoke: SUNY Press.

Nkrumah, K. 1963. *Africa Must Unite*. London: International Publishers.

Nugent, P. 1993. *Arbitrary Lines and the People's Minds: A Dissenting View on Colonial Boundaries in West Africa*. Edinburgh: University of Edinburgh.

Nyaba, P.A. 1996. *The Politics of Liberation in South Sudan*. Kampala: Fountain Publishers.

Nye, J.S., Jr. 2004. *Soft Power: The Means to Success in World Politics*. New York: PublicAffairs.

O' Ballance, E. 1977. *The Secret War in the Sudan, 1955–1972*. London: Faber & Faber Ltd.

O'Brien, J. 1985. Sowing the Seeds of Famine: The Political Economy of Food Deficits in Sudan. *Review of African Political Economy* 12 (33): 23–32.

Oduho, J., and W. Deng. 1963. *The Problem of Southern Sudan*. Oxford: Oxford University Press.

Omenka, N.I. 2010. Blaming the Gods: Christian Religious Propaganda in the Nigeria-Biafra War. *Journal of African History* 51 (3): 367–389.

Omi, M., and H. Winant. 2015. *Racial Formation in the United States: From the 1960s to the 1980s*. New York: Routledge.

Panzer, M.G. 2013. Building a Revolutionary Constituency: Mozambican Refugees and the Development of the FRELIMO Proto-State, 1964–1968. *Social Dynamics: A Journal of African studies* 39 (1): 5–23.

Patey, L. 2014. *The New Kings of Crude: China, India, and the Global Struggle for Oil in Sudan and South Sudan*. London: HarperCollins Publishers India.

Patman, R. 2009. *The Soviet Union in the Horn of Africa: The Diplomacy of Intervention and Disengagement*. Cambridge: Cambridge University Press.

Pax Sudani Network. 1993. Rampant Raids and Cases of Slavery. *Sudan* 3 (3): 37.

Peel, J. 1995. For Who Hath Despised the Day of Small Things? Missionary Narratives, Historical Anthropology. *Comparative Studies in Society and History* 37 (3): 581–607.

Peterson, D., and G. Macolo, eds. 2009. *Recasting the Past: History Writing and Political Work in Modern Africa*. Athens: Ohio University Press.

Petterson, D. 1999. *Inside Sudan: Political Islam, Conflict, and Catastrophe*. Boulder: Westview Press.

Pinaud, C. 2015. "We Are Trained to Be Married!" Elite Formation and Ideology in the "Girls' Battalion" of the Sudan People's Liberation Army. *Journal of Eastern African Studies* 9 (3): 375–393.

Poggo, S. 2011. *The First Sudanese Civil War: Africans, Arabs, and Israelis in the Southern Sudan, 1955–1972*. Basingstoke: Palgrave Macmillan.

Polhemus, J.H. 1977. Nigeria and Southern Africa: Interest, Policy and Means. *Canadian Journal of African Studies* 11 (1): 43–66.

Prashad, V. 2008. *The Darker Nations: A People's History of the Third World*. New York: The New Press.

Prunier, G. 1986. *From Peace to War: The Southern Sudan, 1972–1984*. Hull: Department of Sociology and Social Anthropology, University of Hull.

———. 2004. Rebel Movements and Proxy Warfare: Uganda, Sudan and the Congo (1986–99). *African Affairs* 103: 359–383.

Reno, W. 2001. How Sovereignty Matters: International Markets and the Political Economy of Local Politics in Weak States. In *Intervention and Transnationalism in Africa: Global-Local Networks of Power*, ed. T. Callaghy, R. Kassimir, and R. Latham. Cambridge: Cambridge University Press.

Rolandsen, Ø. 2005. *Guerrilla Government: Political Changes in the Southern Sudan During the 1990s*. Uppsala: Nordiska Afrikainstitutet.

———. 2011a. A False Start: Between War and Peace in the Southern Sudan, 1956–62. *Journal of African History* 52 (1): 105–123.

———. 2011b. The Making of Anya-Nya Insurgency in the Southern Sudan, 1961–64. *Journal of Eastern African Studies* 5 (2): 211–232.

Rolandsen, Ø., and M.W.A. Daly. 2016. *History of South Sudan: From Slavery to Independence*. Cambridge: Cambridge University Press.

Rolandsen, Ø., and C. Leonardi. 2014. Discourses of Violence in the Transition from Colonialism to Independence in Southern Sudan, 1955–1960. *Journal of Eastern African Studies* 8 (4): 609–625.

Rolandsen, Ø., H.M. Glomnes, S. Manoeli, and F. Nicolaisen. 2015. A Year of South Sudan's Third Civil War. *International Area Studies Review* 18 (1): 87–104.

Rone, J. 1995. *Children in Sudan: Slaves, Street Children and Child Soldiers*, 69–71. Human Rights Watch/Africa Human Rights Watch.

Rubin, L. 2014. The Power of a Weak State: Sudan's Relations with Saudi Arabia and Egypt. In *Islam in the Balance: Ideational Threats in Arab Politics*, 62–95. Stanford: Stanford University Press.

Sajed, A. 2016. Peripheral Modernity and Anti-Colonial Nationalism in Java: Economies of Race and Gender in the Constitution of the Indonesian National Teleology. *Third World Quarterly* 38 (2): 1–19.

Salam, A.H.A., and A. de Waal. 1999. *The Phoenix State: Civil Society and the Future of Sudan*. Kampala: Red Sea Press.

Sanderson, L. 1975. Education and Administrative Control in Colonial Sudan and Northern Nigeria. *African Affairs* 74 (297): 427–441.

Sanderson, L.P., and N. Sanderson. 1981. *Education, Religion and Politics in Southern Sudan, 1899–1964*. London: Ithaca Press.

Sapire, H., and C. Saunders, eds. 2013. *Southern African Liberation Struggles: New Local, Regional and Global Perspectives*. Cape Town: UCT Press.

Schwenkel, C. 2014. Traveling Architecture, East German Urban Designs in Vietnam. *International Journal of History, Culture and Modernity* 2 (2): 155–174.

Scott, D. 2015. China's Public Diplomacy Rhetoric, 1990–2012: Pragmatic Image-Crafting. *Diplomacy and Statecraft* 26 (2): 249–265.

Shandy, D.J. 2007. *Nuer-American Passages: Globalizing Sudanese Migration*. Gainesville: University Press of Florida.

Sharkey, H. 2003. *Living with Colonialism: Nationalism and Culture in the Anglo-Egyptian Sudan*. Berkeley: University of California Press.

———. 2008. Arab Identity and Ideology in Sudan: The Politics of Language, Ethnicity, and Race. *African Affairs* 107 (426): 21–43.

———. 2015. *La Belle Africaine*: The Sudanese Giraffe Who Went to France. *Canadian Journal of African Studies* 49 (1): 39–65.

Shubin, V.G. 2008. *The Hot "Cold War": The USSR in Southern Africa*. London: Pluto Press.

Sidahmed, A.S. 1997. *Politics and Islam in Contemporary Sudan*. Richmond: Curzon.

Sikkink, K. 1993. Human Rights, Principled Issue-Networks, and Sovereignty in Latin America. *International Organization* 47 (3): 411–441.

Slate, N. 2014. *The Prism of Race: WEB Du Bois, Langston Hughes, Paul Robeson, and The Colored World of Cedric Dover*. New York: Palgrave Macmillan.

Slobodian, Q., ed. 2015. *Comrades of Color: East Germany in the Cold War World*. Oxford: Berghahn Books.

Sternberger, D. 1968. Legitimacy. In *The International Encyclopedia of Social Science*, ed. D. Sills, vol. 9. New York: Free Press.

Stoler, A. 2001. Tense and Tender Ties: The Politics of Comparison in North American History and (Post) Colonial Studies. *Journal of American History* 88 (3): 829–865.

———. 2009. *Along the Archival Grain: Epistemic Anxieties and Colonial Common Sense*. Princeton: Princeton University Press.

Sudan, Wizarat al-Dakhiliyah. 1964. *The Black Book of the Sudan on the Expulsion of the Missionaries from Southern Sudan: An Answer*. Milan: Istituto Artigianelli.

Thiam, D. 1965. *The Foreign Policy of African States: Ideological Bases, Present Realities, Future Prospects.* London: Phoenix House.

Thomas, E. 2015. *South Sudan: A Slow Liberation.* London: Zed Books.

Tonkin, E. 1992. *Narrating our Pasts: The Social Construction of Oral History.* Cambridge: Cambridge University Press.

Turton, D. 2003. Conceptualizing Forced Migration. Working Paper, no. 12, Refugee Studies Centre, University of Oxford.

Twine, France Winddance. 1998. *Racism in a Racial Democracy: The Maintenance of White Supremacy in Brazil.* New Brunswick: Rutgers University Press.

Unknown. 1985a. Stated Position of the Rebels. *Horn of Africa* 8 (/1): 39–46.

———. 1985b. The New Order. *Horn of Africa* 8 (1): 67–71.

Vambheim, M.M. 2007. Making Peace While Waging War: A Peacemaking Effort in the Sudanese Civil War, 1965–1966. MA thesis, University of Bergen.

Vaughan, C. 2015. *Darfur: Colonial Violence, Sultanic Legacies and Local Politics, 1916–1956.* Oxford: James Currey.

Verhoeven, H. 2015. *Water, Civilization, and Power in Sudan: The Political Economy of Military-Islamist State-Building.* New York: Cambridge University Press.

Voll, J.O., ed. 1991. *Sudan: State and Society in Crisis.* Bloomington: Indiana University Press.

———. 1997. Imperialism, Nationalism, and Missionaries: Lessons from Sudan for the Twenty-First Century. *Islam and Christian Muslim Relations* 8 (1): 39–52.

Voller, Y. 2016. The Egyptian Muslim Brotherhood and the South Sudan Question: Reconsidering Moderation. *International Affairs* 92 (3): 665–682.

Wai, D.M. 1973. *The Southern Sudan: The Problem of National Integration.* London: F. Cass.

———. 1981. *The African-Arab Conflict in the Sudan.* New York: Africana Publishing Company.

———. 1983. African-Arab Relations: Interdependence or Misplaced Optimism? *Journal of Modern African Studies* 21 (2): 187–213.

Wakoson, E.N. 1993. The Politics of Southern Self-Government 1972–83. In *Civil War in the Sudan*, ed. M.W. Daly and A.A. Sikainga. London/New York: British Academic Press.

Wallerstein, I.M. 2005. *Africa: The Politics of Independence and Unity.* Lincoln: University of Nebraska Press.

Wang, J. 2006. Managing National Reputation and International Relations in the Global Era: Public Diplomacy Revisited. *Public Relations Review* 32 (2): 91–96.

Warburg, G. 1995. Mahdism and Islamism in Sudan. *International Journal of Middle East Studies* 27 (2): 219–236.

———. 2003. *Islam, Sectarianism and Politics in Sudan Since the Mahdiyya.* London: Hurst.

Weber, C. 1995. *Simulating Sovereignty: Intervention, the State and Symbolic Exchange*. Cambridge: Cambridge University Press.

Weber, A. 2006. Barbarian Beasts or Mothers of Invention: Relation of Gendered Fighter and Citizen Images: With a Specific Case Study of Southern Sudan. Ph.D., Freie Universität Berlin.

Westad, O.A. 2005. *The Global Cold War: Third World Interventions and the Making of Our Times*. Cambridge: Cambridge University Press.

White, L. 2000. Telling More: Lies, Secrets, and History. *History and Theory* 39 (4): 11–22.

White, L., Stephan F. Miescher, and D.W. Cohen, eds. 2001. *African Words, African Voices: Critical Practices in Oral History*. Bloomington: Indiana University Press.

Williams, C. 2011. Ordering the Nation: SWAPO in Zambia, 1974–1976. *Journal of Southern African Studies* 37 (4): 693–713.

———. 2014. Practicing Pan-Africanism: An Anthropological Perspective on Exile-Host Relations at Kongwa, Tanzania. *Anthropology Southern Africa* 37 (3-4): 224.

———. 2015. *National Liberation in Postcolonial Southern Africa: A Historical Ethnography of SWAPO Exile Camps*. New York: Cambridge University Press.

———. 2017. Education in Exile: International Scholarships, Cold War Politics, and Conflicts Among SWAPO Members in Tanzania, 1961–1968. *Journal of Southern African Studies* 43 (1): 125–141.

Willis, J. 2005. Hukm: The Creolization of Authority in Condominium Sudan. *Journal of African History* 46: 29–50.

———. 2015. The Southern Problem: Representing Sudan's Southern Provinces to c. 1970. *Journal of African History* 56: 282, 300.

Wöndu, S., and A.M. Lesch. 2000. *Battle for Peace in Sudan: An Analysis of the Abuja Conferences 1992–1993*. Lanham: University Press of America.

Woodward, P. 1979. *Condominium and Sudanese Nationalism*. London: Rex Collings.

———. 2003. *The Horn of Africa: Politics and International Relations*. London: I.B. Tauris.

———. 2006. *US Foreign Policy and the Horn of Africa*. London: Routledge.

Yihun, B.B. 2013. Ethiopia's Role in South Sudan's March to Independence, 1955–1991. *African Studies Quarterly* 14 (1 & 2): 35–54.

Yordanov, R. 2016. *The Soviet Union and the Horn of Africa During the Cold War: Between Ideology and Pragmatism*. Lanham: Lexington Books.

Young, T. 1995. A Project to Be Realized: Global Liberalism and Contemporary Africa. *Millennium: Journal of International Studies* 24 (3): 527–546.

Young, J. 1999. Along Ethiopia's Western Frontier: Gambella and Benishangul in Transition. *Journal of Modern African Studies* 37 (2): 321–346.

———. 2012. *The Fate of Sudan: The Origins and Consequences of a Flawed Peace Process*. London: Zed Books.

Zambakari, C. 2015. Sudan and South Sudan: Identity, Citizenship, and Democracy in Plural Societies. *Citizen Studies* 19 (1): 69–82.

Zewde, B. 1991. *History of Modern Ethiopia, 1855–1974*, 83. London: James Currey.

———. 2006. Relations Between Ethiopia and Sudan. In *Ethnic Federalism: The Ethiopian Experience in Comparative Perspective*, ed. D. Turton, 203–230. Oxford: J. Currey.

Unpublished Dissertations and Papers

Abdelhay, A.K. 2007. The Politics of Language Planning in the Sudan: The Case of the Naivasha Language Policy. Ph.D. thesis, University of Edinburgh.

Alexander, J. 2016. Keynote Lecture: 'Telling African Cold War Stories: The Personal in the Geopolitical'. *Africa, Eastern Europe and the Dream of International Socialism: New Perspectives on the Global Cold War* October 28–29, 2016. St Antony's College, Oxford.

Almeida, E. 2000. Was the Colonial Policy of Ethnic Self-Rule Responsible for the Divided Polity in Uganda? Ph.D. thesis, University of Western Ontario.

Gasarasi, C.P. 1988. The Effect of Africa's Exiles/Refugees Upon Inter-African State Relations: Conflict and Cooperation – 1958–1988. Ph.D. thesis, Tulane University.

James, L.E. 2012. 'What We Put in Black and White': George Padmore and the Practice of Anti-imperial Politics. Ph.D. thesis, London School of Economics.

Kindersley, N. 2016. The Fifth Column? An Intellectual History of Southern Sudanese Communities in Khartoum, 1969–2005. Ph.D., Durham University.

Mihatsch, M. 2014. Stories of a Failed Nation: Sudanese Politics, 1945–69. D. Phil. thesis, University of Oxford.

Roberts, G. 2016. Politics, Decolonization, and the Cold War in Dar es Salaam, c. 1965–72. Ph.D. thesis, University of Warwick.

Tounsel, C. 2015. "God Will Crown Us": The Construction of Religious Nationalism in Southern Sudan, 1898–2011. Ph.D. thesis, University of Michigan.

Index

S. C. Manoeli, *Sudan's "Southern Problem"*, African Histories and Modernities, https://doi.org/10.1007/978-3-030-28771-9

S

Zeitfracht Medien GmbH
Ferdinand-Jühlke-Straße 7
99095 Erfurt, Deutschland
produktsicherheit@kolibri360.de